IN THE
FORESTS
OF FREEDOM

IN THE
FORESTS
OF FREEDOM

The fighting Maroons
of Dominica

LENNOX HONYCHURCH

PAPILLOTE PRESS
London and Trafalgar, Dominica

First published in Great Britain in 2017
© text Lennox Honychurch 2017
© illustrations Lennox Honychurch 2017
An earlier version of this book, entitled Negre Mawon: the Fighting Maroons of
Dominica, was published privately by the author in 2014

Typeset in Book Antigua
Book design by Andy Dark

Printed in India by Imprint Digital

ISBN 978-0-9931086-6-2
Papillote Press
23 Rozel Road
London SW4 0EY
United Kingdom
And Trafalgar, Dominica

www.papillotepress.co.uk
@papillotepress

In memory of my father Ted Honychurch (1923-1981) who
gave me my first book on the Maroons as a birthday gift:
'The Fighting Maroons of Jamaica' by Carey Robinson and
who explored with me and my sister the forested
wilds of Dominica, the haunts of the 'Neg Mawon'.

His ashes lie somewhere below the towering peak of
Morne Anglais where he was killed and burned in the forest
in circumstances similar to many of the events recalled
in this book.

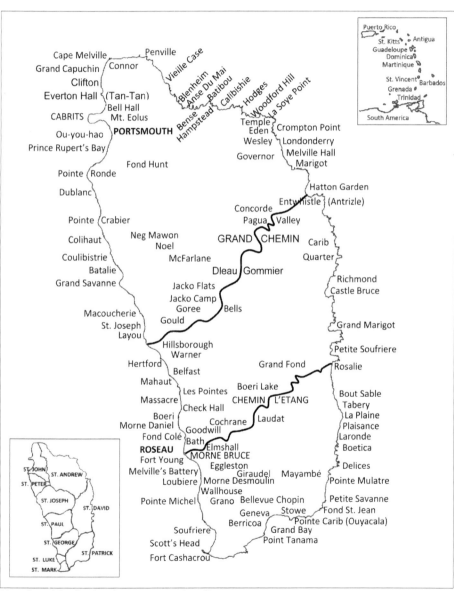

Map of Dominica showing place names mentioned in text.

Contents

The 'Neg Mawon Emancipation Statue' unveiled on Emancipation Day, 1 August 2013

1

A lasting memorial: the leaders of liberty

A speech for the unveiling of the 'Neg Mawon' emancipation statue delivered by the author at Peebles Park, Roseau, Dominica, 1 August 2013

Your Excellency the President and Mrs Williams; Acting Prime Minister Hon Ambrose George; Minister of Culture,Youth and Sports Hon Justina Charles, other members of Cabinet and the House of Assembly; Mayor of Roseau Cecil Joseph; distinguished guests; brothers and sisters all of this Commonwealth of Dominica.

In a socio-historical study of Dominica carried out in 1984 the Haitian historian Jean Casimir noted that Dominica shows the effects not so much of a plantation society but of a Maroon society. He argued that a late and weak plantation system in Dominica had resulted in a less colonised and thus less regimented and more open modern society.[1] Briefly, Dominica was the last island in the Caribbean to be colonised. Its rugged mountainous nature enabled it to be one of the last places of refuge for the the region's indigenous people, the Kalinago. When the British took over the island in 1763 there were already more than 300 Maroons living in small settlements in the interior. As British and French planters opened up more land for sugar and coffee and imported more enslaved labour so did the Maroon numbers increase. Plantations and villages clung to the coast while inland a vast jumble of forested ravines, cliffs and river valleys combined to create a complex natural maze which confounded the British forces who attempted to reduce the Maroons by any means possible.

The call of the conch shell, the *kon lambi*, echoed across the valleys sending messages and warnings from camp to camp, from one 'Neg

Mawon' leader to the other. The name 'Maroon' had come from the Spanish word *cimarrón* meaning 'fugitive, runaway, living on mountaintops' (from the Spanish *cima* meaning 'top, summit'). It was adopted by the English and anglicised into 'Maroon'. For the French Creoles it became 'Neg Mawon'; in those days the French word *negre* did not merely mean black man or Negro, it also referred to a slave.

This memorial that we are about to unveil recalls the 'Neg Mawon' chiefs such as Balla, Congo Ray, Gorre Greg, Jacko, Cicero, Pharcel, Zombie, Jupiter, Juba, Mabouya, Sandy, Quashie, Nicko, Hall and many others. There were also women among them: Charlotte, Calypso, Angelique, Marie-Rose, Tranquille, Rosay, Victorie and Rachel, and hundreds of others with unrecorded names who, from the 1760s through to the first stage of emancipation in 1834, held out against the plantation forces that were pitted against them.

It is significant that most of the senior chiefs had been born in Africa for unlike the Creole, Dominican-born slaves these Africans had once lived in and experienced a society other than the plantation society. They knew that an alternative system existed and they had no difficulty imagining that it could be recreated here on the other side of the Atlantic.

In one way I had hoped that this statue would have been erected in a prominent place in the mountainous heartland of our island home. For in those hills the statue would overlook the mighty green citadel of jagged peaks that was the place of liberty and freedom. It was a sanctuary for those who escaped the system and fought to overturn the institution of enslavement that had been imposed upon them. For, up there, among those forested mountains, was truly their land of Zion.

Instead, this symbolic representation of Maroon heritage has been placed here on this hill in the centre of the nation's capital. Within a few hundred yards in every direction there are places that were, for many of the Maroons, familiar: the site of arrival, the site of sale, the place of punishment and the point of death. For this area was indeed their Babylon. Just down the hill in the harbour below us anchored the slave ships that had completed the treacherous Middle Passage across the Atlantic Ocean from the coast of west Africa. There, on that coast, renegade chiefs, not unlike the drug lords and cocaine dealers of today, had connived with European traders to engage in human trafficking in return for the equivalent of bling and ill-gotten gain.

Along the Bay Front stood the warehouses and open yards, the taverns and main marketplace where the sales of the newly arrived slaves were transacted. The last of these buildings to survive is the barracoon building near the end of Dame Eugenia Charles Boulevard on the junction with Hillsborough Street.

Besides being a place of sale, the Old Market was the scene of horrific public punishments and executions. After the great Maroon conflict of 1814, the cobblestones are said to have run with blood, so much so that the populace refused to continue to draw water from the public well and it had to be filled in and covered over.

Right next to us at Fort Young, the Maroon chief Balla was brought in half dead from the heights of Layou in 1786. According to the British Governor, John Orde, 'Balla refused answering almost any questions that were put to him… he called upon his captors repeatedly to cut off his head, telling them that they might do so, but that Balla would not die – his Obi or charm and his child were the only things that he expressed much anxiety about. The former he wished to bury, the latter, a boy of about five years old he bid to remember [that] the Beckeys or White Man had killed his father.'[2] Balla was taken to the marketplace to be displayed in a narrow iron cage called a gibbet and took a week to die. The people sang a refrain '*Balla mort, Bwa gattay Oh.*' ('Balla is dead, the woods are spoilt.') And, as for his son, Governor Orde took the little boy to England where he was sent to school and where he disappeared into the social whirl of Regency London.

But perhaps the greatest tragedy of the whole Maroon campaign was that many of the 'Neg Mawon' lost their lives at the hands of their own people, the so-called 'trusted Negroes' who joined their masters' Ranger Corps. You can go to the National Archives on Kennedy Avenue in Roseau and see the receipts for rewards and bills of freedom paid to Rangers in return for killing the aged and respected chief Jacko, on 12 July 1814, and other chiefs.

A couple of hundred yards to the south of us is the House of Assembly, which in those days also served as the Court House. There, and at Fort Young and also at the Market House, which still stands overlooking the present Old Market, is where the 'kangaroo court' trials of the Maroons took place. The planters produced and quoted legal and religious books to justify the power that they had seized in this colonial society. For we must be frank about this: the Judaic Christian Bible was just as much a tool of colonisation and control as were the draconian laws, the land titles and the maps of appropriation and possession.

That House of Assembly echoed with Biblical quotations plucked from the Old and New Testaments to justify the institution of enslavement. Among the most favoured passages used by the planter-legislators was Leviticus 25:44-46: 'Your male and female slaves are to come from the nations around you; from them you may buy slaves… and they will become your property. You can will them to your children as inherited property and can make them slaves for life…'

In exhorting their human property to accept their state in life, they turned to passages such as Peter 2:18: 'Slaves, submit yourselves to your masters with all respect, not only to those who are good and considerate, but also to those who are harsh.' And when they were debating the Amelioration Acts in the 1820s, aimed at reducing some of the greatest abuses of the system, they turned, in their defence, to Exodus 21:20-21: 'If a man beats his male or female slave with a rod and the slave dies as a direct result, he must be punished, but he is not to be punished if the slave gets up after a day or two, since the slave is his property.'[3] It is fitting to note that as the tide against slavery began to swell, other verses from that same Bible were used by the Anti-Slavery Movement, Methodists and Moravians prominent among them, to ask, 'Am I not a man and a brother?' It is truly a religious text for all seasons.

When full emancipation was granted on 1 August 1838, exactly 175 years ago today, it was far from the end of the struggle. The Emancipation Act granted compensation not to the former slaves but to their masters for the loss of their property. The slave holders of Dominica received £275,547 from the British government while the 14,175 former slaves were left with absolutely nothing to start out their lives as free people. This must be taken into account when considering Dominican society today for, when seen in that light, it is remarkable what has been achieved in areas such as education, home and land ownership and self-government, given that the majority of our ancestors started off with nothing.

In the decades following emancipation, a raft of laws, such as the wide-ranging vagrancy acts, were passed to keep control of the masses. The aim was to deprive them of land so as to tie them to reliance on the estates, to limit the right to vote and to determine everything in their lives from the rates of their labour to the nature of their sexual activity. The so-called obeah laws were a front for a government policy of de-Africanisation of the population. Carve a mask or a statue out of wood and you could be charged with the possession of an instrument of obeah.

Many of these post-emancipation laws of control still litter our legislation. On independence, we maybe should have done as Nelson Mandela did in South Africa: sweep everything away and start afresh to meet the needs of a modern nation state. But we were too timid, maybe we are still too timid, and that unlike what the Haitian historian Jean Casimir said of Dominican society, we have been too well and thoroughly colonised to 'free our minds of mental slavery'.

However, it must be said that we were bold enough to go directly into independence as a republic, the only Commonwealth Caribbean country to do so (Trinidad and Guyana became republics some years after their independence). Even today, we are the only member of the Organisation of Eastern Caribbean States (OECS) where our head of state, elected by our own representatives, sits among us, as he does today, and participates in the life and aspirations of our people rather than being a governor-general representing a distant figure 5,000 miles away.

So the message of this statue does not end with the end of slavery. It does not even end with political independence. Its message carries on, to look back and remember, but also to look forward to influence our present ideals and those in the years ahead. Together with the nearby cenotaph commemorating Dominicans who died in the two world wars, this statue represents a spirit of determination against all odds, a spirit of togetherness in the *koudmen* tradition of the 'Neg Mawon', a spirit of self-reliance and a respect for the forested citadel of this island that has given its natural resources for our survival and for the continued protection of our people.

2

An island citadel: understanding the Maroon landscape

Climbing along a sharp-edged ridge above the rain forest in the centre of Dominica adventurous hikers push aside the branches of the thick smooth leaves of the *kaklin* and the stiff fronds of the mountain palm (*palmiste*) to look out towards Morne Diablotin, the island's tallest peak. There is nothing to indicate that they are on an island. No blue triangle of sea breaks the waves of green ridges that encircle them. Every ridge is a different shade of green and within each wave rise trees that spread contrasting tones into dark ravines or against the skyline. Shadows and sunny highlights shift as the breeze ripples across the canopy. They see no one else although someone could always be there. They could walk for days and meet no one, although someone may have seen them pass.

———————————

It is in this landscape that the story of the 'Neg Mawon' of Dominica unfolded as a displaced and enslaved people fought upon this forested island to create a free and self-sufficient society during an intense 70-year-long struggle (1764-1834). Those seven decades of internal conflict began in earnest the year after the British took possession of the island following the Treaty of Paris in 1763. From 1778, when the French recaptured Dominica, Maroon activity intensified, overflowing into the period of British repossession. The momentum was briefly broken by an unsettled lull between 1787 and

1791 while the Maroons regrouped. Against the backdrop of the French Revolution and Napoleonic wars, spanning the decade of the 1790s and climaxing in 1814, the Maroons shook the British hold on Dominica to its foundations. It forced the colonial power into a 20-year period of amelioration of slave laws that led to the first stage of emancipation in 1834.

From the very beginning, the Maroons' long-term objective was to overturn a system that kept their people in bondage. But defeating slavery was not the end. In the years after emancipation the descendants of Maroons pieced together what cultural elements they could to mould a new more equitable community out of the shattered remains of their ancestral experience. Even the much later achievements of self-government and political independence do not close the story begun centuries before by men and women struggling to be free.

The island upon which all this took place provides a spectacular stage for the human drama in which three ethnic groups, Kalinago, African and European, converged to engage with each other to manipulate

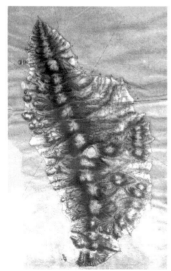

possession and control of this rugged space. To fully comprehend the powerful hold that the Maroons of Dominica had upon this plantation colony during the last half of the 18th and the early 19th century one must understand the nature of the island and particularly its volcanic origins. Aerial and satellite photographs of the central mountains show the complex formations that aided the escaped slaves for the terrain of deep valleys and ridges was an excellent hideout for any force. The Kalinago people had used it to their advantage for some 200 years throughout the 16th and 17th centuries during the long offensive to hold on to their

An early 18th-century map of Dominica with an imagined interior

island delaying attempts by Spanish, French and British settlers to colonise it. Once again, in the 18th and 19th centuries, the luxuriant forests would offer protection.

Approaching the island from the sea in 1887, the

South coast of Dominica from the Martinique Channel

British historian James Anthony Froude contemplated the land mass that rose before him: 'Grenada, St Vincent, St Lucia, Martinique are all volcanic, with lofty peaks and ridges; but Dominica was at the centre of the force which lifted the Antilles out of the ocean, and the features which are common to all are there in a magnified form. The mountains being the tallest in all the group, the rains are also the most violent, and the ravines torn out by the torrents are the wildest and the most magnificent. The volcanic forces are still active here. There are sulphur springs and boiling water fountains, and in a central crater there is a boiling lake.'[1]

Froude's observations came many decades before geologists had fully accepted the theory that the earth's surface is composed of independent, slowly shifting tectonic plates, which move against each other creating uplifted mountain ranges and arcs of volcanic activity. Froude rightly suggested that Dominica was at the bow of the Caribbean tectonic plate 'at the centre of the force' thrusting up and outwards into the Atlantic Ocean. As a result, it is the most mountainous in the Caribbean chain and has the highest concentration of live volcanoes on earth. Nowhere else will you find an area of less than 300 square miles with nine live volcanic centres crowded together. A base of molten magma lies beneath the main volcanic domes that make up the backbone of the island with the northernmost, Morne Aux Diables, having a separate magma chamber.

Dominica rises sharply out of the sea. The east coast is hammered by the powerful ocean swells of the Atlantic. Here, constant erosion has carved out precipices interspersed with occasional coves and long beaches of black volcanic sand. These gaps between the towering walls of rock are swept by high waves and dangerous undercurrents that make the landing of boats well-nigh impossible. During the colonial period, the plantations on this windward coast were isolated and lacked proper communications by land or sea. Only here and there did the planters use shelves of rock as at Glacee near Boetica, or walls and a crane as at Rosalie, or the shelter of islets such as at Castle Bruce, to load and ship supplies and produce. Elsewhere, the boatmen counted the waves and then rowed their canoes frantically through the lowest swells to drive themselves up onto a beach, jumping out to secure their boats before the next wave came crashing behind them. Such were the landing places at Bout Sable and Plaisance Bay, La Plaine, or at Pointe Mulatre, Delices. As a result, east coast plantations were most prone to attacks by Maroons who descended in armed parties from their camps in the hills cornering the isolated settlements between an inhospitable ocean on one hand and impenetrable terrain on the other.

On the north-east side of the island, the coastline makes an abrupt turn to the west at Crompton Point. From there, all along the north coast, the bays and headlands face due north towards the French islands of Guadeloupe, Mariegalante and Les Saintes. Here the land slopes more gently and the bays are better protected so that several of these coves such as those at La Soye, Calibishie, Batibou and Anse Du Mai provide reasonable landing places for small craft. The favourable setting attracted wealthy British investors who established a line of large plantations comprising Blenheim, Hampstead, Hodges, Woodford Hill, Temple, Eden, Londonderry, Melville Hall, Governor and Hatton Garden, all served by streams to power their sugar mills. From the 1760s to the 1890s, sugar cane fields on these estates spread in a continuous undulating carpet from one end of the north coast to the other.

The west coast, in contrast, is sheltered from the Atlantic swells by the island itself. Precipitous cliffs also form most of the shoreline but the intermittent sandy bays and coves are well protected. This leeward coast was therefore the favoured zone for plantation settlement because it was more secure from natural and manmade threats. A visitor to one of these west coast estates in 1803 noted in a letter to a friend that 'the Estate is situated to the leeward of the Island and Managed at less Expense and Risque than a windward Plantation.'[2] The calm lee waters ensured that communication by sea between neighbouring estates and the main ports of Roseau and Portsmouth was easy.

During the 18th and 19th centuries the most productive sugar estates on the island occupied the narrow valleys along this coast while coffee was grown further inland at higher elevations where the climate was cooler and more moist. Cultivation petered out beyond 1500ft above sea level in most places. Behind this was uncharted territory. Early maps of the island left the interior as a vague space of imagined mountains and rumoured lakes. It was Terra Incognita. Until the first aerial photographs were taken in the 1950s Dominica's hinterland remained a mysterious place of forest spirits and luxuriant rain forest visited occasionally by hunters and woodcutters, builders of Kalinago canoes and commanded by people of African descent escaping their enslavement. The high rainfall and jagged landscape that provided little level ground for plantation agriculture and made road building difficult deterred the planters. Even when bridle tracks for horses and pack animals were constructed, the transportation of produce was hampered by landslides and flooded ravines. The Kalinagos even had a special phrase for this phenomena, *Tacoulouloútoni tóna*, the damage wrought by powerful rainstorms causing rivers to rise rapidly and overflow their banks stripping everything away before them, tossing giant boulders in a *bouleversement de roches* that reconfigures the landscape.[3]

Of even greater concern to the colonists during the years of slavery and marronage was the personal safety of the European occupants of any estates so far inland. During heightened Maroon activity such isolated estates were in the frontline of attack. Because of their close proximity to the Maroon camps the plantation managers and overseers were also the first to come under suspicion by Maroon leaders for having divulged information to the authorities about their location and movements. Death and destruction was the form of retribution for any of these suspects. Death threats and actual attacks were the methods by which the Maroons forced the abandonment of such estates. In doing so, they created a wider buffer zone between their camps and the larger and more secure plantations along the coast.

This harsh terrain ensured that 'Plantation Dominica' extended little more than two miles from the coast. This left thousands of acres in the interior, amounting to nearly two-thirds of the island, as untouched as it had been from before the time of Christopher Columbus. This was Maroon Country. It was a state within a state: an African state that existed within the colonial European state of coastal Dominica.

These forested highlands of Maroon Country have distinct geographical features. There are six main vegetation zones on Dominica from the seashore to the mountain tops but, botanically, Maroon Country was divided into the three highest zones: virgin rain forest rising into mossy montane

Maroon country: looking towards Morne Diablotin

thicket and eventually opening out onto craggy elfin woodland at the highest elevations. The last two types make up the cloud forest around the main mountain summits.

Maroon Country was dominated by six volcanic massifs: in the extreme south-east between Delices and Grand Bay, there is Morne Perdu Temps (referred to in the 18th century as Morne Paix Bouche). Moving north, there is a cluster of three peaks comprising Morne Anglais, Morne John and Morne Watt. To the east of this group are the

Grand Soufriere Hills including Mount Sinai and Morne Gouverneur overlooking Delices and La Plaine. Then comes the massive combination of Morne Micotrin and Morne Trois Pitons.

Between Trois Pitons and Morne Diablotin further north is the heart of Dominica, a wide gap made up of a maze of plateaus and river gorges that have been carved out of the 'welded tuff', the compacted debris from the eruptions of the two volcanoes. In this space stands Morne Laurent, better known as Morne 'Neg Mawon' (Maroon Mountain). The largest and most famous Maroon camps, such as Balla's Grand Camp, Jacko's camp, Fond Zombie and McFarlane camps were found in this zone. Morne Diablotin, the island's highest peak, rises to 4,747ft and it dominated the northern section of Maroon Country with encampments and hideouts recorded all around its flanks such as Gros Bois behind Melville Hall, Noel overlooking the north-west and another Morne 'Neg Mawon' overlooking Colihaut.

Then there is the northernmost massif of Morne Aux Diables rising to 2,826ft. This, however, did not see much Maroon activity because it was surrounded almost to its summit by the farms of French and free coloured smallholders. Besides, the western slopes of this mountain were in full view of, and in close proximity to, the large Cabrits Garrison, which at the height of its activity was manned by 700 soldiers. Similarly, in the south, the volcanic massif of Morne Plat Paye was not favoured by the Maroons because it was surrounded by the mainly French-owned coffee estates behind Pointe Michel, Soufriere, Bellevue Chopin, Geneva and Tete Morne.

To the European settler arriving on the island this vast interior was an untamed wilderness of 'nothing more interesting than trees' as the French priest Père Labat described it when he walked through it in 1700.[4] However, the indigenous Amerindians and, later, the African Maroons saw it as a storehouse of useful plants for medicine, food, shelter, boat building, bow-and-arrow fabrication, basket making and cultivation. The soils provided clays for pottery and the rivers supplied freshwater fish, crayfish, snails and crabs for the pot. Birds such as *ramyé* (scaly-naped pigeon, *Columba squamosa*) and *pedwi* (ruddy quail-dove, *Geotrygon mystacea montana*) were hunted with bow and arrow while the terrestrial agouti (*Dasyprocta antillensis*) and marsupial manicou (*Opossum didelphis marsupialis insularis*)[5] provided meat to go with provisions of wild yams. One British soldier, active in the forest during the Maroon conflicts, commented on the significance of the wild yam known as *wawa* or *ouaoua* (*Rajania sintenisii*) to the Maroon diet. 'This is one of the main victuals keeping them alive in the forest,' he noted irritably, 'without such sustenance they could be easily reduced.'[6] If one knew what to look for, and how to prepare it, Maroon Country in the high woods, referred to in Creole as *la gwan bwa*, provided the basics for survival.

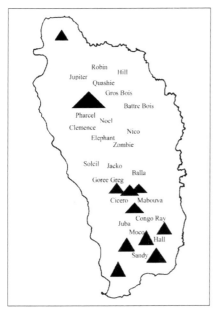

Known Maroon camps and chiefs (1763-1834).

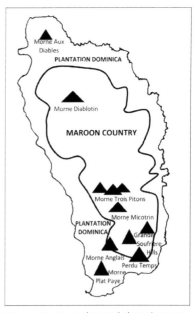

Maroon country and coastal plantation zones

3

The First Maroons:
the Kalinago foundation

It was dawn when the great canoes came over the east horizon, their bows rising and dipping with the swell and cutting through the crested waves, each vessel driven by huge white wings of cloth spread out before the power of the wind, all painted with the blood-red crosses of their sailors' faith. Peering through the thick foliage of the windswept littoral forest the islanders watched in awe as the strange craft came nearer to the coast.

Agile Kalinago youth ran along the precipitous cliff-side pathways that threaded up and over the rugged headlands jutting out into the Atlantic Ocean. Leaping over volcanic rocks and between the trees they kept pace with the 17 ships which skirted the inhospitable shoreline as if looking for a landing place. But there was no sheltered bay along this windward coast that was large or safe enough to accommodate such a fleet of caravels, and by noon the Kalinagos saw the seaborne apparition disappear northwards like a flock of low-flying pelicans towards the flat island of Aichi and mountainous Karoukera and perhaps even further on to Borenquin and Aiti.

Unknown to the Kalinagos as they watched the ships sail by that morning, their island, which they knew as Wai'tukubuli, had been claimed by the admiral of the fleet as the property of a distant king and queen and had been renamed in a foreign tongue for an alien god.

To the strangers aboard the caravels, in their reckoning of time, it was Sunday, 3 November 1493 when they approached the island that one of them described as 'all very mountainous, very beautiful and very green down to the water's edge'.[1] And with the self-confident ignorance characteristic of colonisers through the ages, they assumed this jumble of peaks rising out of a restless sea was nameless, or perhaps had a name unworthy of attention, so they christened it in Latin, *Dies Dominica*, for the Day of their Lord. Already the strangers had determined that the people of this newfound Dominica were called Caribees or Caribales or Cannibals; but for many years the Kalinagos were unaware of this new identity that had been thrust upon them. Some time went by before they saw such ships again but by then news had already reached them of the pillage, fire and killing wrought by these pale hairy strangers covered in shells of metal that reflected the sun. It was Taino refugees, fleeing massacre and enslavement on the larger islands, who brought them news of this greed-fed madness driven by a thirst for the shining yellow metal found among the rocks and streams of the Greater Antilles.

———————

From the time of Columbus' arrival, the Amerindian islanders put up a spirited resistance to colonisation and enslavement. Spanish raiders swept through the flatter more accessible islands of the Lesser Antilles from about 1503 to near the end of the century. They were armed with guns, swords and hunting dogs and with declarations or *cedulas* and *requerimientos* issued by the joint Spanish monarchy of Isabella of Castile and Ferdinand of Aragon. These edicts permitted Spanish colonists to seize all natives on the islands south of Puerto Rico as far as Trinidad; to wage war upon, enslave and sell duty free any Kalinagos 'because the inhabitants of those islands are given as slaves for their resistance to Christians and because they are said to eat human flesh'.[2] This propaganda was begun by Columbus based on mis-information received from the Tainos of the Greater Antilles during his first voyage; it was used to justify Kalinago enslavement and massacre by perpetrating a slander that was to hound the Kalinagos for centuries. The captured Amerindians were taken to the slave markets of San Juan, Hispaniola and Cuba and forced to work in mines and on haciendas and were put to dive for pearls off the islands of Margarita and Los Roches along the Caribbean coast of South America. The Spanish objective was not merely to procure slave labour but also to clear the islands of what they saw as dangerous neighbours.

Many Tainos and Kalinagos simply died of disease, that invisible, unintended weapon brought from Europe in the form of smallpox and measles. Disease often travelled ahead of the raids, carried unknowingly by natives who had been in contact with Spaniards. In this way, whole communities of indigenous people fell victim before the conquistadors' actual arrival in their villages to inflict the coup de grace.

Thanks to the topography of Dominica (and St Vincent to the south), the Kalinagos could retreat into the mountains from where they resisted Spanish slave raiders. Their Kalinago ancestors had named this island for its mountainous terrain, first seen rising steeply out of the ocean as they had approached it on their way up the Lesser Antilles from South America. Raymond Breton, the 17th-century French missionary, recorded the name as Ouáitoucoubouli, composed of the words *ouaitúmti*: it is tall; *nócoubou*: my body; *li*: her or, in the modern version, Wai'tukubuli: 'tall is her body'.

As early as 1499 the Kalinagos of Ouyouhao (today's Prince Rupert's Bay in northern Dominica) launched a furious attack on a landing party led by Admiral Alonso de Ojeda that included Amerigo Vespucci, after whom the Americas was named. So significant was this experience that it was recorded in an engraving by the foremost illustrator of Spanish

Kalinagos and European seafarers meet

17

conquest Theodore De Bry. The Kalinagos' guerrilla-style warfare, waged in a familiar landscape, gave them every advantage. 'They shoot so quickly that they can loose ten or a dozen arrows in the time it takes to load a gun,' commented one observer.[3] In any case the Spaniards quickly found out that enslaving a Kalinago was a tough and largely unrewarding business. Numerous Kalinagos escaped and made their way back to their islands strengthened in their resolve not to make any concessions to Europeans.[4]

The Kalinagos developed a robust disrespect for the Christian crucifix which they saw as a symbol of Spanish cruelty. As late as the 1690s the Kalinagos of southern Dominica repeatedly destroyed any cross raised upon their land. The French priest and adventurer Père Jean Baptiste Labat also noted that although the Kalinagos felt that crucifixes in their huts would sometimes protect them from evil spirits they could also cause them bad luck in hunting and fishing. In such cases, he reported, 'They will then burn the cross and smash it to pieces.'[5]

Mariners who landed at Dominica took the precaution of being well armed because of the unpredictability of the reception by the Kalinagos. Some reports spoke of spirited attacks with showers of arrows from the islanders while sailors were drawing barrels of water from the rivers. Other accounts indicated no action at all except for an ominous silence broken only by the rustling of trees in the wind. English accounts from the late 16th century, particularly those of Sir Francis Drake, George Clifford 3rd Earl of Cumberland and Sir Anthony Shirley, gave reports of peaceful trading with

Admiral Ojeda and crew, including Amerigo Vespucci, land on Dominica, 1499, and meet resistance from Kalinagos. (Theodore de Bry)

the Kalinagos, who by that time had become increasingly dependent on European trade goods, particularly iron tools and cotton cloth.

In 1700, during an expedition to visit the Kalinagos and explore the wild eastern side of Dominica, Père Labat noted their passion for liberty: 'There are no people in the world so jealous of their liberty, or who resent more the smallest check on their freedom. They laugh at us for obeying and respecting our rulers, and say we must be their slaves, and that since we allow them to give us orders we must also be cowards... Our Caribs... have always been a bellicose people, who are proud and indomitable, and prefer death to slavery'.[6] During this visit to the island, Labat estimated the number of Kalinagos in Dominica to be no more than 2,000 'and of these, two thirds are women and children'.

Labat is also an important voice in defending the Kalinagos against the accusation of cannibalism: 'It is a mistake to believe that the savages of our islands are cannibals, or that they go to war for the express purpose of capturing prisoners in order to devour them. I have proofs to the contrary clearer than day.'[7] They did, however, keep smoked body parts preserved in their huts as trophies of victory to excite raiding parties prior to their departure and to strike fear into their enemies. The fact that this practice was talked about, exaggerated and repeated down the centuries proves the effectiveness of it as a fear tactic that made Europeans hesitate to go among the Kalinagos.

Cultural exchange

Nevertheless, long before the actual colonisation of the island by Europeans, an intriguing collection of different nationalities and ethnic groups was to be found in Kalinago villages during the late 16th and early 17th centuries. There were Africans who had travelled back with Kalinago seafarers after their raids on neighbouring islands or European deserters from ships that had stopped briefly in Dominica to refresh their crews. Others had escaped from slavery or indenture on plantations as far away as Puerto Rico. A few were survivors of shipwrecks. This form of marronage was not peculiar to Dominica. At the Cape of Gracias à Dios on the Spanish Main there were Africans living among the Amerindians who had landed from a shipwreck; these Africans 'being bound for Terra Firma in a ship that carried them to be sold in those parts, they killed the Captain and mariners, with design to return unto their country. But, through their ignorance in marinery, they stranded their vessel hereabouts.'[8] A shipwreck of Africans on the shores of Bequia in the Grenadines in the 1640s and slaves escaping by boat from Barbados later in that century created a similar situation in St Vincent.

In 1569 it was estimated that there were more than 30 Spaniards and 40 Africans living among the Kalinagos in the vicinity of Ouyouhao. Among them was an African woman called Luisa de Navarette, who was captured by Kalinago raiders during an attack on Puerto Rico in 1576 and brought to Dominica where she lived for four years. She was picked up by a passing Spanish ship, taken back to Puerto Rico, and there recounted her experiences to the Bishop of San Juan in 1580 giving details of her life with the Kalinagos and recalling the language and customs that she had adopted.[9]

While new colonies were being settled to the north and south of the island by English, French and Dutch investors, Dominica continued to stand green and defiant in the centre of the chain of the Lesser Antilles. Enslaved Africans shipped across the Atlantic to work the cane fields and sugar factories on these new settlements risked their lives to escape across the sea towards the mountainous island on the horizon as colonisation intensified after 1625 when the English adventurer Sir Thomas Warner established a colony in St Kitts, henceforth described to generations of schoolchildren across the region as 'the mother colony of the British West Indies'.

One of the earliest English writers on the Caribbean, John Davies, translating the observations made by the Frenchman Charles de Rochefort, noted the increasing number of Africans among the Kalinagos during the following century: 'In Dominico… there are some

Caribs who have many Negroes as slaves… Some of them they got from the English Plantations and some from the Spanish ships heretofore cast away on their coasts, and they are called Tamons, that is Slaves: they are so well ordered, that they serve them in all things about which they are employed, with as much obedience, readiness and respect as if they were the most civilised people in the world'.[10]

This description of Africans as serving as 'slaves' to the Kalinagos is now disputed. Judging from other literature it is more likely that the Kalinagos were incorporating this other ethnic group into their kinship system for the survival of both.[11] Certainly, the Amerindians passed on much of their knowledge of the island environment and survival techniques to the Africans. From their word for the colour black *tiboulou*, they called the Africans *tiboulotie* in the men's language and *meguerou* in the women's language.[12] The latter word may have been influenced by the Spanish, *negro*, since they were first aware of them in the company of Spanish soldiers and sailors, although they may have been in contact with Africans who made it across the Atlantic before

Columbus.[13] As the Kalinagos observed the ethnic mix taking place between Africans and Europeans in the early years of colonisation, they gave their own name, *cachionna*, to 'a child born of a white man and a black woman'.[14]

The Kalinago names of places, plants and animals survive today thanks to the 16th and

Early Maroons adapted their West African forest traditions to the island environment

17th century period of contact and cultural exchange; and in the 21st century Dominicans remain the greatest users of Kalinago words in the world. Their speech is filled with references to Kalinago place names such as Colihaut, Calibishie, Coulibistrie, Bataka, Batali, Salybia and Boeri. They also refer, for example, to *cirique* and *touloulou* (crabs), *acouma*, *balata* and *coubari* (trees), *zanana*, *cashima*, *cowossol* and *zicaque* (fruit), *yen-yen* and *ariri* (insects), *sibouli*, *vivaneau*, *balaou*, *couliou*, *titiwi* (fish), *batu*, *cali*, *canáoa* (fishing equipment) and even the national bird, the sisserou.

Much research has been done on the Creole languages of the colonial period that developed from a mixture of European and African languages. However, except for the work of the British linguist Douglas Taylor, there has been very little investigation into the Kalinago loan words adopted in pre-colonial Dominica.[15] The Africans who arrived among the Kalinagos came from a wide variety of West African language groups. If they had arrived in Dominica before the 1690s, the basis for communication would have been through the Kalinago language. The strange new places, plants and animals were introduced to them by the Kalinagos using the pre-Columbian Arawakan names.[16] With the commencement of plantation slavery on the island in the early 18th century, the Africans who were already in Dominica passed on these words to the ever-increasing number of new arrivals coming off the slave ships. French woodcutters, white indentured labourers and army deserters among them would have picked up those names as well.

Unlike the other island states in the Lesser Antilles, the pre-Columbian Kalinago contribution to the Creole culture of Dominica remains extremely strong. It was the 19th-century British author and traveller Anthony Trollope, who most succinctly summarised the meaning of Creole while on a voyage through the islands in the 1850s: 'It should be understood that a Creole is a person born in the West Indies of a race not indigenous to the islands. There may be white Creoles, coloured Creoles, or black Creoles. People talk of Creole horses and Creole poultry; namely those which have not themselves been imported, but which have been bred from imported stock.'[17] He could have added music, dance, language, food and architecture, but even as he wrote the extended use of the word was still evolving. Spawned during the early period of contact and culture exchange in the

Caribbean the process of 'creolisation' went from strength to strength.

In Dominica it had its roots in the early process of contact and cultural exchange that was taking place as West Africans adapted their continental experience to the more compact tropical island world of the Kalinagos. This interaction between two alienated groups was evolving a form of creolisation on the periphery of European influence. It is true that the Kalinagos were already adopting Spanish and Portuguese loan words into their language such as *boulatta* for *plata* (silver) and *cábrara* for *capra* (goat) as well as trading cassava and tobacco for useful European goods.[18] Similarly, the African arrivals had also been open to various European influences on the 'slave coast', the Middle Passage and during their brief plantation experience. But once together on the island the cross-cultural interaction was essentially between each other.

The Kalinagos must have soon recognised the diversity of societies and class hierarchies among the new African settlers. Roman Catholic missionaries in the French colonies at the time had already recorded 13 different African language groups in the neighbouring islands and a similar variety would have been present in Dominica.[19] As the years progressed, traces of African languages, such Yoruba, Twi, Ewe, Fon, Ibo, Ibibo, Nembe, Ashanti, Kru, Wolof and several others, survived in the island's Creole culture.[20] Clues to these connections have lingered in a word here, a song pattern there, or a character of the spirit world whose African roots had survived. The name of the popular delicacy, the *titiwi accra*, for instance, is composed of the Kalinago word *titiwi* for the small river fish (*Sicydium punctatum*) and the Yoruba àkàrà (a fried bean-cake). It is symbolic of the cross cultural linkages that took place between Africans and Amerindians during the two centuries prior to formal European colonisation.

4

The neutral island: creating a Maroon base

A fleet of some ten dugout canoes, each bearing 20 Kalinago paddlers and supporters landed on the long, grey, sandy beach in front of the fledgling town of Basseterre, the main settlement on St Kitts called Liamuiga by the Amerindians. They had come from as far as St Vincent, the island that they still knew as Yurumei, and had been joined on their way by islanders from Wai'tukubuli. The Kalinagos had been drawn to Liamuiga by the news that one of their main patrons, Phillipe de Lonvilliers de Poincy, governor general of the Compagnie de Sainte Christophe, was dying and that before he departed this world he wished to make a treaty to protect the last Amerindians on the islands. Leaving their canoes on the beach, they began to walk up the long gentle slope towards de Poincy's baroque chateau in the hills above Basseterre. The band of 200 Kalinagos on the move attracted the stares of enslaved Africans bent in labour among the fields of cotton, tobacco and the newly introduced sugar cane, which grew in a lush carpet from the hilltops down to the seashore. When the Kalinagos reached de Poincy's chateau, a small group of French and English settlers was waiting on the terrace to guide them into the presence of the great man. At the end of a large, marble-tiled hall sat de Poincy propped up by damask pillows in a large armchair. Weakly, he raised his silver-headed staff and beckoned the assembled company towards the table in front of him.

I t was 31 March 1660. This Treaty of St Christopher signed between the English, French and marked with tribal icons and symbols by 15 of the most prominent Kalinago chiefs declared that the islands of Dominica and St Vincent were designated as 'Neutral Islands' not to be occupied by any European power, but to be left to the Kalinago people forever. Within a few days de Poincy was dead, breathing his last on 11 April 1660. Eight years later, on 3 January 1668, another treaty, agreed aboard a ship anchored in the harbour of Charlestown, Nevis, reconfirmed this. On deck as witnesses were the governor of the English Caribbees, Lord Francis Willoughby, and his French counterpart, Joseph de la Barre, governor of the French Isles of America, in the presence of Kalinago representatives from Dominica and St Vincent. In the following century the Treaty of Aix La Chapelle of 1748 reinforced the terms of neutrality.

On one level it was an idealistic project aimed at saving the 'disappearing other', in this case the Kalinagos, and it was influenced by the philosophical theories current at the time. Various concepts of people living in 'a state of nature' were being discussed by the greatest minds in Europe. There were conflicting views based on the arguments raised mainly by Thomas Hobbes (1588-1679) and John Locke (1632-1704). This would later lead to the philosophy of Jean-Jacques Rousseau (1712-1778) who advocated that man in a state of nature is a 'noble savage' and that civilisation is the corrupter and destroyer of true values. In arguing his case, Rousseau used the Kalinagos living in tune with nature on the islands as examples of this theory. He had studied descriptions of the Kalinagos of the French Antilles in the books of Jean Baptiste Du Tertre, superior of the mission of the Dominican Order based in Guadeloupe, to come to his conclusions contained in his 'Discourse on the Origins and foundations of Inequality among Men'.[1]

However, there were other reasons for declaring these islands neutral. The earliest treaties coincided with the introduction of the sugar cane industry to the eastern Caribbean from the 1650s. Prices for sugar were good and many planters in the 'old colonies' of St Kitts,

Nevis, Antigua, Montserrat, Martinique, Guadeloupe and Barbados thought that if more islands were taken and opened up to sugar plantations, there would be a glut on the market and their sugar revenues would fall. The supporters of the neutrality agreements also had their eyes on the security of the islands in the neighbourhood and felt that by consigning the islands to the Kalinagos and leaving them in peace the sugar colonies would be safe from attack and the days of surprise raids and the destruction of settlements would be over.

In the midst of all this emerges the early Dominican patriot 'Carib' or 'Indian' Warner. Officially, his name was Thomas Warner. Born in St Kitts, he was the son of the English colonist Sir Thomas Warner and a Kalinago woman called Barbè originally from Dominica. Young Thomas grew up in his father's house along with his English stepmother, Rebecca, and his English half-brothers, Philip and Edward. However, on the death of his father in 1648 Thomas was banished from the Warner household by his new stepmother, Anne, Sir Thomas's second wife. Taking this rejection as a deep and lasting insult (in a manner that the Amerindians of the islands were famous for), he retreated to live among his mother's people on the west coast of Dominica.

There, at Boeri, in the area known today as Canefield and Massacre, Carib Warner settled and adopted the ways of the Kalinagos and rose to be their chief. With his accession to this position the neighbouring European colonisers now had a formidable foe. He was one of the most unusual characters of the 17th-century Caribbean. This young man, a mixture of European and Kalinago, had grown up surrounded by the elite of French and English colonial power in the region. As a result, he had an intimate knowledge of the ways and the languages of both these European tribes. Each side actively wooed his friendship, scheming to engineer their influence over him and thereby their control over Dominica. Neither nation was quite sure of his allegiance: 'he was a Carib first and last.'[2] Carib Warner played them as good as he got: turning a blind eye when his warriors raided the fledgling English settlements of Antigua and Montserrat, manipulating a French attack on St Lucia, playing cat and mouse to ensure that Dominica would survive against the tide of colonisation as a virtually independent Kalinago state.

When a new English governor, Francis Willoughby, 5th Baron Willoughby of Parham, was sent out to Barbados in 1663 he was given instructions by the court at Whitehall, London, as to how to 'treat with the natives'. On 16 June that year, along with other directives, he was given 'Power to treat with the natives, especially those of St Vincent and Dominica, or if injurious or contentious, to pursue them fire and sword.'[3] Willoughby chose the path of diplomacy. He offered Carib Warner the position of lieutenant governor of Dominica on behalf of England. This he accepted thereby shielding his people from that enemy while he could concentrate on engaging the French. However, the English in the Leeward Islands, particularly his half-brother Philip in Antigua, did not agree with the Barbadian tactic of peace and cooperation. As far as the Antiguans were concerned it was all very well for Bridgetown to be so magnanimous but Barbados was over 100 miles away to windward safe from any attacks whereas Antigua and the Leeward Islands were close enough to Dominica to be in constant danger. Indeed, the Kalinago raids against Antigua, Barbuda and Montserrat continued. The English also had cause to complain of the Kalinago alliance with the Maroons, for the governor of Antigua, William Stapleton, reported to London that of the 1,500 Kalinagos active against the colonists, some 600 were African bowmen.[4]

Several Englishmen were killed, pioneer settlements were burned and their women and children were seized and taken back to Dominica as hostages. In response, the English in Antigua led by Philip Warner planned to end Carib Warner's designs for an idealistic Kalinago utopia once and for all.

In late 1674, Philip led a raiding party to Indian Warner's village at Boeri. Feigning friendship, he invited the chief and his men to come on board his sailing ship for a party. At the height of the feasting, with most of the Kalinagos senseless with rum, Philip slit his half-brother's throat as the signal to commence an attack. After killing all of the Kalinagos on board, Philip and his motley gang went ashore, massacring the villagers, raping women and children and burning homes and canoes. The French, ever ready to give the English bad publicity, christened the site of the village, Massacre, the name that survives to this day. An earlier French massacre of Kalinagos at Anse du Mai in 1635 gets little attention.

The assassination of Carib Warner did little to stop the Kalinago raids on the Leeward Islands which continued into the 1680s. But it did rob the Kalinagos of an exceptional leader. It is probable that Carib Warner would have helped ensure that Dominica did in fact remain a neutral territory outside of the colonial scramble that was intensifying around it. By then, however, it was not only the Kalinago presence with which the Europeans would have to contend. Dominica and St Vincent had become free zones for African refugees fleeing the increasing number of sugar plantations in the region. The Kalinagos were one thing, but to have an island refuge for escaped African slaves in the midst of what was fast becoming an extensive slave zone stretching from Brazil to North America, was a completely different state of affairs in the eyes of the European colonists.

The Kalinagos of Dominica were already trading on the fringes of the plantation system taking local produce across the sea channels in their canoes and selling it in the towns and villages on the neighbouring French islands. They caught the edible *crapaud* (frogs) or 'mountain chicken' as well as land crabs and traded these delicacies, along with cassava flour and other food stuffs, and items such as baskets and canoes in exchange for knives, cutlasses, axes and hoes, tools that were much in demand among them.

After 1650, forests on the other islands were increasingly cleared to plant sugar cane and to obtain wood to burn as fuel in the boiling houses that produced the sugar and rum. The French government forbade their countrymen in Dominica to grow and process sugar cane. Not only did they want to stem any competition in the market, but more importantly, sugar processing required serious investment in buildings, machinery and labour. It was not advisable to put that kind of money into sugar when the island was technically neutral and its European ownership was sure to become the subject of future dispute. Soon the planters of Martinique and Guadeloupe were running out of accessible forests near the coasts on their own islands and they needed wood for timber and fuel for their sugar boiling houses. It was seen as cheaper to deforest the coast of Dominica than to trek further inland on

Mural by Dominican artist Earl Etienne on a wall in Massacre depicts the site of the assassination of 'Carib' Warner in 1764

29

their own islands to obtain supplies of lumber and firewood. As a result, lumberjacks arrived on Dominica to negotiate with the Kalinagos for rights to cut and ship wood in exchange for tools, mirrors, scissors, cloth and casks of rum.

The woodcutters and timber merchants brought African slaves with them to help cut and saw wood. The timber works were basic campsites of thatched huts and Kalinago *ajoupas* and in the circumstances it was easy for slaves to escape into the bush. In fact, when marauding privateers threatened to raid their camps the timber men actually encouraged their slaves to run away temporarily on *petit marronage* so that they would not be captured and taken aboard ship as booty. The enslaved Africans were the only pieces of their 'property' that could move on their own to escape seizure but often the Africans never returned. To disappear on *petit marronage* was to escape for a short period with the intention of returning to the saw mill or to the plantation. To go on a *grand marronage* was to leave with the intention that the escape would be permanent, withdrawing one's labour, creating a loss to the 'master' on his investment in purchase money, disrupting plantation production and seeking long-term liberation.

With Dominica nominally a Neutral Island under the control of the Kalinagos, both the English and French competed for woodcutting rights among the Amerindians. As a result there was much tension between the three groups and it was made more confusing because the Kalinagos of the east coast more often sided with the French whereas those on the west coast sided more with the English. When some French prospectors shifted from timber working to farming at the end of the 17th century there were an unknown number of African Maroons living in Kalinago villages or in their own camps in the mountains. Often they camped in the forest singly rather than in groups as in one case in 1657 when hunters reported that they had come across an *'Ajoupa d'un Negre Fugitif'*, a lean-to hut in the Kalinago style, in which they found cassava, potatoes, calabashes with food and water and a fire; an example of the cultural exchange that was taking place as a result of the contact between Africans and Kalinagos.[5] Not only did they cultivate self-sufficient farms in the forest but the Africans also became involved in trading produce and canoes with the French islands so much so that the Council in Martinique issued a decree that trading with African Maroons on Dominica was a criminal offence.

It is clear that the treaties of neutrality for Dominica that were intended to protect the Kalinagos actually created a distinct advantage for the Maroons, providing them with a 100-year period, from 1660 to 1761, to establish a strong base on the island while its neighbours were being transformed by colonisation.

5
The first plantations: Jeannot Rolle at Grand Bay

The canoe could barely be seen in the middle of the channel. It was an unpainted wooden dugout with six Kalinago paddlers spread out amidships. In the stern was the *gouverneur*, the man controlling a large paddle by the same name who steered the vessel. In front of him was an awning made of bent saplings and woven palm thatch to provide shelter from the sun. Sitting in the shade was Jeannot Rolle, a man of African descent dressed in a well-worn French-style suit common in the 1690s: beige breeches, a stained white shirt with ample sleeves and a blue waistcoat trimmed in gold braid. Secured firmly on his head and tied under his chin with string against the wind was a black tri-cornered hat bedecked with two faded ostrich feathers. The canoe and its passenger and crew appeared and disappeared on the crests and troughs of the Atlantic swells that swept through the Martinique Channel. Ahead stood Dominica, Point Tanama and the bay of Berricoa. The *gouverneur* set his paddle for the landing place in the lee of Point Ouyacala, now known as Pointe Carib. As the bow touched the narrow beach, the Kalinagos leaped into the surf and held the canoe steady so that the African could step easily onto dry land. Chief Ouraragan of the Berricoa region was awaiting him and they greeted each other as old friends.

J eannot Rolle was the first person to establish a permanent plantation on Dominica and to import enslaved Africans to work. He was a free black man or, as the French records have it, *un negre libre* from Martinique. This is unique in the Caribbean. The Martiniquais historian Professor Léo Elisabeth stresses the point that Dominica was the only plantation colony in the Americas to be established by a black man.[1] This set the tone for the internal tensions on the island between whites, free people of colour, enslaved blacks and the Maroons that dominated its social history. As whites departed the island in increasing numbers following economic depression caused by coffee blight and the decline of the sugar industry in the 19th century, a tense relationship developed between the emergent coloured elite and the black working class; this lingered on well after emancipation and even into the political machinations of the late 20th century.

Map of Grand Bay (1765) shows Jesuit plantation

Martinique had been claimed and colonised by France in 1635. It immediately started to develop all the social and economic trappings of a fledgling Caribbean dependency dominated by the European metropolis. Plantations began to spread along the west coast, while the east coast was briefly set aside as an area reserved for the indigenous Kalinago islanders. An administrative and commercial centre was established at St Pierre on the north-west coast. French settlers and their white indentured labourers, *les engagés*, who had signed their lives over to a master for five to ten years, arrived to carve out plantations. The slave ships began to sail in from Africa and disgorge their human cargoes.[2]

By the end of the century, the Kalinagos of Martinique had been pushed out of the windward side, the *côte au vent*, and those who did not integrate themselves into the periphery of the colonial society retreated to Dominica. Africans escaping slavery in Martinique soon followed them across the channel after the French settlers, led by Governor Du Parquet, made an agreement with the Kalinagos on Martinique on 28 October 1657 in respect of their relationship with '*les Negres Marron*'. After an exchange of gifts it was agreed that hostilities between the French and Kalinagos would end on condition that they no longer harboured escaped slaves.[3] The alternative for the African fugitives on Martinique was to make the perilous journey towards the towering green island on the northern horizon.

With the east coast of Martinique secured, coffee and sugar plantations soon fringed the entire island and French colonisation moved into top gear with all of the social and ethnic changes that came with it. Mulatto children were being born as French planters and indentured servants, whether by rape or consent, had sex with female African slaves. (As Gordon Lewis points out, in a very real sense the history of the Caribbean slave regime is the history of the sexual exploitation of black women.[4]) At the same time, a handful of enslaved Creole Africans, born on the island and Christianised by Roman Catholic missionaries, gained their freedom. Jeannot Rolle was one of those and he appears to have been closely associated with the Jesuit priests at their mission in St Pierre. It was the Jesuits, the first

'Petits blancs' French settlers

missionary order to settle in the French West Indies – arriving in Martinique in 1640 – who started the first sugar plantation there, and by 1650 they had become the second largest slaveholder on the island. So important is Jeannot Rolle and the Jesuits to the development of marronage and the course of Dominica's early history that it is important to go into some detail about this enterprise.

Rolle was born in St Pierre in 1661 and as a young man he was operating as a wood-worker and tradesman along the north coast of Martinique across the channel from Dominica. He developed a friendly relationship with the Kalinago people who came across from the Berricoa Grande Baie area in their canoes to trade with plantations. Rolle learned their language and gradually gained the esteem of their chief, Ouraragan, who invited him to make a trip across the channel to visit Dominica in 1691. While at Grande Baie he got permission from Ouraragan to make canoes and cut timber for sale in Martinique.

He returned to Dominica soon afterwards and many years later he gave an account of his pioneering adventure to a Jesuit priest who wrote it all down.[5] 'When I landed at Grande Baie, which was a complete forest without any habitations except for those of the Caribs, which were twenty to thirty families thereabouts... they permitted me to work on constructing two canoes with my two slaves... and they helped me to get wood and to drag the timber to the coast with the help of taffia [raw rum].'

The sale of the canoes in Martinique was profitable and Rolle was able to purchase some more slaves 'to assist with the work at my chantier [saw pit].' He returned to Grand Bay and eventually made an agreement with Ouraragan to set up a base for small-scale timber production. 'After about a year I was a bit more confident with the Caribs and I got their permission to bring my wife and my little family from Martinique and also permission to build "une Grande Carbette" like theirs for my family and I proposed to them that they sell me 14 or 15 "carres" of land.'

Chief Ouraragan agreed to the request but on two conditions: no crucifix to be erected and no horned cattle to be imported. The agreement of sale was certified on a piece of paper 'upon which they painted bows and arrows and *"quelques autre barbonillage"* using roucou dye [red] and guinipa fruit [black].' However, Rolle was a very religious man with a firm belief that he was being guided in his enterprise by 'the Holy Spirit'. In defiance of the Kalinagos' wishes he erected a stout wooden cross but this was burned down along with his *'grande carbette'* and all his belongings, the remains of which were tossed into the sea. 'The Caribs saw my cross as a victory of the Christian faith and made war on my settlement and to save myself I had to hide in the woods with my family and slaves.'

The attacks were repeated every time Rolle sought to erect a new cross, including one made from the trunk of a lépini tree (*Zanthoxylum caribaeum*) and covered with large thorns that were used in the corners of wooden houses to, it was believed, keep out evil spirits.[6] 'Every time I made a new cross I made them stronger and stronger,' Rolle boasted. As the conflict continued, he fortified his little plantation compound with wooden palisades and defended it with the help of his armed slaves. Eventually he directed his men to produce a stone cross chiselled out from a single rock and measuring seven feet and '11 ponces' wide.

He further angered the Kalinagos by defying the second point of their land agreement when he brought oxen from Martinique to haul the finished product, which he placed on a low hill 225 paces from where it was made. Every so often, the Kalinagos would launch a token attack against it and fire arrows at his cattle. But it still stands overlooking the cemetery at Grand Bay.[7] It is also the oldest surviving symbol of Christianity in Dominica. Jeannot Rolle died in 1753 at the age of 92 and was buried at the foot of his cross.

By 1715, the French poor whites of Martinique and Guadeloupe, made up of smallholders and *les engagés*, who together were generally referred to as *les petits blancs*, were also crossing the sea channels to seek opportunities on Dominica. The expansion of sugar plantations on the French islands were pushing them off their smallholdings and the arrival of enslaved African labour in ever increasing numbers was reducing the unemployed white servants to destitution, so much so that some of them in Martinique mounted a revolt called '*la Gaoulé*'. Commenting on the situation some years later, the British governor, Sir William Young, observed that, 'It is well known that many of the present inhabitants [of Dominica] who were driven thither by poverty and necessity are now become, from the lowest degree of indigence, possessors of good estates; and it is notorious that by far the greater number of French now inhabiting Dominica, and possessed of plantations and negroes, were obliged to quit Martinique and Guadeloupe from similar causes.'[8]

Shortly after erecting his stone cross, Rolle appealed to the superior of the Jesuit Order in Martinique, Fr Antoine La Valette, to come over and bless his 'Belle Croix' as it became known. He also offered the Jesuits part of his estate to start a mission in a bid to convert the neighbouring Kalinagos to Christianity. The mission soon became a cover for the establishment of a plant-

Jeannot Rolle's cross, Grand Bay

ation worked by the first significant numbers of enslaved Africans to be imported, estimated at about 200 strong. They were purchased in Barbados and landed at what became known as Les Jesuits in 1749 being put to work clearing land, planting tea, indigo, coffee and cocoa. Soon the Order was plunged into financial and political disgrace in France and was suppressed in 1764. Three years later the Jesuits were expelled from the French mainland and its colonies, and the plantation at Grand Bay was sold to English creditors.

From the 1720s major changes had been taking place in Dominica as the number of French settlers increased and the community became more organised. With the astounding rise in profits from the sale of sugar by the end of the 17th century, greedy eyes were now turning towards the uncolonised Caribees. Equally covetous of these Kalinago homelands were the British in Barbados and the Leeward Islands. As the pressure for Britain to capture and take over the Neutral Islands intensified, a small section of the Barbadian plantocracy lobbied for them to be left in their 'natural state' arguing their case in terms of 'protecting' the indigenous people. 'Savage as they are, they understand that there can be no room for Indians to hunt, or ramble, where canes are planted. It will surely prevail to suffer [to let] the

Native Caribbeans to live and enjoy peaceable the districts that they have reserved unto themselves.'[9] But this statement may not be as sincere as it first appears. The planter who wrote it, to the Secretary of State in London, may have just been using another tactic to persuade the British to leave the Neutral Islands alone for economic reasons so as to maintain the dominance of the Barbados sugar trade.

However, by the 1750s the sugar producers on the older colonies realised that the demand for the commodity in Europe was growing to a point where their earlier fear of a glut and drop in price was unfounded. Besides, the fresh fertile soils of Dominica, St Vincent and Tobago could make up for the exhausted soils of the old colonies where sugar cane had sapped its nutrients for more than 100 years. Dominica was seen as a tempting piece of real estate just waiting for exploitation. It was the view of many potential colonists that settlement of the island was being prevented by treaties of neutrality whose terms were impossible to impose and police. All this for the sake of an estimated 800 indigenous occupants who had been joined by escaped Africans and some renegade whites who had 'gone native' and were living among the Kalinagos in their scattered villages along the coast.

The arguments in favour of maintaining certain islands as neutral and those against caused deep divisions between the idealists in Europe and the plantation society in the Caribbean. (Such a division would recur later in the century between those in Britain calling for the abolition of the slave trade and those on the ground in the Caribbean campaigning to maintain the commerce in human beings.) In 1730 the French and English governments agreed that they should call for the official evacuation of all their nationals from Dominica to fulfil the terms of neutrality. But when agents of both nations went among the small scattered settlements of their compatriots to read the declarations of evacuation few of the settled lumbermen paid any attention. The French increasingly continued to woo Kalinago friendship and became even more brazen as the woodcutters gradually became permanent settlers. The Treaty of Aix la Chapelle, at the end of the War of Jenkins's

Ear and the War of the Austrian Succession in 1748, once again declared that Dominica was neutral. But regardless of what was decided by officials in their palaces across the Atlantic Ocean, on the ground in La Dominique, the French were digging in for the long term.

Another call for evacuation in 1751 fell on deaf ears for even as the official agents were reading out the declaration they saw that French settlers had constructed a secure little fort on the hill behind Roseau. It was a small battery mounted with three nine-pounder cannons surrounded by a stone wall the height of a man. On a hill even higher above, on what is now called Morne Bruce, one leading settler called

Louis Robert de Longpré had constructed a well-built house and a platform in front of it facing the sea. On this he had mounted four new nine-pounder cannons and a store of ammunition.

During this hiatus most of the slaves on the Jesuit plantation in Grand Bay took the opportunity to escape into the surrounding mountains. The exodus increased when the British captured Dominica in 1761 and officially took over administration of the colony in 1763. Numerous Maroon camps were established during that two-year

Free people of colour in Dominica
(Agostino Brunias)

hiatus as the island changed hands. Colonial security was lax and the enslaved labourers were wary of what treatment they would receive under new foreign owners. The British settler, planter, magistrate and historian Thomas Atwood suggests that the move from French to British control at Les Jesuits and the wider shift from casual small-scale settlement to industrial plantation agriculture was the main reason for the upsurge of marronage. 'Many of the negroes purchased from the Jesuits, either as an attachment to them or dislike to their new masters, soon after betook themselves to the woods with their wives and children, where they were joined from time to time by others from different estates. There they secreted themselves for a number of years, formed companies under different chiefs, built good houses and planted gardens in the woods, where they raised poultry, hogs, and other small stock, which, with what the sea, rivers, and woods afforded, and what they got from the negroes they had intercourse with on the plantations, they lived very comfortably, and were seldom disturbed in their haunts.'[10]

The Maroons had not yet taken to attacking settlements and using weapons for these were not easy to obtain, and the initial period of transfer posed little threat to their freedom. But within a decade there was a radical change in the situation as the building of forts and coastal batteries, an increase of troops based in purpose-built garrisons, the introduction of sugar cane cultivation and the consequent importation of Africans on a much larger scale meant that Maroon activity took a new turn. For the British, it was a repeat of their experience in Jamaica just over 100 years before when, following their capture of the island from Spain in 1655, the slaves on the small scattered Spanish haciendas took to the hills and formed a crucible of resistance which grew into a force that seriously challenged Britain's hold on its prized colonial conquest in the Greater Antilles. This, too, would happen in Dominica.

6

The British take over: Maroons consolidate

From their smallholdings on the highest slopes of Morne Anglais, then known as Couliaboune, a group of Maroon farmers looked down upon Roseau 2,000ft below. The town was really just a village gathered around the main landing place and open market where canoes and small boats were dragged up on shore. On a slight hill behind the settlement stood the small French church with its rough plank walls and thatched roof. These Maroons had cut their gardens out of the forest in the slash and burn method, planting their food crops among the ashes of fallen trees just before the rainy season. Their people had been here for roughly 60 years, raising their families and seeing their grown sons moving to open gardens in other parts of the forest. They had lived largely undisturbed, even trading their produce with vendors from Martinique. They made and traded canoes like the Kalinagos did,

The British capture Roseau, 6 June 1761, and take Dominica

although legislation had been passed in Martinique outlawing such commerce with *les negres maron de la Dominique*.

That day, 6 June 1761, the sea off Roseau was busy with large sailing warships and small boats. In the late afternoon cannon fire echoed up the mountain and it was clear that some battle was in progress. In the days that followed the Maroons of Couliaboune would learn the outcome of that short engagement and eventually discover how it was destined to wreck the life of bush farming and secure settlement that they had created for themselves in the forest. It would disperse their families, ruin their crops and force them to shift from one temporary encampment to the next, constantly on the move for fear of their lives.

From 1756 to 1763 Dominica was caught up in the Seven Years War. Developing from a dispute over military and naval bases, the conflict was not limited to the West Indies alone and the French and British forces had clashes on their home grounds, and in Canada and India on land and sea. Early in the war, incidents occurred off the coast of Dominica between English and French ships. By October 1759 Commodore John Moore had written to his Prime Minister, William Pitt, stating, 'Dominica is absolutely under the direction of the Governor of Martinique and is developing into an island of consequence... Dominica is troublesome to the British and since the French in Dominica are not neutral I would advise that the island be treated as it deserves.'[1]

In 1761 Pitt wanted Dominica seized before the hurricane season and on 3 May, 2,000 experienced soldiers under Lord Andrew Rollo sailed from North America to Guadeloupe. There, Lord Rollo and his men met other ships under Sir James Douglas, and their large fleet of four war vessels carrying 100 cannons along with four transport ships packed with men sailed towards Roseau.

Rollo sent two officers ashore with a letter calling for the surrender of the island. The French commander Louis Longpré stoutly refused and hastily manned the defences with members of the local militia. But in the face of the vast British force they were powerless. At four o'clock that afternoon, on 6 June, Rollo landed his troops at Roseau. By six o'clock the small and heavily outnumbered militia of French settlers had surrendered.

At noon the following day, the plunder of Roseau was ended by official order. All French inhabitants were directed to surrender and take an oath of submission. The British invaders left a small force to occupy the island until the end of the war when their possession of Dominica was confirmed by the Treaty of Paris in 1763. Under the terms of the treaty, the neutral islands of Tobago, St Vincent and Dominica were 'ceded' to Britain and sometimes referred to as 'the Ceded Islands'; no mention was made of the historic neutrality agreements for the security of the Kalinagos.

The first action taken by the British Crown on Dominica was to survey the island and divide it into lots for sale to British purchasers. Those French people who already occupied plots were allowed to remain but they could only hold their land as tenants to the British Crown and had to pay an annual rent. The land commissioners who came out to survey and sell the island in lots only left one plot of 134 acres for the Kalinagos labelling the plot CHARAIBS. A few years later it was increased to 277 acres.

The mountainous interior posed a major challenge to the surveyors. In most cases, the main massifs were ignored and left undivided but elsewhere the surveyors simply drew numbered squares on the main map (called the 'Byres Map' after the head surveyor John Byres) even if these were over precipitous terrain that they had never actually seen. Most of these lots in the interior remained unsold and many that were bought were never occupied due to their inaccessibility. Around the entire coastline of the island the surveyors set aside a zone 66 yards wide called the King's Three Chains which was reserved as public land set aside for wharves, gun batteries, warehouses and the like. In the years after slave emancipation this strip of land would be a contentious issue between freed slaves and the government.[2]

Both the Kalinagos and the Maroons were unaware of these official sub-divisions of the island but over the next few years they would come to realise the implications of what the surveyors had produced as they saw land being cleared and settlements established in territory that was once sovereign to them. This had now been appropriated by others.

A new government

In 1764, the British established the federal colony of the Southern Caribbee Islands which consisted of Dominica, Tobago, Grenada and St Vincent and the Grenadines. It was administered from its head-quarters in Grenada by a governor, General Robert Melville, with lieutenant governors in each unit.[3] Soon the planters of Dominica were demanding their own separate assembly (not for the last time was a federated government of the Caribbean broken up) and Sir William Young became the first governor of the new colony, sworn in on 17 November 1770. Even in his official affairs, Sir William ensured that the finer trappings of the British aristocracy were transported across the Atlantic and planted upon the rain-drenched volcanic island amid the brutishness of a colonising plantocracy. Years later, his son, also named William, recalled of his father that 'He recommended, he solicited; he invited to settlements in a wilderness with the voice of music and fine arts; he made jovial parties of colonisation… and few who ventured within the charm of his society could not long resist his example or his persuasions, to enlist in the undertaking…'[4]

The governor sent out from England was head of the colony's government and commander in chief. He was assisted by a nominated Council made up of prominent residents on the island. Below the Council was the House of Assembly, which, composed of elected representatives, two for each of the ten parishes, turned out to be a cumbersome and cantankerous system given to divisiveness and much ill will. Using the Westminster-style House of Assembly, laws were passed to ensure that Roman Catholics could not hold public office. Free non-whites were barred from almost everything except commerce, land holding, militia duties and paying taxes. The enslaved were kept firmly in their place and the Maroons, that alternative society regarded as the greatest threat of all, was to be brutally suppressed.

With the new legislature in place one of the first laws passed was 'An Act for the suppressing of Runaway Slaves, and for the better government of Slaves and for preventing Slaves being fraudulently carried off the Island.'[5] On 21 February 1772 the Council noted with concern to Sir William Young that 'the number of Runaway Slaves is of late much increased in the island and that there are several encampments formed in the woods, particularly in the Fonds of Maho, at Coulaboonne, Pointe Mulatre and Point Jacko by which inhabitants of the neighbouring plantations are much alarmed.' They appealed to Sir William to 'put the Slave Act into immediate Force' although they considered that the act was 'insufficient for the speedy and effectual bringing in such Runaway Slaves we do further recommend... additional officers, men of property... and Free Negroes and Free Mulattoes... and such white volunteers as will go out upon this service.'[6]

On 12 March 1772, the governor in turn exhorted the members of the House of Assembly that 'the expeditions resolved on against the Runaway Negroes will speedily require your presence and your influence in your respective quarters [of the island].' On 16 August 1773 the legislation 'for suppressing the Runaways' was 'strengthened' and again on 7 December 1775 additional offences and punishments were instituted. The most notable amendments were aimed at 'such White Persons or Free Persons of Colour who shall be found trafficking or having any dealings with or associating with or comforting, aiding and abetting or concealing of any Runaway Slave or Slaves.'[7]

Maintaining a sufficient number of white people to serve as elected members, jurors, public officers and militiamen was always a matter of concern given the racial basis of selection to these posts. In the face of the upsurge in the number of enslaved blacks and the paucity of whites, Sir William Young attempted to ensure that a sufficient number of whites were available when, as chairman of the Land Commission, he declared that 'For every hundred acres cleared lands the purchaser is obliged to keep thereon, one white man, or two white women, under penalty of forty pounds a year for each man and twenty five pounds for each woman defective.'[8]

A militia was established to maintain internal order and to assist the regular troops with the defence of the island from external enemies. It included 'all description of white men, and free people of colour, from the age of eighteen to fifty years old who are able to bear arms, and have resided thirty days at one time in the island'.[9] Drill practice and parade was once a month, although sometimes, when danger threatened, the militia met once a week or even more often at the discretion of the legislature. In the unstable years that lay ahead, the militia was kept busy against the Maroons, only being called out on three occasions to confront invading French forces.

A change in agriculture

The population and agricultural figures for Dominica when the British took over in 1763 indicates that the French, mostly peasant farmers working alongside their slaves, had already established a productive

little colony. Although it was divided into numerous scattered *l'habitations* with an average of less than two slaves per 'French habitant', the volume of coffee and other crops produced was impressive. [10]

Here is the demographic and productive state of the colony that Britain had captured in 1763. It was described as follows:[11]

Ruined watermill at Geneva estate, Grand Bay

1,718 French inhabitants
500 free negroes and people of colour
5,872 slaves including 3,145 working adults and 2,113 children
50-60 Carib families
3,027 acres of land occupied
271,650lb of cocoa
9,973 barrels of manioc
1,690,368lb of coffee

This was a self-sufficient informal society growing crops for local consumption while the excess was exported to neighbouring islands. Farms were cultivated by whites, free people of colour and African slaves with smuggled produce of the Maroon gardens also contributing to the output. However, this agricultural balance was upset when the British introduced sugar cane and forced on Dominica a mono-crop economy for the international market. It would make the island almost entirely dependent on imported food and goods for the rest of time. It also established a mindset that economic development could only be achieved by plantations. It deprecated smallholders, and it was not until the 20th century, after 160 years of plantation domination and failure, that the important role of the peasant proprietor, later known as the 'small farmer', began to be recognised once more.

The Swedish scientist and anti-slavery advocate Carl Wadström, who passed through the West Indies on his way from an expedition in Africa in the 1780s, decried the introduction of sugar into the Ceded Islands, declaring that 'in no age or country was ever avarice more completely disappointed, or humanity more shockingly outraged than in the... ill judged introduction of the sugar cane into all or most of the British West

Ruined aqueduct arches at Wallhouse estate

Indies, especially the Ceded Islands... its premature and forced cultivation has, within our own memory, swept masters and slaves, the oppressors and the oppressed into one common grave.'[12]

The British imposition of sugar cane also changed the landscape. Thousands of acres of forest from the river banks to the mountain tops were stripped for sugar.[13] The large investment in mills, distilleries, boiling houses, managers' residences, slave quarters and slave hospitals that sugar required were put in place. The owners' houses were usually built on a ridge directly above the sugar works with a view of the surrounding valley. Some had walls on the edge of cliffs like gun batteries in case of attack. This can still be seen in the layout of such estate buildings at, for example, Macoucherie, Rosalie, Pointe Mulatre, Stowe, Hillsborough and Blenheim. None of them could be called 'Great Houses' in the manner of those in Jamaica or Barbados. Most of the actual owners fled the colony after French occupation in 1778 and left managers and attorneys in charge of the dirty and dangerous business of plantation management in Dominica. As a result, minimal funds or effort was lavished on such estate houses and those few that do survive are modest buildings.

In the plantation factory yards or 'works', the boiling houses had to be tended round the clock when the crop was being processed. The furnaces had to be constantly fed with wood and 'bagasse', the crushed cane stems that were added to the fuel. Extra forest land was stripped for firewood. Mills powered by cattle, wind and water turned the heavy iron rollers that crushed the canes. Water mills were the most efficient but also the most expensive to construct. Part of the cost included building canals to conduct water from nearby streams to the mill house, and arched aqueducts survive on some estates such as Wallhouse, Geneva, Rosalie and Canefield.[14]

Slaves working in the boiling houses were subject to constant danger. In the heat of crop time the iron rollers sometimes crushed exhausted slaves as well as the cane. There was always an axe ready in the mill house to sever the arm of a slave whose hand had slipped into the rollers. Little could be done when someone fell into a boiling cauldron of sugar cane juice or was hit by the twirling sail of a windmill. Such were some of the many hazards of sugar production.

During the 1770s, sugar incomes grew rapidly as the British plantations came into full production. In 1767, Dominica produced just over 981,596lb of sugar. By 1774 production had reached a plateau of 5,988,036lb. To move from less than one million pounds of sugar in 1767 to more than five million in so short a time, shows the speed of the sugar takeover. The British also entered the coffee business which had been dominated by the French. Production rose from 652,892lb in 1767 to 2,818,506lb in 1776.[15] The increase of almost 500 per cent in both crops also reflected the increase in the labour force and by extension the overspill into the Maroon camps.

With the arrival of the British, the system of African enslavement that they had developed in the Caribbean since taking St Kitts in 1625 and more so after settling Barbados in 1627 was imposed lock stock and barrel on Dominica during the 1760s. A prefabricated society was offloaded. Within a decade, all of the trappings of a British West Indian colony were in place – but it had arrived too late to survive intact. Too much had

Marketplace: sale of enslaved man

happened in Dominica in the years before their arrival to make this British enterprise an easy undertaking. The Kalinagos had continued to hold on to the island for too long. The African Maroon 'settlers' had established their holdings in the hills too early. The free blacks and mulattos had established themselves as equals to white French peasant proprietors. The agriculture that they had developed was a small-scale mixed crop economy. The social structure of this small farming society was in for a radical change. Even so, Britain found it near impossible to smother the previously established community with its own.

The new colonial power had arrived with high hopes. For more than a hundred years Britain had not gained any new real estate in the Caribbean since capturing Jamaica in 1655. As Sir William Young noted: 'Since our conquest of Jamaica from the Spaniards, in the days of Oliver Cromwell, down to the present times, there has been no such opportunity of improving private fortunes.'[16] By the 1760s British investors were thirsty for new sugar islands in which to put their money and the Ceded Islands provided that chance. This new money came from the profits of the fledgling British industrial revolution; money gained by the Anglo-Irish landlords exploiting Ireland; new Scottish money in a new United Kingdom and planters from the 'Old West Indies Colonies' such as Barbados and the Leeward islands seeking to expand their sugar empires. Yet Dominica defied them. Although they did make some profits at peak times, between the 1770s and the 1830s, it was at a horrendous cost in lives and money lavished on the purchase and maintenance of an enslaved workforce, on procuring manufacturing equipment, on constructing sugar and coffee works and on military hardware and manpower for both internal and external defence.

Hardly any slaves had come directly from Africa to Dominica before 1765; the long established and prosperous sugar islands of Barbados, Antigua, St Kitts, Guadeloupe and Martinique were far more attractive to the slave merchants. The small numbers of slaves brought to Dominica during the French days were usually trans-shipped from these larger trading centres and many who came to the island were already West Indian born. Slave figures for Dominica rose dramatically after the British took over in 1763. The island became even more deeply embroiled in the slave trade when Roseau and Portsmouth were declared free ports in 1766 and were open to trade with ships of all nations. Under this system thousands of slaves brought to Dominica hardly touched the shore but were resold for shipment to other colonies as far as the Carolinas and New England.

As the sales of land progressed there was a marked influx of white

British plantation owners, managers and overseers who started opening up extensive areas of virgin forest to grow sugar cane and coffee. The numbers of slave arrivals rose in tandem with these developments. From a figure of 3,145 adult slaves in 1763, there was an increase to 8,496 adult slaves in 1766 while land clearance and first plantings were still taking place, escalating during the 1770s as sugar cane and coffee production came on stream. The slave population reached 22,083 in 1805, and peaked at an all-time high of 24,000 in 1812 but had decreased to 14,175 by the time of emancipation in 1834.

The French in Dominica had followed a general code of slave law, Louis XIV's 'Code Noir' of 1685. This celebrated and detailed code was often disregarded yet it made clear the legal status of slaves whose ownership and sale was to be regulated. Now French slaveholders in Dominica had to conform to a mixed and continuously amended collection of British slave laws enacted by the local Assembly. In any case, barring some differences such as access to the Christian religion and the admission of evidence from a slave in court, the basic intention of slave masters of both nationalities was to maintain as tight control as possible over what they considered to be their property and to get the most that they could out of their investment.

Like all other commodities, the price of a slave fluctuated during the 70 years of British slave commerce on Dominica depending on supply and demand, based on the conditions of peace or war or military occupation as it affected shipping and colonial trade in the region. In

Mount Anthony, a British coffee estate near present-day Cochrane

the early years of plantation settlement it was considered more economical to buy fresh slaves often rather than to expend funds on maintaining their health and longevity. However, as the 18th century progressed slave prices rose and the planters placed greater emphasis on building plantation hospitals, hiring doctors and improving nutrition through the granting of land for garden plots so as to augment food rations and extend the life span of their human property.

By the end of the 1790s, just a few years before the abolition of the slave trade in 1807, the price of a healthy male African landed at Roseau or Portsmouth was put at £70. In the 1820s, during a downturn in the economy, laws were passed to restrict the number of slaves being

transferred to more prosperous British colonies so as to guard against a shortage of labour and an increase in local prices. Even today, certain expressions linger in the Creole language that are rooted in the

The British establish a sugar economy: feeding the mill rollers with cane

commerce of slavery: if something is considered to be unreasonably expensive, one occasionally hears the comment, 'Man, he wanted *tet neg* for that thing' meaning that it was as expensive as the head of a slave. In the countryside, particularly along the dry scrub woodland of the west coast, there grows a thick prickly vine that forms a barrier to easy movement in the bush. Its Creole name is *awéte neg*, being a plant that would block the passage of an escaping slave.[17]

Generally, the planters saw this labour force as an undifferentiated mass when in fact, as Carey Robinson has pointed out, 'the people who came in the ships did not think of themselves as "Negro slaves" but as members of the clan or nation from which they came. Just as Scotsmen thought of themselves as Scots, and Irishmen as Irish, the Africans thought of themselves as Ashantis, Mandingos, Fantyns, Ibos, etc.'[18]

Dominica had been the last island in the Caribbean to be officially colonised thanks to the resistance of the Kalinagos and the difficult topography of this the most mountainous land mass in the region. As a result, Dominica had a shorter period of British plantation slavery than anywhere else, although for the 75 years it lasted, from 1763 to full emancipation in 1838, it was as intense as elsewhere. The history of Dominica is not the history of Jamaica or Barbados or St Kitts or Antigua. It may follow the general pattern of West Indian plantation systems after 1763 but it takes a course all of its own in many ways.

One feature of this was that there were already many slaveholders of African descent in Dominica before the British took over. Dominica had the highest percentage of 'free coloured' slave masters of any of the other colonies except for Grenada. One of the most prominent black slaveholders was John Baptiste Louis Birmingham who, before he left Dominica for Trinidad in 1818, owned as many as three plantations worked by 175 slaves. Much of this he lost when he was found guilty of smuggling slaves to Trinidad in contravention of the terms of the 1807 legislation which abolished the slave trade and limited the movement of slaves within the region.

Dominica's late colonisation meant that free blacks and 'people of colour' or mulattos, as well as poor whites, the so called *petits blancs*, had secured landholding rights prior to the British subdivision of the island. Plantation registers for the parishes in the south and east record the original land owners from Martinique such as Anselm, Durand, Darroux, Laurent, Laronde, Fontaine, Moise, Bellot, Giraudel, Sorhaindo, Peltier, Tavanier and others. Similarly, in the north and west, the registers reflect arrivals from Guadeloupe, with names such as Royer, Le Blanc, Brument, Dubois, Foi, Lamothe, Sharplis, Sabroach, Vidal. In most cases the land they claimed in the early 1700s still belongs to their families.[19] By the time that the first stage of eman-cipation came along in 1834, most of the descendants of these *petit blancs* families had mixed to become classified as 'people of colour'. When compensation was granted to slave owners for 'loss of their property' under the terms of the Emancipation Act of 1833, the names of most of these families are listed as beneficiaries.

Another peculiarity was that, with the permission of their masters, domestic and skilled slaves were allowed to buy and own slaves themselves. So one Veronique, a Creole slave of Geneva estate, purchased an African she named Francoise, whom she rented out to earn money on the side.[20] At Londonderry estate, the plantation house-keeper, a domestic slave called Mary, owned ten slaves. When the master of Londonderry, John Simpson, died, it was revealed in his will that Mary should be given her freedom and continue to own her ten slaves. He also freed 'her four children' who were to be given £500 each on his death, making the bequest without revealing that he was actually their father.[21] Other similar cases scattered across Dominica contributed to further divisions among the enslaved population besides those created by the social stratification of the plantation workforce into groups such as field slaves, drivers, skilled slaves, boatmen, domestics and quasi-military rangers.

Overshadowing all of this was the division between French and British influence on an island where the population operated under normal circumstances in a state of dual nationality. Such a situation created competing loyalties among the enslaved towards either of the two European groups that further weakened any cohesiveness of purpose when it came to revolt. Any Maroon leader embarking on a campaign to attack and overthrow this system had to steer a delicate strategy of inspiring commitment to his cause among people with many divided loyalties.

The changes wrought by the arrival of the British also led to an intensification of marronage as many newly arrived Africans took to the hills as soon as they could do so. With the development of plantations all over the island the enslaved labour force soon constituted an overwhelming majority of the island's population. As elsewhere in the region during the slave era the European minority lived in constant fear of revolt and, to ensure their safety, the plantocracy maintained a rigorous discipline. Disobedience, slackness from exhaustion or mere errors of judgment were severely punished. These plantations were operating under a system of labour that was effectively based on the industrialisation of human energy whereby production was controlled with a finely calculated regime of time and motion exploiting the very limits of human endurance. The basis for this had been argued quite bluntly by both French and British planters in the older colonies as early as the 1660s. 'They [the Negroes] are to be kept in awe by threats and blows; for if a man grow too familiar with them, they are presently apt to make their advantages of it, and to abuse that familiarity.' Yet the writer urges a manipulative balance, for he continues: 'If treated with excessive severity they will run away... into the Mountains and Forests where they live like so many beasts; then they are called Marons, that is to say, Savages.'[22]

During the first British period (1763-1778), numerous Maroons were captured and brought to jail in Roseau. Conditions in the jail were appalling and the lists of captured Maroons show that many died in prison soon after their arrival.[23] The provost marshal's reports to the Assembly's Public Accounts Committee during the 1770s lists payments for carrying Maroons from the places where they were captured to their placement in the public jail and for settling fees for doctors' bills, trials, burials or advertisements for their capture. The large number of Maroons whose names are followed by the words 'died in gaol' hints at the conditions of their capture and of herding them through the forest to Roseau as well as the conditions in jail. Some entries suggest this: 'October 2nd 1776. To cash paid for taking up a Negro by Richard Barry who died in gaol 16s 6d. To gaol fee for ditto with advertisements: £6 6s 6d. To cash paid for bringing him: 33/- (plus Doctor's Bill 33/-) = £3 6s 0d. To gaol fees for a Runaway Negro committed by Alexander Stewart on Mr. Grey's Estate, taken up at Prince Rupert's on 10th August and died in gaol 14th September with taking up advertisements and burying him: £8 19s 3d.'[24]

This was the start of what would become a massive drain on the colony's treasury in a campaign against the Maroons which would last for several decades. Letters written by planters to each other also tell something of the private commercial activity that became a side effect of marronage. On October 27 1778, planter and attorney general Charles Winston wrote a letter to accompany a slave he sold to Thomas Campbell, in which he intimated, 'the Reason of my selling the Fellow is that he is disliked by the rest of the Negroes on the Plantation & he is addicted to running away.'[25] Notices appeared regularly in the newspapers announcing rewards for the recapture or return of 'runaway slaves'.[26] The payment of such fees and the monetary transactions related to marronage became an increasingly significant fringe business as Maroon numbers grew during the first British period of occupation.

Establishing a military state

To keep Dominica under her rule Britain had to defend the island against both her internal and external enemies. In the hills were the growing numbers of Maroons and out at sea were the French. Along with the surveyors and commissioners who came out to plan and organise the sale of land, engineers were commissioned to produce plans for the defence of the colony. Colonel James Bruce, Royal Engineer, was head of that particular project in Dominica, and in March 1770 he dispatched a report to London giving his suggestions, maps and designs for fortifications needed on Dominica. Among these were the drawings for batteries and forts for the defence of Roseau and two large garrisons, one at Morne Bruce in the south and the other at the Cabrits, also known as Prince Rupert's, guarding the north.[27] The presence of such military might was not only to secure the island against French invasion but to so visually dominate the landscape as to inhibit any tendency for the slaves to consider revolt. When the Cabrits garrison was being strengthened in the 1790s, the governor impressed on the secretary of state for the colonies in London the role that this fortification was to play: 'From such a Garrison half a battalion with a proportion of Artillery would be necessary... to awe the Negroes and maintain due Subordination in the Colony.'[28]

To maintain communications along the west coast between the two garrisons Bruce organised a line of signal stations. A gun was fired to attract attention and then three flags were raised, each one representing a number. A book of figures noted what each set of numbers meant. By firing the gun and raising the same colour and design of flags, the signal man on duty at each station would send the code along to the next station. It was said that a message could get from Scotts Head in the south to the Cabrits in the north in less than half an hour by this method. If, for instance, there was a slave uprising in the south, Scott's Head station would signal to Fort Young and the gun and flag signals went on to Morne Daniel, Layou, Grand Savannah,

Fort Shirley: looking towards the mountains of 'Maroon Country'

Pointe Crabier, Pointe Ronde, the Cabrits and finally to Cape Melville at Capuchin. During Maroon activity, these signal stations also served as lookout posts for any activity in the district. At the time of the Second Maroon War (1812-14) some signalmen stationed in their isolated locations were credited with capturing Maroons.

It took the British colonists ten years to get all of the trappings and systems required for a fully working sugar colony in place. Between 1765, when lands were first sold, and 1775 when most of the sugar plantations were producing full crops, the planters had been very busy. Enslaved labourers were imported; tracks and landing places to the properties were built; forests were cleared mainly using French and Italian contract labourers; fields were marked out; the first sugar canes were planted; sugar factories were constructed and the first canes were reaped.

The planters focused on the business of establishing their enterprises and, in the spirit of Governor Young, made 'jovial parties of colonisation' often lightheartedly playing at being Maroons themselves. According to one resident, the white families 'proceed into the country on *marooning parties,* as they are called; that is parties of pleasure hastily resolved on, and immediately carried into effect. They generally resort to the woods or to a river's side… the company set out some riding, and others walking, servants following with baskets of meat, wine, &c. Having selected a spot on the river's bank, and an arbour and seats having been formed, breakfast was prepared; after which the ladies read, worked and played at cards. The men fished and shot ramiers, the local pigeons.'[29]

Any major action against Maroons apart from apprehending obvious escapees could wait until later. Meanwhile, the Maroons for their part withheld any attack hoping perhaps that the uneasy peace would continue so that they could maintain their free communities and gardens in the mountains.

Slave villages and Maroon camps

Like the Kalinagos before them, the enslaved Africans who had escaped to freedom in the mountains relied on natural materials to

construct their huts and shelters and to produce utensils for their households. On the plantations, the cabins were thatched with sugar cane leaves while in the forest a wide variety of palm, heliconia, *woseau* and *zel mouche* leaves were used for this purpose. The walls were made of woven *gaulettes* which are thin saplings. The *gaulettes* were

Maroon camps were strategically placed to deter attacks

woven into panels which were held in place by wooden house frames made of round wood posts. In some cases the panels were plastered with clay and on plantations they were usually painted with white lime wash. This kind of wattle and daube construction is found in a wide range of cultures, the Dominican version being adopted from west African patterns.

Calabashes and carved wood spoons and forks provided implements for eating and on some plantations in the north-east of the island there is evidence of locally produced clay bowls. Around each hut there were small beds planted with 'bush teas' and herbs for medicines and food seasoning as well as fruit trees and banana and plantain plants. On the edge of the plantations, on steep and stony land unsuitable for sugar cane and coffee fields, the enslaved were granted plots to make their 'gardens' which they would tend during their off time. These were prized concessions that provided food to supplement plantation rations and sell at Sunday markets. They represented a significant if limited opportunity for independence in a life dominated by intense control so much so that access to gardens and time to tend them became contentious issues in master-slave relationships.

The Maroon camps were military-style strongholds that took advantage of the steep topography of their location. Several were situated on top of plateaus surrounded on at least three sides by precipices. These plateaus had been formed during periods of volcanic eruption when the heated ash or pyroclastic flow spread out around the volcanic domes to form layers of 'welded tuff' hundreds of feet thick. Over thousands of years, streams and rivulets eroded deep ravines out of the compacted and welded ash. This created a complex network of natural citadels standing high above the rivers. They were covered in thick forest that added to the security of the encampments.

The Maroons selected the most secure of these plateaus upon which to place their fortified settlements. Steps were carved into the cliff sides to access the camps and these were designed so that anyone above could have a clear view through the trees of who was approaching.

Sections of the steps were carved deep into the rock so that any group coming up would be forced to climb in single file making it easier to subdue their attackers. One fine example of this is the chiselled stone staircase leading to the site of the camp of Chief Jacko at Jacko Flats above the Layou River near to the community of Bells. Although these 'Jacko Steps' were made more accessible during the late 19th century well after slavery was abolished, the precipitous route that scales the cliff face follows the original approach to Jacko's camp providing a vivid example of such defences.

Together with the natural precipices and deep ravines, the plateaus were defended by palisades made of logs with sharpened tops stuck into the ground. The gated entrances were guarded by booby traps similar to the pig traps that are used by Dominican hunters today. Huts were grouped within this protected space and were surrounded by the same small gardens that were found on the plantations while the larger gardens for food crops were cut out of the forest some distance from the camps as would have existed in the interior rain forest zones of west Africa. In many ways, the camps were west African forest communities transported in the minds of the enslaved and recreated in the jungles of Dominica.

Communication between the camps and bands of Maroons moving through the forest was facilitated by the blowing of conch shell trumpets fashioned out of the Queen conch, *Strombus gigas*, known locally as *kon lambi*. The large sea shell had been used by the Kalinagos for centuries, providing food, shell tools and jewellery. By cutting off the pointed tip of the conical spire a hole is created and by blowing powerfully through the spiral labyrinth within it the sound is amplified to cover a wide area. Messages were transmitted by blowing different rhythmical calls with prearranged meanings that, in the case of the Maroons, conveyed information relating to a variety of situations such as the location of troops and their numbers, the arrival of allies, deaths, victory and celebration. The sound of the conch shell trumpet reverberating across the forest canopy struck terror into the colonial forces as it signalled the presence of Maroons without revealing their exact whereabouts and, unless African interpreters were on hand to translate the calls, they were at a loss to know the message. The supply of conch shells from the coast to the interior was of just as much concern to the colonial authorities as the movement of food supplies and arms and ammunition. The last uprising where conch shell calls were used to pass messages of revolt was the Land Tax Riot at La Plaine in 1893, although general messages were still being passed in this way from village to village well into the 20th century.[30]

Kalinago and African Maroon relationship

The Kalinago spirit of liberty and passion for the defence of their homeland had been matched with the African determination to escape the bonds of slavery. In earlier years they had developed a symbiotic relationship of cooperation for survival in the face of a common enemy. The tightness of this relationship loosened, however, from 1700 onwards, once the Kalinagos had no need to resist the French or English. By then, the Europeans had given up any thought of enslaving Kalinagos and those on Dominica were free to live their lives as they pleased. They were forced to shift their settlements to the more rugged parts of the east coast and interacted with the plantations to supply fish, game, baskets and canoes while generally remaining aloof from the colonial conflicts over the mountains.

The cave of Vonte Zara at the junction of the Pagayer and Layou rivers was a regular hide-out for Maroons

In 1791, Thomas Atwood would write: 'There are not more than twenty or thirty families who have their dwellings on the east part of the island, at a great distance from Roseau where they are seldom seen. They chiefly live by fishing in the rivers and the sea, or by fowling in the woods, at both of which they are very expert with their bows and arrows... they are very serviceable to the planters near their settlements who they chiefly supply with fish and game. They are also very ingenious making curious wrought panniers, or baskets... It is much to be regretted that since this island has been in possession of the English, so little pains have been taken to cultivate an union with these people, as they might be capable of essential service to its internal security, especially against the accumulation of runaway negroes in time of peace; and in war they might be induced to join in its defence, should it be invaded. Yet they are permitted to roam wherever their fancies take them, as much unnoticed as if no such people were in existence. They are men as well as we, are born with the same degree of sensibility and by proper encouragement, might be of material benefit to a country which was originally their own.'[31]

In that same year a free mulatto called Jean Louis Polinaire talked about the African slave 'Janvier, *belonging* to Mr Laronde, and a Caraib, named Bigaire, *who lives* on Mr Laronde's Estate'. He makes a clear distinction between the slave that is owned by Mr Laronde and the Kalinago who just lives on his estate.[32] After the British arrived in 1763, there were several instances where Kalinagos sided with the Europeans. Along the east coast, Kalinago families often farmed extra land on the outskirts of plantations with permission of the owners.[33] In 1791, a Kalinago man went to the plantation owner James Bruce and informed him where to find Jean Louis Polinaire who was wanted for treason and inciting rebellion. Bruce rewarded him with gold currency. In 1805, Kalinagos guided Governor George Prevost across the island during the French attack on Roseau. There is no record of a single Kalinago being captured or on any 'wanted' list of rebels during the entire Maroon period. On the contrary, during the Second Maroon War (1812-1814), a Kalinago private in the 4th West Indies Regiment was killed and had his heart ripped out of his chest on the orders of a Maroon chief when he took a message from the British governor to a Maroon camp.[34]

At this time, over ten years after Atwood's account, it was still the case that 'A few families of Caribs, or free Indians... inhabit the mountains and occasionally visit Roseau, to sell their bows and arrows and other curiosities. They are very quiet and inoffensive, live entirely by themselves, and have never at any time, given any disturbance to the planters... and mix neither with negroes or people of colour.'[35]

It is tempting to jump on the bandwagon of the radical nationalist activists of the 1960s and 1970s and conjure up a picture of the proto-nationalist Kalinago and African Maroons joining in common cause against the colonialist oppressors. In fact, by the 1760s, the Kalinagos of Dominica, like the 'Yellow Caribs' of St Vincent, had no need to fight wars with the colonists. They had lost the battle to hold on to their islands. Now they were left unto themselves to engage with the plantations in domestic trade and occasionally hire out their canoes for loading produce. There was no advantage to them to side with Maroons. Their own niche of freedom, engineered by isolation and non-confrontation, had been achieved.

A Kalinago settlement in the 1770s
(Agostino Brunias)

7

The French return:
Maroons gain strength

The enslaved Africans on the French coffee estates in the south-west of Dominica from Roseau to Cashacrou and in the hills behind observed an increase of visitors dropping in at the modest plantation homes of their 'masters' in July and August of 1778. These strangers from Martinique were clearly interested in local news, asking questions, rolling out maps, expressing thanks and moving on. During field practices and parades of the local British militia in Roseau, similar types of men were noticed scattered through the crowd who usually gathered on such occasions. Some of them were known from previous visits to the island, prominent among them being a certain Monsieur Gabrouse. At the same time, free people of colour from Martinique were consulting with the Maroon leaders gathered in camps in the south-central forests behind Morne Anglais. Something was definitely up.

On the evening of 6 September, the French planters held a party in the village of Cashacrou which the British had recently renamed Scott's Head. Having a party during the hurricane season was somewhat unusual; one did not want to tempt the wrath of God. They had invited British soldiers from Fort Cashacrou, situated atop the nearby point, and they were lavish in their supply of the best rum, gin and brandy. The French hosts insisted that the troops on guard duty should not be left out and they went up to the small fort to entertain them as well. At the height of the festivities the French filled the touch holes of the cannons with sand to prevent them from firing. In the excitement, two British soldiers lost their balance on the ramparts and fell to their deaths on the rocky shore below.[1]

———————————

T he French had kept their eyes on Dominica since losing it in 1761 and took the earliest opportunity to launch an attack. Many French inhabitants had been informed of the impending assault and Maroons in the hills had pledged their support to the French cause. The information garnered by M Gabrouse and his spies during the previous months had been put to good use.[2]

The French offensive began between three and four o'clock on the morning of Monday 7 September 1778. They had chosen the hurricane season and a night of the full moon in the belief that the English would not expect an attack during that period. The fleet of four frigates, ten armed sloops and schooners, and about 20 troop transports carrying almost 3,000 men crossed the channel from Martinique under the command of Marquis de Bouille. Along with the regular troops this number included more than 1,000 'renegade white men, negroes, mulattos and the outcasts of society'.[3]

Their first obstacle was the fort at Cashacrou. But thanks to their preparations of the night before it was easily taken. At the capture, a celebration signal was fired and this was the first notice that the British in Roseau had of the attack. The rest of the action that day was swift. The militiamen of Roseau were called to arms while women and children were guided into the hills by their slaves. The French members of the militia did not assist in the defence of the town and the number of active men was less than 100. The guns on forts and batteries surrounding Roseau were in bad repair, especially those on Melville's Battery where the gun carriages were so rotten that they were soon in pieces and the guns had to be rested along the wall for shooting.

Nevertheless, the French did not march on Roseau easily. By mid-day all the troops had landed and were pushing towards the town from

Pointe Michel. After three unsuccessful attempts, they took Loubiere, two miles from the capital, and headed on for Roseau. Led by Maroons and French-speaking slaves who knew the country, the 'renegade' French supporters clambered up through the forest and plantation fields behind Loubiere to occupy the ridges below Giraudel and Eggleston overlooking Roseau by late that afternoon. Having gained possession of the heights above the town, it appeared to the British governor, William Stuart, that the enemy was waiting for darkness to make their final attack. Realising that his force was small, and understanding that Maroons were among the French forces waiting in the hills, he therefore decided to surrender the island to the French.

The opposing commanders, Governor Stuart and Marquis de Bouille, met at Government House to sign the 27 Articles of Capitulation, which laid down the terms of the British surrender. As soon as a new form of government had been settled, de Bouille appointed the Marquis Duchilleau to be governor of the island and returned to Martinique. The blue flag bearing the *fleurs-de-lis* and the coat of arms of his most Christian Majesty King Louis XVI was hoisted on the flagpole of Fort Young. Dominica would be under French occupation for the next five years.

French assault on Loubiere, south of Roseau, 1778

The French hoped that they would hold on to the island. Under the command of Marquis de Bouille, directing operations from Martinique, about 3,000 French troops were brought in. Orders were given that the plantations supply cattle every day to feed them and the colony's livestock was quickly depleted. Slaves were hired to work on improving roads, aqueducts, forts and coastal batteries. French authorities renamed Fort Young, Fort de La Reine, and made major improvements to the barracks, ramparts and storerooms. Up at Morne Bruce and at the Cabrits Garrison they set to work as if they were there for the long term. However, their project received a serious setback when a powerful hurricane lashed the island on the night of 29 August 1779 severely damaging buildings on the fort; another hurricane hit the following year, 30 September 1780, with even greater damage. The inhabitants of Roseau had hardly recovered from the destruction of their homes and business places by the storms, when a huge fire swept through the town on the evening of Easter Sunday 1781. More than 500 houses were consumed in a few hours along with merchandise, household goods and so on to the value of some £200,000. Like so much else during the French governorship of Dominica, the British blamed the fire on Duchilleau.

During the occupation, the importation of new slaves declined to a trickle. Between 1778 and mid-May 1783 no slave ship arrived directly from Africa to Dominica except for one vessel that came to trade in 1781. It was known that the island was experiencing hard times and due to the uncertainty over which colonial power would gain the island at the peace treaty, traders knew that planters would not be keen to invest in new labour under these uncertain conditions.[4]

Circumstances for the Maroons to operate improved during the French occupation of 1778-1784. The bickering between the two groups of Europeans which lasted throughout those years enabled the Maroons to further consolidate their forces and launch raids on British estates almost with

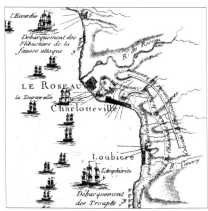

Map of French attack shows lines of Maroons in hinterland

impunity. From time to time statements were made by senior officers of the French occupation forces that deliberately incited the slaves to rebel against their British masters. An increasing number of slaves took to the woods and started to harry the plantation owners, stealing, burning and fomenting divisions among those who remained at their tasks. The French looked on and made little attempt to help the British settlers; they even went so far as to arm the Maroons while demanding that the British hand in their arms.

Many plantation owners abandoned their estates and retreated to Roseau or left the island all together. The upper-class, better educated planters who had been entertained and encouraged to invest by Governor Sir William Young in the 1760s and 1770s were the first to go. Except for a handful such as Clarke, Laing, Stewart, Greg, Bruce and Laidlaw, the British who remained in Dominica were a gaggle of uncouth, ill-educated, infighting band of overseers, managers and attorneys. However, regardless of class, their joint attitude to the Maroons was one of unbridled hatred, for the resistance fighters in the hills were seen as the most serious threat to British investments and accumulation of wealth. Thomas Atwood not surprisingly blamed the Maroons' change of mood on the French, when he compared the state of the Maroons before and after the occupation: 'They were not however often guilty of any material mischief, and had never committed murder till the reduction of the island by the French; but soon after that happened the depredations of the runaways began to be of a more serious nature; for they robbed, and destroyed property and at length killed some English inhabitants.'[5]

As an Englishman, Atwood failed to consider that the reason for the upsurge against the British in Dominica during the five years of French control was caused by the pent up anger that had been building since 1763 and the changed conditions of the enslaved under King Sugar and Britannia's rule. When the British residents complained to Duchilleau that something must be done, the French commander found himself in a tight spot because he had engaged some of the Maroons to help defend the island. He had ordered that they be given muskets and ammunition for that purpose. His response to British demands was to suggest an amnesty between the two groups:

'Gentlemen of Council. The reiterated complaints which I receive concerning the runaways, invite me to propose to you a grant of general pardon to those who will return to their masters, directing them to receive their said slaves without inflicting any punishment on them.

'I submit, Gentlemen, to your opinion and your knowledge of the country, the advantages or inconveniences which might result from this measure and I will with eagerness subscribe to whatever you think proper to be done, to bring them to their duty again, to lessen their number and to prevent the continuance of their depredations…'[6]

The Council debated the issue of a pardon but came up with no concrete agreement. Complaints continued to pour in from planters throughout the island reporting the robbing of ground provisions, plantains, bananas, and small stock.

Marquis Duchilleau was paranoid about a British insurrection against his occupying forces. This was despite the fact that the much reduced population of English, Scots, Irish and Welsh scattered across the island were far outnumbered by Frenchmen. He thought that it would strengthen his position to disregard the 18th Article of the Terms of Capitulation, which clearly and simply stated, 'The Inhabitants shall keep their arms; Granted on condition that they serve not against the King of France.'[7] He disarmed the British, distributing their arms to the Maroons, with whom, so the British claimed, he had actually entered into a treaty of assistance. According to Atwood, Duchilleau 'gave them the muskets and bayonets which he took from the English inhabitants, with powder and balls; and also furnished them with the same provisions as was allowed to the French soldiers.'[8]

The French approach to internal security appeared aimed at unnerving the British. As far as the occupying forces were concerned, the more of their enemies that were pressured to quit the island the better. Yet a major side effect of this tactic was the way that it emboldened the Maroons. Armed with muskets, bayonets, pistols and cutlasses, they continued to sweep down from their fortified camps in the central mountains and raid plantations in several parishes, carrying off stores and cattle, enticing other slaves to join them and sending threatening messages to planters. On the four-mile stretch of road between Roseau and Mahaut that ran through the plantations of Goodwill, Canefield, Check Hall, Les Pointes and Belfast, the Maroons even robbed travellers in broad daylight.

The British residents were horrified by the murder of planter Robert Grahame in his dwelling as he pleaded on his knees to 'spare his life and take his possessions'.[9] This happened as a result of an earlier attack when the manager of the estate, Hugh Gould, had opposed the Maroons and drove them away. Exasperated at this they returned a few days later in greater numbers determined to kill him. However, Gould had gone away on business leaving Grahame in charge. Although missing their intended target, they chose to leave an example of their power in the district by killing Grahame 'as he was begging for mercy, using him in the most shocking, barbarous manner while he was dying...'[10] After stripping the house of everything of value, they set it on fire. The area, in the heights of the Layou valley, is still called Gould today.

The Maroon chief implicated as the mastermind of that attack was Goree Greg. His name comes from two sources: Goree because he is supposed to have been put on a slave ship at the slave trading islet of Goree off the coast of present-day Senegal; and Greg because the Greg family owned Hillsborough plantation from which he had escaped. Even today, people of the district refer to the plantation as 'En Greg' and the beach along its shoreline as 'Bord la me Greg'. The forested heights behind Gould are still called Goree (or sometimes Coree) after the Maroon chief's camp once located there.

British reports claim that Governor Duchilleau had actually threatened some of their English, Irish and Scottish compatriots that if they dared to attempt anything against the Maroons he would imprison them, or send them off the island. At the same time, he is supposed to have acknowledged, 'The runaways were his friends.' This could have been simply British propaganda, but it did appear that

Maroon chiefs were emboldened by the French governor's cavalier attitude. They were fearless in their attacks, coming in large groups to attack whichever plantations they chose in daylight. Sometimes, to further taunt their former oppressors, they came down with conch shells blowing and French colours flying, close to Roseau, within sight of the French soldiers.

On 1 June 1781, the British residents petitioned Duchilleau to allow them to get arms to defend themselves but the commandant refused their requests although some French troops were dispatched against the Maroons on the pleas of the legislators at least as a show of force. A number of Maroons up the Layou Valley in the hills behind Gould were taken and speedily executed. However, a neighbouring planter, William Atkinson, writing to London the following year, considered that this token example 'has hitherto had no good effect on them'. Others complained 'of the parties that used at times to be sent out after them in the woods… being composed only of People of Colour [who] were no ways industrious in that service, and actually never apprehended one of them'.[11]

By this time, Duchilleau was the object of intense hatred by the British for other grievances besides his perceived leniency on the Maroons, and the feeling was mutual. Even de Bouille in Martinique realised that changes had to be made. The replacement sent to Dominica, the Count de Bourgon, allowed the planters and inhabitants to subscribe a sum of 500 Johannes (Portuguese gold coins commonly called Joes) for the 'suppression of the runaways' after successfully petitioning de Bouille for guns.

With arms and ammunition now available, one English estate manager, John Tombs, responded to an attempt by Maroons to rob the buildings under his charge and actually took some of them prisoner. Recalling the case of Grahame, he was apprehensive that they would return in greater numbers to seek revenge and retribution for the loss of their companions and their loot. To learn their intentions, he sent 'a trusty negro' into the woods with the ruse that he would act as if he was escaping from the plantation, angry at harsh treatment meted out on him by Tombs.

Meanwhile, Tombs accumulated several blunderbusses and muskets and instructed other slaves on the estate how to use them. For several days they practised their moves in anticipation of an attack. Then the

slave in the forest sent a message as to the date and time of the intended raid. It would be at night time when they thought they would take 'Mas Tomb' in bed and the news was that they intended to put him to death 'in a most cruel manner'.

The Maroons found their way through the forest with lighted torches, *les flambeaux*, made out

Maroons with lighted torches move through the forest

of *bwa chandelle*, which they extinguished as they got near to Tombs' house. As soon as the lights were out 'their guide, the faithful spy' absconded and in the darkness joined his 'master' to warn him of the Maroons' approach. With his men at the ready in the windows and doors of the estate buildings, Tombs' offensive worked as planned and he got much the better of the brief engagement. An unknown number of Maroons were killed or wounded (the exact figure is unknown because of the Maroon custom of taking their dead and injured with them as they retreated). But the cries and groans coming out of the night indicated that casualties had been high.[12]

Knowing that the British whites now had arms and were prepared to use them regardless of French directives, the remaining years of French occupation were uneventful in terms of Maroon activity.

Meanwhile, the intercolonial conflicts were continuing across the region at a time when the British Empire in the Caribbean was on its knees. For a time in 1781 Britain held only three islands in the West Indies: Jamaica, Antigua and Barbados.

The Battle of the Saintes

Then, on 12 April 1782, the slaves working on plantations on the northwestern slopes of Morne Aux Diables from Bell Hall north to Grand Capuchin and Connor estates were diverted from their early morning labours. Spread out below them was a mass of ships moving in formation across the sea channel towards the French islands of Les Saintes on the far horizon. Just as he began his breakfast at his house on Grand Capuchin estate, planter John Mair made a note that two mighty naval squadrons of France and Britain were commencing an engagement. It would result in the largest naval battle in the history of the Caribbean. During the entire day slaves on his plantation provided food and drink for the neighbouring planters and their families who gathered at Grand Capuchin for a ringside seat.[13] The bombardment echoed up the surrounding slopes and the engagement could be viewed from as far as Morne Diablotin where it would have been possible for Maroons perched on their clifftop lookouts to cover the encounter as well. The two European tribes were once again at war.

The Royal Navy's conquest that day strengthened the British hand in the Caribbean. At the peace negotiations which led up to the Treaty of Versailles in September 1783, Dominica was handed back to Britain mainly as a result of this victory at the Battle of the Saintes. The French would have liked to

The Roseau bayfront and harbour with slave ships offloading when trade recommenced after 1783

retain Dominica and offered Tobago to Britain instead. But the British knew that although the island tended to be an economic liability with a complex and volatile society, it stood between two French colonial strongholds and would be a strategic post for British forces. They wanted Dominica as a wedge between Martinique and Guadeloupe while the French wanted the island so that it could then have three colonies in a row thereby splitting the British Windward and Leeward Islands further apart. As a future British administrator put it: 'It was not for its commercial value as a British colony that we conquered and held Dominica, but rather to bedevil the French in a military sense by cutting their great West Indian colony in two.'[14]

Yet, once it had been conquered, the planters and their financial backers in London could not afford to lose the millions of pounds that they had already invested in Dominica since 1763. During those 20 years they had neither sufficient time nor the ideal conditions to fully recoup their investments and British interests were served on many levels by holding on to Dominica.

British forces landed at Pointe Michel in January 1784 and camped there until the French government and its soldiers were ready to depart from Roseau. As French troops left the island they laid down barrels of gunpowder and blew up as many of the military works that they had constructed as possible so as to reduce any free advantage to the British army.

As the news of the British reoccupation reached the Maroon chiefs it appeared to the colonists that 'they were resolved to recommence their depredations... they bid defiance to every measure, and had the audacity to threaten [that] they would repel any attempts to be made to reduce them.'[15] A return to British rule would mean the commencement of an all-out war against them. In the name of 'peace and civilised order' the brutal discipline on the plantations would be intensified. Retribution for any liberties taken during the French occupation would be set in motion and the laws and public punishments against them would be strengthened. It was clear that the years ahead would be challenging and the chiefs wasted no time in moving to preempt any action by the planters that would threaten their survival.

8

The First Maroon War: the Balla uprising

When British troops arrived to reclaim Dominica in January 1784 '... multitudes of negroes, lined both sides of the way as they entered the town.'[1] Just by observing the British celebrations as they took back control of the island, the slaves and Maroon leaders were aware that the English speaking plantocracy had reclaimed their colonial possession and its plantations with a renewed sense of purpose and jingoistic determination. 'As soon as the British troops were in possession of the fort, they hoisted the standard of England on the flagstaff... and being elated with joy on the occasion, the English inhabitants were so eager to lend their assistance to hoist it, that they were nearly pulling the halliards, by which it was raised, to pieces, and breaking down the flagstaff by the force of their numbers.'[2]

Immediately after the French forces went aboard their vessels in Roseau harbour, the new British governor, Captain John Orde, was welcomed ashore. He had served in the Royal Navy since joining in 1766, had commanded ships and seen action in several parts of the Atlantic and Mediterranean and had visited most of the colonies of Britain's fledgling empire. The Admiralty and the Board of Trade were of the view that this experience would put him in good stead to command what was already known to be a difficult posting. Amid shouts of 'Long live King

Sir John Orde, governor of Dominica 1784-93 (George Romney)

George', he was escorted by the inhabitants to the Court House where he took the usual oaths of a new governor.

However, once the celebrations had died down and the reorganised English and Protestant legislature got back to work, Orde found out how short-lived the hospitality had been. He learned how difficult the men who had to vote money for his schemes could be and, from the very start, he did not have much luck with his secretaries; they were too free with his secrets, too deeply involved in local feuds – and there were many of these. Within months of taking office Orde became unpopular, both with the Assembly and the public.

Apart from the political bickering and the problems of reviving trade and production, the government of the colony also faced two major challenges: providing for refugees who had arrived from the former British colonies in North America and raising a local army to make war against the increasing numbers of Maroons.

American colonists, who were loyal to the British Crown, had fled from the newly declared United States of America and ventured to establish new settlements in Jamaica, the Bahamas, Dominica and St Vincent. Those who came to Dominica – nearly 600 of them – required land and funds to get started, and the Assembly, eager to increase the depleted white population and get more men to join the militia, was willing to grant favours.[3] With the American Loyalists came another group who would ultimately affect the Maroons: enslaved Africans who had fought during the American War of Independence on the side of their Loyalist 'masters' and who also had to leave the newly declared United States. They came to the Caribbean as the South Carolina Corps and gave the British army the idea of forming black Regiments to defend the islands. The establishment of such slave Regiments in 1797 along with a Black Ranger Corps was to be a serious blow to the Maroons for they would have to fight black forces as well as whites raised against them.

At the time of Orde's arrival, the established planters had renewed investments in their plantations, reorganised their sugar production and expanded into coffee as the French had done. The markets for both of these crops were doing well during that decade. The enslaved African labour force to put all of this into operation had to be increased and, as a result, the importation of enslaved Africans surged from late 1783 when news of the treaty that would return Dominica to British rule had been confirmed. Just as a new wave of African arrivals in the 1760s led to a sudden increase in Maroon numbers so too did this second wave of slave imports.

Maroon leaders such as Jacko, Balla, Congo Ray, Pharcel, Mabouya and Cicero[4] (otherwise known as 'Sussex') had arrived with the first wave of British slavers after 1764, and in the 1780s a new influx of younger leaders such as Noel, Quashie, Elephant and Moco would become senior chiefs in later conflicts. The long-term effects of this would be felt in the escalation of Maroon pressure on the plantocracy punctuated by the First Maroon War of 1785-1786, the New Year's Day Revolt of 1791 and the Second Maroon War of 1812-1814.

Over this period new names of Maroons of both sexes appear in the reports sent in by parish militia leaders, commanders of Black Ranger Corps and regular soldiers hired to scour the interior of the island for Maroons. Besides those already mentioned are names such as Hall, Gros Bois, Dick, Liverpool, Ledger, Louis Moco, Bibiane, Agathe, Angelique, Presente, Caesar, Calypso, Marie Rose, Yellow, Cork, Contabrie, Tranquille, Quaco, Alexis, Jupiter, Juba, Zombie (otherwise known as 'Townside'), Clemence, Brutus and Petite Jacques.

But the decision to become a Maroon was not an easy one. Liberty in the forest came at a price. The danger of being caught and punished was one thing, but living in rain-drenched conditions, constantly on the look out and on the move and with only seasonal food supplies for nourishment, had to be taken into account. However harsh plantation conditions may have been, there was a certain stability to be considered when comparing the two options. Ethnic, language and social differences within the slave society also affected the slaves' decision to join the Maroons.

Orde faces the Maroons

When Governor John Orde took up office he faced planters who had just come through several disasters during the French occupation and they now had to concentrate on the serious Maroon threat. In trying to deal with the crisis in Dominica they repeatedly referred to the situation in Jamaica where the British had been battling Maroons since the 1650s. Indeed, throughout the 18th century, the Dominica Maroons were rated only second in organisation, discipline, strength and unity of purpose to their counterparts in Jamaica.[5]

However, towards the end of the Maroon era, Robert Heron, a British MP, informed the House of Commons that the situation in Jamaica was by no means the same as in Dominica. In his anti-Maroon tirade, defending the harsh action taken against them, he claimed that the Dominica Maroons were worse. 'They were not like those in Jamaica; the Jamaica Maroons are a body of men originally composed of the Coromantyne Negroes, who fled from the Spanish at the first conquest of the island by the British and establishing themselves in the difficult country in its centre, sometimes recruiting their number by runaway slaves, at other times giving them up, were acknowledged by repeated treaties, and obtained a political existence. The Dominica Maroons, on the contrary, more numerous and far more savage, consisted entirely of runaway slaves, never acknowledged by any treaty or truce whatever. It is very difficult for us to conceive that in an island only 29 miles by 12, there should be a territory in the interior so strong, that I believe it would occupy more days to traverse its breadth than the distance contains miles; this country the Maroons inhabited, they cultivated some provision grounds, but their chief dependence was on plunder, robbery their subsistence their occupation murder.'[6]

By 1785, a string of Maroon camps had developed in the centre of Dominica. Each was led by a chief. In the southern camps there were Congo Ray, Balla, Zombie, Jupiter, Juba, Cicero and Hall. Above Grand Fond was the camp of Mabouya and in the higher reaches of the Layou valley there was Jacko, Goree Greg and Sandy; above Colihaut was

Pharcel. The Maroons had organised themselves into social and political units headed
by chiefs, subchiefs and captains, and their
camps were also inhabited by women and
children. Each chief had special gun bearers
who acted as loyal valets seeing to their
needs. Then there were recruiting agents
who urged slaves on the estates to join their
camps. Governor Orde wrote to London
that in Dominica he had 'an internal enemy
of the most alarming kind'.[7]

Morne 'Neg Mawon', with the
Laurent River

Within months of the British reoccupation
of the island, Chief Balla, an African-born
slave from Belfast plantation on the west coast, got news that the
planters were raising their own little army; this was because they could
not depend on the regular troops stationed at the garrisons at Morne
Bruce and at Prince Rupert's Bay. The British army had a policy of
reserving their forces for external action only. It expected the local
Assembly to make their own arrangements for internal defence against
the Maroons. If regular troops such as the 30th or 15th Regiments were
used in such circumstances they would have to be paid for by the
legislature from the local treasury and supplied with rations, clothing,
ammunition, arms and shelter at no cost to the army. Similarly, the
burden of launching a local force to take on this campaign would rest
squarely with the Assembly.

To facilitate this, a bill was prepared in 1785 to raise a fund for
financing a 'Legion' by imposing extra taxes on possessions, produce,
and on each person according to their profession or economic status.
The extra levies imposed for this special fund were set in place for three
years and based on the first year's receipts of £17,014 7s 10 ½ d from
May 1785 to May 1786, the colony amassed an estimated £51,043 for its
anti-Maroon campaign over that period. Such a figure represented a
significant diversion of money away from commercial investment at a

time of financial stress and it showed how the continued pressure by the Maroons on the plantocracy hit at the very economic stability of the colony besides creating a climate of fear, death and physical destruction.[8]

As news of this offensive reached Balla at his jungle headquarters near Morne 'Neg Mawon', he appears to have held consultations with Pharcel, Cicero and Congo Ray to argue for the creation of a 'Grand Camp' in the middle of the island to counteract the government's plan and meet force with force. He wanted to match the Legion's numbers and launch an attack against the plantations with all haste so as to catch the British off guard before they had time to fully organise their colonial forces.[9]

Down in Roseau the legislature lumbered through the parliamentary process of getting the Legion up and running with lengthy debates and resolutions communicated by messengers between the Assembly, Council and governor as if they were in London replicating the process between the Commons, Lords and monarch. Eventually the necessary legislation was approved and the first funds were collected to finance a Legion of 500 men: free people of colour, Europeans and 'trusty' enslaved Africans belonging to various plantations. The planter's army set up three camps at strategic points: in the south to cover the parishes of St Patrick and the less volatile mainly French zones, of St Mark and St Luke; in the north, behind the large British estates of Hatton Garden, Melville Hall and Londonderry, to overlook the parishes of St Andrew around to St Joseph that skirted the base of Morne Diablotin.

The third and largest base was encamped on the 'Lake Road', still known today in Creole as the Chemin L'Etang, between Rosalie and Roseau. This was to monitor the parishes on both sides of the island including St George and St Paul on the west and St David on the east. However, it was a long time before they could accomplish anything significant against the Maroons, who were continuing their raids on estates. This was largely because of the very different methods of fighting between the two forces. The Legion used more formal

European military tactics while the Maroons were experts in guerrilla warfare. Towards the end of 1785 and at the beginning of the following year there was a major test of strength and skill between the two forces.

Apart from the Lake route, there was only one other significant track that crossed the island through the forested interior. That was the 'Grand Chemin' from the mouth of the Layou river on the west coast to Pagua Bay on the north-east coast. It had been opened up under the direction of the French before 1761 and was based on an earlier Kalinago trace across Dominica. (Even in the 21st century, part of the trans-insular road from Roseau to Douglas-Charles Airport at Melville Hall follows this track in the vicinity of Bells, D'Leau Gomier and down the Pagua valley to the Atlantic side of the island.) A few other French tracks went up the valleys to connect small coffee estates to the coast or crossed narrow parts of the island such as Loubiere to Grand Bay, Anse Du Mai to Portsmouth and Penville to Capuchin. Most of these tracks were almost impassable and elsewhere the island was completely without roads. This provided an uncharted battleground where only those who knew the ways of the forest could succeed and here the Maroons were superior to the organised military tactics of the 18th-century colonists.

In addition to the challenges of the thick jungle and difficult terrain there were also the seasonal changes to contend with. Torrential rains and the threat of hurricanes affected campaigns against the Maroons during the rainy season from June to November. During the first months of the year planters and their slave gangs were consumed with harvesting and processing sugar cane at 'crop time' and this provided an opportunity for the Maroons to disrupt production.

Balla's major attack on the windward coast estate of Rosalie is an example of their well laid plans. News had reached Balla that a Maroon from his camp had been recaptured by the government and had been disciplined by William Stuart, the former governor of Dominica. Stuart was part owner of this 2,081 acre plantation with investors O'Hara, Clarke and Browne (all of whose names survive in the names of the tributaries that flow into the main Rosalie river). Chief Balla decided to punish Stuart for his unofficial action and thus send a message to other planters across the colony by attacking this prominent plantation. The Maroons of Balla's camp had blocked the Chemin L'Etang above Grand Fond with large trees and they had piled boulders tied with stout vines on clifftops above the paths where soldiers would have to march in single file. Guards had been set to warn them of the Legion's movements. Sweeping down from the hills in the dark, a band of some 100 Maroons plundered the sugar works and plantation house at Rosalie, murdering the manager, the two overseers, a carpenter, and the

chief driver and threw them into the flames of the burning buildings. Even today, the hill directly behind the ruins of the manager's house is still called 'Neg Mawon'. For two days Balla and his men ate, drank and revelled at the estate, most of which they had destroyed by fire. With

Rosalie estate, 1776, a major sugar producer

Chemin L'Etang blocked and guarded by Maroon lookouts, news of this Maroon victory reached Roseau via the southern tracks days before the Legion based at Laudat knew a thing about it.

This defeat of the colony's ambitious and costly plan caused the Legion to be blamed for slackness and it was only with the assistance of some private individuals that any counter attacks were successful. Among these helpers was an English carpenter called Richardson, who was employed in January 1786 to rebuild the works at Rosalie. As the priest-historian Father Raymond Proesmans described it: 'Richardson met the captain of the camp at Laudat and this captain told him, "I am rather small today because I got a good shaking up from Roseau". So the carpenter said, "Oh you want to catch them? You talk as if it is going to be easy. We do not want to go with an army like you have, we want a

THE FIRST MAROON WAR: THE BALLA UPRISING

little group of men that are really decided and ready to die if necessary".'[10]

Leading a small group of Legionnaires moving through the forest in the manner of jungle guerrillas rather than formal 18th-century soldiers, Richardson guided the expedition across the difficult terrain towards the encampment of Balla. They must have roughly followed the course of the modern Rosalie to Pont Casse road and then swerved north to the mountain where Balla had his camp, near the summit of Morne 'Neg Mawon', the steep-sided mountain that dominates the gentler sloping land just north of Morne Trois Pitons. Atwood described the approach to the camp as being a staircase with steps very far apart. These are similar to those described for the camp of Jacko overlooking the Layou river and it appears that this form of military earthworks was replicated in other Maroon camps across Dominica. Scaling these heights was a severe test for

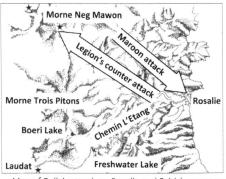

Map of Balla's attack on Rosalie and British response

the legionnaires as Atwood recounted: 'Having travelled all night through the woods wading through rapid rivers, crossing over steep mountains, and encountering many rivers in their way, by noon next day they came to the mountain whereon was the encampment of Balla. This they ascended with great difficulty it being cut into steps of a great height above each other, which had been done by the runaways for their own convenience as being the only possible way to ascend the mountain.[11]

Although Richardson and his band reached Balla's camp, their main objective failed for most of the Maroons fled the settlement during the surprise attack. However, in the panic of the escape a number of women and children were left in the camp and captured by the Legion. Among them were Charlotte, Calypso, Angelique, Marie-Rose,

Tranquille, Rosay and Victorie, who were reported to be the women or wives of Balla, Sandy and Goree Greg. Among the children was a boy described as 'Balla's little son'.[12]

The women were taken to Roseau where they appeared in court in early February 1786. The House of Assembly and Council had quickly passed temporary legislation enabling the captives to act as witnesses since under normal circumstances the evidence of blacks was not permissible in court. The judge offered the women leniency if they gave accounts of all that they knew about the Maroons. As a result, they revealed valuable information at their trial. One of them, Rosay, gave a rough census of Maroons in Sandy's camp while others added facts concerning the position and size of certain other major camps in the south and central mountains.[13]

Rosay's evidence about Sandy's camp gives an idea of the typical composition of these forest forts: 'Men: Sandy, owner Granault; August, owner Granault; Louis, owner Granault; Laurent, owner Granault; Yellow, owner Granault; Cork, owner Dr. Nelson; Constable, owner Lefalier; Congo, owner Laudat; Dominique, owner Forneau. Women: Calypso, owner Granault; Charlotte, owner Granault; Angelique, owner Normand Loubiere; Marie-Rose, not known to her, Corne and child Jean, owner Dr Nelson; Tranquille and children, owner Fourneau; Victorie, Rosay, owner Fourneau.'[14] Based on the names of the owners

it appears that these Maroons had come from all over the island, from plantations in the parishes of St Peter, St George, and St Andrew. Once the captured women had served their purpose in court they were returned with their children to their former owners even though their offspring had been born in

Aqueduct arch at Rosalie today

the forest. 'You know how slavery went. The child belonged to the mother, so who owns the mother owns the child.'[15]

In the same month, Chief Cicero was captured at Fond Boeri, near the Boeri Lake, by a free black man called Augustine. The chief's mountain retreat had been revealed by a fellow slave called Petite Jacques, and Augustine acted on the tip off so as to get a share of the reward. 'The examination of Cicero, otherwise called Sussex, belonging to Mitcham's estate, Parish of St Patrick, says he was absent from the said estate upwards of three years and in the woods part of the time in the Camp of Congoree and Balla; says that he was at Rosalie at the attack made there. But says he was forced to go; was taken by a free Negro named Augustine and others on 17 February 1786 at Fond de Boeri.'[16] Other information reveals that at the time of the Rosalie raid Cicero was Balla's gun-bearer and that he was also at an earlier attack 'on Mr. Haddock's estate'. 'He was one of the most active everywhere; collected Negroes for the purpose and was instrumental in incorporating the camp of Balla and Congoree; set fire on the order of Balla to the Negro Houses at Rosalie and carried one of Congoree's guns at the attack on Tana' (at Tanama Point overlooking Grand Bay).[17]

When Cicero was dragged before the court, Petit Jacques gave additional evidence against him and thus the respected Maroon strategist was found guilty of not only being involved in the attack on Rosalie but on other estates as well and was condemned to death: 'He shall be carried back to the common gaol of this island there to remain until Saturday fourth March 1786, and from thence be carried to Woodbridge Bay beyond the French houses on the Kings 50 paces and there be jibbeted alive.'[18]

The scene of Cicero's execution was Fond Cole, a mile from Roseau, and there he was left broken and exposed on an ox cart wheel atop a pole as a lesson to others. The following day was the main market day, and anyone going into Roseau to sell their produce would have seen the body. The man who had helped to capture him was paid a reward of £33. As Father Proesmans said, 'The text which I have seen says £33,

£33 which he received. And I found it criminal that they just had to put it £33, like Judas got 33 pieces too…'[19]

On 17 March 1786, the House of Assembly passed a resolution offering rewards to those who killed or captured the key Maroon chiefs still at large. 'That the Governor in Chief be authorised to offer a reward of Freedom and the sum of £16.10s to any Slave and the sum of £150, to any white or free person who shall apprehend or bring in the head of Balla, Farcelle, Congaree or Mabuyah over and above the rewards already given by Law. And that this House will make provision for the payment of such rewards and expenses. And also for the payment of some Blankets that have been furnished to the Slaves employed against the runaways to be repaid for by the respective Owners out of their hire.'[20]

That same day a bill was introduced 'to Alter and amend the Act for the more effectual Suppression of Runaway Slaves' which strengthened the powers against Maroons and imposed more stringent punishments on plantation slaves who aided them in any way. Maroon camps were attacked and severely mauled, some 150 of the fugitives being killed or captured. Later that month three more chiefs were taken: Balla, Goree Greg and Sandy. In response to the reward that was offered, Balla was betrayed by a slave of Belfast estate and was shot and injured by a party of black legionnaires who brought him into Roseau.

Orde, writing to the Secretary of State Viscount Sydney, on 16 April, gave his account of Balla's last defiant stand. It is just one example of the hundreds of detailed reports on the Maroons that were sent to London by the governors of Dominica during the 30 years of intense Maroon resistance: '… good fortune has given us possession of the Principal Runaway Chief, Balla, many of his followers are killed and taken, many have surrendered and the rest are greatly dispersed and distressed… Balla … would not suffer himself to be taken until so wounded that he could not fly. The behaviour of this deluded wretch at his death proved him as hardened as previous conduct had done – he refused answering almost any questions that were put to him, though perfectly in his senses – he called upon his captors repeatedly to cut off his head, telling them that they might do so, but that Balla would not die – his obi or charm and his child were the only things that he expressed much anxiety about. The former he wished to bury, the latter, a boy of about 5 years old he bid to remember, the Beckeys or White Man had killed his father.'[21]

Balla, in the manner of Cicero, was taken to the public marketplace in Roseau and exposed in an iron frame or gibbet, rather like a cage, and took a week to die. The slaves sang a mournful Creole lament '*Balla mort, bwa gatay*.' ('Balla is dead, the woods are spoilt.')

Throughout March and April of 1786, hired soldiers, militiamen and black legionnaires continued to scour the mountains for Maroons. Commanding officers sent letters to Governor Orde in Roseau via slave runners keeping him abreast of their progress in the forest. On 22 March, for instance, Captain Garret, commander of the North Legion Rangers, reports from Hatton Garden estate about his exploits on the slopes of Morne Diablotin 'between the heads of the Layou and Cashibona Rivers'. There, he said, 'I discovered two huts on the opposite side of the Mountain, which our guide told me he believed to be the camp of eight Runaways commanded by Gro Bois... I soon entered the encampment and from the number of Pickets, and Pitts with which I found it surrounded, I was immediately convinced that it was Farcell's Camp.'[22]

The force captured one Maroon who gave his name as Fortune 'the property of Mr. Younge at Grand Baye'. Again, this shows the wide area covered by the Maroons since this camp was in the north and Fortune had come from the extreme south of the island. Maroons of this camp had taken up positions behind trees and bushes and succeeded in wounding three of the Colony Troops while four members of the 30th Regiment were seriously injured by sharp wood pickets, a form of hunters' trap still used today to catch wild pigs.

The camp had been warned of the soldiers' approach by three Maroons, who they had pursued the day before '... in consequence of which, all their women and baggage had been immediately sent from camp, and only the men left with Arms to oppose us. That Farcell's party consists of fifty Men, a number of women and Children, that they have many Fire Arms… he never saw more than two hornfull's of powder and very little ball.'[23]

Meanwhile, Rangers were on the look out for the Maroon called Pharcel, who was considered to be one of the main chiefs in the Morne Diablotin area above Colihaut. One slave called Joseph, who was tried

on 6 March 1786, was accused of harbouring Maroons of Pharcel's camp and supplying food to other camps and was convicted and sentenced to death. Despite all his master's efforts to save him, he was brought back to Colihaut where he worked and was burned alive at the stake five days later on 11 March. The site of this and other public executions

The burning of Joseph at La Place Dam, Colihaut

at Colihaut was in the open square in the centre of the village. It is known today as La Place Dam, but the origin of the name is from the French, La Place Des Armes, where members of the St Peter's parish militia did their drill every month and where the Sunday market was held.

These events came towards the end of the First Maroon War, and eventually, satisfied that their objective had met with some success, Governor Orde wrote to the Assembly: 'Gentlemen. I have the pleasure to inform you that in consequence of the capture and surrender of the Runaway chiefs: Balla, Goree Greg and Sandy and the destruction and dispersion of so great a part of their followers as has lately taken place, the council and myself have determined that keeping up so large a Force as was hitherto employed against them, will no longer be necessary.

'I have therefore with their advice directed it to be reduced… and so to be continued until Farcelle and his followers (who are still formidable) shall be broken up – until the Legislature shall determine upon some permanent establishment better suited to the present circumstances …'[24]

In the same letter, Governor Orde urged that the slave laws should be revised and made more 'humanitarian' in order that slaves might not be so tempted to escape. In 1788, after much cajoling by the governor and his superiors in London, the local legislature passed a set of bills that grudgingly set down some regulations for the administration and protection of the enslaved. On 17 December 1788 the Council informed the House that a bill was passed entitled 'An Act for the encouragement, protection and better government of Slaves'. One of its clauses declared that there should be a limit on the number of lashes given as punishment to any slave and this was set at 39 strokes; even so it was at times disregarded with the knowledge that juries, packed with planters, would treat any convictions lightly even if not dismissing the case.

It was a mixed bag of legislation. On 4 December 1788, a bill was presented in the House to appoint a company of Rangers. This formalised the bands of 'trusted slaves' that had been raised by planters to assist the campaign against the Maroons in 1786. There was also a bill to revise and amend the Militia Act 'for the better administration of a Militia in this Island'. Both of these were aimed at consolidating the planters' forces against the Maroons.

Among these acts of 1788 was the first legislation attempting to outlaw the practice of obeah. It was really an attack on a wide range of African religious traditions, which were seen by the planters as 'dangerous superstitions'. Obeah was also viewed as a means of rallying slave support for rebellion and of creating networks, rather like secret societies, that linked slaves across plantations.[25] As the philosopher and historian Gordon Lewis pointed out, it was part of the remembered African background.[26] In the death throes of Chief Balla, Governor Orde had, as already noted, commented about the chief's concern for his 'Obi charm' hanging around his neck.

Maroon warriors underwent complex rites in order to persuade themselves that they were physically immune to white Western guns and ammunition. This legislation was aimed at stamping out all such delusions. As the preamble to the legislation put it: 'It frequently happens that slaves assume the art of witchcraft, or are what is commonly called Obeah or Doctor Men, and, under the pretense of a gift of supernatural powers, do influence the minds of weak and credulous slaves, and frequently stimulate them to acts of mutiny or rebellion against their masters, renters, managers, and overseers and administer certain drugs and potions of a secret and generally a poisonous nature, as well as to slaves, as to free people of every description.' This was the earliest slave law in the West Indies to explicitly link poison with obeah. Punishments ranged from execution or, at the discretion of the judiciary, to suffer 'banishment and flogging on the bare breech.'[27]

Obeah laws were amended and upgraded in various forms over the years well after slavery was over. This is particularly true of the Obeah Act of 1904, which remains almost unchanged on the island's statute books today; indeed attempts for its removal would, in some quarters, be strenuously resisted. In effect, the 1904 Act outlawed a particular type of religious belief. It also denied the Africans the practice of their art forms, mainly in woodcarving, since they could be punished for making 'an instrument of obeah' if they carved a mask or a figurine. It was part of a policy of the de-Africanisation of the people.[28]

9

A new challenge:
the French ascendancy

Between 1789 and 1799 France was torn by revolution. This period of rapid change and political intrigue led to much bewilderment among the French inhabitants of the West Indies and to restlessness among the free coloured people and slaves. The time it took for letters, military orders and news to cross the Atlantic Ocean further confused the issue. By the time that orders had been received from Paris and had been replied to, about five months had passed. There were disturbances in all French colonies. In Haiti, of course, it had its most violent and long-lasting effects.

One of the most misleading statistics quoted in outlines of Dominican history is the respective length of French and British occupation of the island. Judged simply on that basis, Dominica should be among the more Anglophile of the West Indian islands, having had only five years of French control since it was ceded to Britain in 1763. But the island's position between two of the most important and valuable colonies of the French Empire created a constant imbalance between British occupation and French influence.

The majority of the European population on Dominica was French and by cultural transfusion so were their slaves. The movement of people and the business and family connections which were maintained between the islands defied the state of war, peace, or treaties between the colonial powers. The culture of the permanently resident French families on their scattered estates triumphed over that of the British officials huddled in Roseau or of the transient attorneys who managed the British estates for their mainly absentee owners in London, Glasgow, Edinburgh or Belfast.

Balla's rebellion, following so closely after five years of French occupation and the side effects of the American War of Independence (1775-1783) completely unnerved the British plantocracy in Dominica. It was considered that the island had suffered most severely of all their Caribbean colonies during those years. In 1785 the House of Assembly and Council made an appeal directly to King George III, through Governor Orde, for military hardware to compensate for that which had been lost during the French occupation. The armaments arrived shortly after Balla's demise. In spite of the Governor's optimistic outlook in his letter to them expressing pleasure that certain major Maroon chiefs and their supporters had been captured and surrendered, both branches of the legislature wrote again to the king in mid-April 1786 expressing their concerns. While thanking him for 'your Majesty's Gift of one thousand stand of Arms and Accoutrements', they made it clear that his loyal subjects were labouring 'under the severest load of accumulated Misfortunes' and proceeded to provide the King with a litany of Dominica's woes:

Cudgelling match between French and English slaves
(Agostino Brunias)

'The poverty of its inhabitants, caused in a great Measure by the heavy Expenses and Labour attendant on clearing and settling Land in standing wood and in many cases by the Infertility of the Soil; Its subsequent Capture by the Arms of France; The visitation of Providence in two dreadful Hurricanes in 1779 and 1780 and a Fire that consumed the Town of Roseau in 1781 added to the Rebellion of our

Slaves which at this moment exists, are calamities that would have conquered the Spirits of any other Subjects, than such as looked up to the Blessings of a British Government and confided in the aid and relief of a benevolent and gracious Sovereign.' The flattery aside, they threw themselves upon his mercy and implored the king for further aid 'particularly from the pressure of public Debts…and such relief and assistance as to Your Majesty's Royal Wisdom shall seem meet.' On behalf of the planters they petitioned for 'a remission of the balances still due on their estates'[1] but further support was slow in coming and, by 1790, only 50 plantations were in operation while some 30 had been abandoned.

The Mulatto Connection

As the British sold off parts of their estates, the mulattos[2] or free coloured tradesmen from Martinique and Guadeloupe bought and developed them. Dominica offered them opportunities denied to them on their own islands and the French of all colours took advantage of the loopholes available in the colony of another nation; they were considered to be notorious smugglers through whom sugar of French origin entered England thus evading the strict trading and navigation laws then in force. The French mulatto population also had other more personal reasons for investing in Dominica during the late eighteenth century. The Code Noir of 1685 had given them all the rights of free men, but that had been gradually eroded to a point in 1766 when the French colonial planter councils persuaded the government to pass laws restricting their rights.

Already denied any political rights, these well educated and well off owners of slaves and property could no longer be officers in the militia or hold legal posts. Even the wearing of certain clothes was banned. Mulatto men were forbidden to carry swords, in a period when the wearing of a sword was the sign of a gentleman. In 1787, the French colonies were granted assemblies but the mulattos were barred from membership. These new regulations were an irritant to men who regarded themselves as being more French than African.

In British Dominica, there was greater latitude regarding personal affairs of the free coloured and although political activity and positions of public office were similarly restricted, landholding was permitted with full freehold rights. A wide range of commercial activities was also open to them and special mulatto militias existed. This did not mean that the mulattos were any less patriotic to France. They were pragmatists who balanced their state of virtual dual nationality to their own advantage whenever possible. Yet as far as the British were concerned, their presence was of economic advantage in a colony that needed every penny of taxes, export duty and private enterprise it could muster, regardless of the colour of the entrepreneurs. Indeed, as the number of whites on Dominica declined rapidly after full emancipation of the enslaved in 1838, the prominence of people of colour in politics, commerce, landholding and the social structure of the island grew rapidly, and by the 20th century they commanded a powerful network of control over the black working class. One elite had simply been replaced by another.

As conditions on the plantations deteriorated, French Royalists who came to Dominica for safety from the unstable situation in Martinique and Guadeloupe, were armed to assist the British in the defence of the island. By 1793, it was estimated that between 5,000 and 6,000 Royalist refugees, white and coloured, had arrived in Dominica. However, Republicans, French whites and mulattos sympathetic to the French Revolution, were also entering the island adding to the large French population already established; and they too were quietly taking sides. Secretly printed pamphlets were being circulated. *'L'ami de la Liberté - l'enemi de la licence'*, they proclaimed ('the friend of liberty – the enemy of the law'). This paper was of grave concern to the Assembly for its minutes of 25 January 1791 noted: 'Encouragement is given to slaves and opinions promulgated in their favour so dangerous to lives and properties of their Masters... it appears that [the publication] is one of the principal causes to which the present disaffection amongst the

Negroes may be attributed.'[3] It was widely assumed that the author was planter and printer John Lowndes, proprietor of Mount Anthony estate near today's village of Cochrane. He was an eccentric character who, more than once, had been brought before the courts for libel and had served time in the local jail for what he had published.[4] The landing of free mulattos on Dominica's shores and their movements along the bridle paths and countryside was by now a matter of grave concern to the governor and Assembly. The 1786 action against the Maroons had only achieved a brief respite for now their numbers and movement in the mountains were intensifying once more.

The planters were now facing a three-pronged attack, from mulattos, Maroons and France, a situation which tormented the British in Dominica for more than 20 years. When Governor John Orde had addressed the House of Assembly in 1786 on his satisfaction at the surrender of the Maroon chiefs 'and the destruction and dispersion of so great a part of their followers', he was not to know that a spark was being lit in the streets of Paris, the flames of which would rage through France and across the Atlantic to the broad plains of Haiti, the towns and villages of Guadeloupe, and from there scorch the tenuous British hold on Dominica. The effects of this were to make the last years of John Orde in Dominica the most miserable of his life.

10

The New Year's Day Revolt: Maroons and 'the Rights of Man'

The British plantations on Dominica enjoyed their main holiday of festival and feasting on the days between Christmas and New Year's Day. Immediately after that, the busy preparation for 'crop time' would begin on the sugar estates. However, as the sun rose on New Year's Day 1791 over the wide valley along the shores of Grand Bay and further east over the sugar and coffee fields of Bagatelle and in the areas of Delices and Boetica no one stirred in the slave compounds. 'Negro drivers' came around the crowded huts to urge the slaves under their charge to get a move on. Then managers, attorneys and overseers arose from their quarters. But the bells and conch shell horns that called the slaves to work went unheeded.

In January 1791, a rebellion began at Grand Bay in the parish of St Patrick and spread to the east as far as Rosalie. Popularly called The New Year's Day Revolt, it was the first of a new form of uprising, inspired not merely by the yearning for freedom but fed also by French revolutionary ideas. Its leader was a free Martiniquan mulatto called Jean Louis Polinaire, a carpenter by trade. His attempt to mobilise and control the southern and eastern parishes was part of a plan to take over the whole island – by starting a chain of rebellion from the windward areas.

Polinaire's family had been in Martinique for several generations. His mother and her forbears had been enslaved Africans. On his father's side he was descended from French settlers who had come out from Europe to engage in plantation business. There were many young men like him scattered around the French Antilles. They were skilled tradesmen and educated contributors to the social and commercial life of the colonies. Nevertheless, because of their ethnicity, they were restricted by law from participating as fully free citizens.

As they read the works of the philosophers of the French Enlightenment such as Voltaire, Jean-Jacques Rousseau, Denis Diderot and Charles Louis Montesquieu on human liberty, equality and fraternity, they looked around at their own condition in the Caribbean and began to ask questions and demand change. Although Polinaire himself may not have been able to write and his reading skills may have been basic,[1] he absorbed the new philosophy of equality and rights during gatherings organised by the more educated people of his class and colour in Martinique. Some, like Polinaire, went further and sought to organise actual revolt for despite the Declaration of the Rights of Man and Citizen, passed by the French Assembly in 1789, it was clear that 'Man' did not yet include the enslaved.

Polinaire considered that he would have little chance of success of fomenting revolt in Martinique where, in spite of a cluster of forested mountains in the northern half of the island, the extensive plantations were in close proximity to each other and the powerful planters had an iron grip on their slaves. They also had the backing of a strong military presence in forts and coastal batteries across the island. More significantly, Fort Royale (the pre-revolutionary name for the capital Fort de France) was a heavily defended base for the French navy. Besides, the white population were by and large supporters of the Royalist cause in France and had no sympathy with the revolutionary ideas that were being promoted in Martinique by the free *gens du couleur*, who were mainly gathered in the old island capital of St Pierre.

A veritable civil war broke out between town and country. During the latter part of 1790, St Pierre was blockaded by land and sea and free black and mulatto revolutionaries were attacked and killed. Those who could do so escaped in canoes across the channel to Dominica, landing secretly in places such as Stowe, Fond St Jean, Petite Savanne and Pointe Mulatre along the south coast. This was a well-established route that had been plied by smugglers from Martinique and vice versa since the 1760s.

Polinaire was one such refugee who crossed the 25 miles of open ocean to escape the volatile situation in St Pierre. He saw Dominica as a safer base from which to spread his message and he landed into a situation where conditions were conducive for successful revolt. The European population in Dominica was not only divided by national allegiance between the British and French, but there were political tensions between the planters and the colonial administration. In addition, the many *petits blancs*, smallholders of both nationalities, felt disadvantaged by the social and economic divisions within the white community. And not least, there were increasing numbers of slaves escaping from plantations and filling the Maroon camps.

In at least one case, inspiration for revolution came directly to Dominica from the unfolding rebellion in St Domingue. A free mulatto called Bonhomme, originally from St Domingue and educated in France, lived for a time in Dominica. According to the historian Anne Pérotin-Dumon, Bonhomme remarked to an English colonist in Dominica that the prediction of Abbé Raynal, the philosopher of the French enlightenment, about the rise to power of a black Spartacus in the Caribbean had come true. If blacks in St Domingue organised themselves and were determined, Bonhomme was quoted as saying, 'they were going to take power and replace the whites'. Unlike Polinaire, whose naive vision for Dominica included a role for sympathetic whites, Bonhomme argued not to integrate with whites but to overthrow them, not to join with the minority of citizens but to create a new majority whose ruling elite would be free coloureds.[2] It appears that Bonhomme eventually escaped from Dominica as the local revolt of 1791 collapsed and made it across the northern channel to

Mariegalante where he attempted to foment a similar insurrection there. He was, however, arrested soon afterwards and hanged as an alleged conspirator in 'a plot' planned for Christmas Day 1791.

As always, the physical nature of Dominica conspired to assist such causes. Improvements to the weak colonial defences that had enabled the French to take the island in 1778 were still under construction. The topographical division between the east and west coasts caused by the steep backbone of impassable mountains made a clear separation between windward and leeward that could be exploited. A fractured population alienated by differences in ethnicity, nationality, religion, language and separated by landscape lacked any unity of purpose. By Polinaire's assessment all this pointed to a society ripe for revolution. For a time in 1790 he worked at his trade of carpentry while gauging the state of the colony and conducting clandestine meetings with slaves and Maroon leaders.

French refugees such as Polinaire and Bonhomme had to take oaths of allegiance to the British Crown to be permitted to stay and work in Dominica. This was usually seen as a mere formality and a source of income for the registry, but as Polinaire was to find out, anyone who had sworn loyalty to King George III and later turned against the British colonial government or disturbed the peace in its colony of Dominica, could then be charged with treason.

Planters plot Orde's demise

British Governor Orde obtained the King's permission to return to England in 1789 'to make some arrangements relative to his private affairs'[3] but he also took the opportunity to consult with his superiors in London and to take some rest after five years of unrelenting political upheaval in the colony. He also took with him the son of the Maroon chief Balla who had been captured with his mother in the forest camp and who was present at his father's interrogation in Roseau three years before. Orde had taken the boy as his slave, raising him as his personal pageboy at Government House and took him to England to give him an education. Once in London, the youth disappears from the record but there are hints that he was sent to school and, like the sons of some African chiefs, he became an exotic character of London's Regency society. Orde was not alone in this. Some years earlier the Earl of Halifax, then at the head of the Board of Trade, had saved 'two black princes of Annamaboe'[4] from slavery in the West Indies and 'had them clothed and educated in a suitable manner'. They were 'in fashion at all assemblies…were received by the king and visited Covent Garden' before returning to Africa.[5]

On 9 August 1790, Orde was created Baronet Orde of Morpeth, Northumberland, which came with a knighthood. This elevation of status was a reward to the governor for his exemplary performance of his duties under difficult circumstances. But it was also aimed at sending a message to the irascible planters of Dominica that he was an officer in whom the Crown was well pleased. Even so, the factions railed against Orde and hoped that the British government would replace him with someone else. While he was abroad, Dominica was administered by Colonel James Bruce of the 70th Regiment, a senior planter, a member of the Executive Council and deputy provost marshal. The news of Orde's imminent return drove the governor's enemies into a frenzy and they plotted to ensure that he was prevented from landing, even to the point of planning to drown him as he disembarked.

The slaves overheard the planters plotting Orde's demise. From what they understood, the governor had been given orders by the King to improve the conditions of the slaves and allow them more time to work their gardens but that their masters were opposed to his return on those grounds. As the slaves perceived, the king and the governor were acting in their favour but the planters were trying to prevent the governor from doing so. Such a misunderstanding was a common feature of slave revolts in the British West Indies during the late 18th and early 19th centuries.

The myth of a benevolent king betrayed by others recurs throughout history and it is not surprising that it should repeatedly appear in the Caribbean. After all, African-born slaves had come from a culture of chiefdoms and monarchies. They had been raised on the concept of the benign chief who must be trusted and obeyed but whose munificence was often undermined by scheming minions. At the commencement of the Haitian Revolution, rebel slaves did not generally wear the French revolutionaries' tricolour cockade. To them it symbolised the emancipation of the whites only. Instead, they wore the white cockade, signifying loyalty to King Louis XVI.[6] 'Weirdest fantasy of all, many of the revolting slaves at the outset regarded themselves as the staunch vassals and champions of the King of France. They mixed up this idea with that of their personal emancipation, which they imagined he had ordered and that the colonists were selfishly withholding.'[7]

In Dominica, this myth was further distorted as slaves got snippets of news about the activities of the anti-slavery movement in England and the work of abolitionists such as William Wilberforce and Thomas Clarkson. The Society for Effecting the Abolition of the Slave Trade had been formed in 1787, while the French equivalent, the Societé des Amis des Noirs, was established the following year. Sailors in port and soldiers stationed on the forts discussed the growing tide of popular support for abolition and the sympathy of some members of parliament in London for their cause. The fact that Roseau and Portsmouth had been reopened as free ports, welcoming ships of all nations, was a major factor in facilitating the transfer of international news circulating the docksides, taverns and 'tippling houses' exchanged by European seamen who frequented all of the main port cities across the Atlantic world. Slaves doing plantation errands in Roseau and vendors taking part in the Sunday markets in the capital returned to the plantations with versions of the news that they had heard while in town. Domestic slaves, the 'house slaves' serving at the planters' tables, would have overheard conversations about current affairs, most of which decried the abolitionists and what they saw as the conciliatory attitude of the Crown government. The basic message picked up by the slaves from all this jumble of information was that administrative orders coming from the king in England via the governor were beneficial to them, but what came from the local planter assembly was bad.

Polinaire himself later confirmed that this had been the origin of the revolt: 'The Origin of the Revolt was, that Mr. Anketell, accompanied by Mr. Hall, and afterwards other gentlemen, came to the Windward of the Island, to get the Signatures of the Planters, to prevent the return of Governor Orde to this Country, saying that if Governor Orde returned to this Country, he would protect the Negroes and Mulattoes, which would make as much trouble here as at Martinico. That the Negroes understood that it was the intention of the Inhabitants, to fire on the Vessel that Governor Orde should come in and sink her sooner than let him land.'[8]

As it turned out, Orde landed in Roseau without incident apart from some jeering from onlookers as he made his way up the hill to Government House. Polinaire's plan was to conspire with the slaves on plantations along the south and east coasts to disrupt the plantation routine as a form of protest action. Its aim was that Orde, seeing their support for him, would implement the concessions that he had

supposedly been directed to make to the slaves. If they were not granted, this was the sign to launch a general uprising. Then, with the cooperation of the Maroons in the hills, they would overthrow the planters, attorneys, overseers and slave drivers to take control of the plantations of the windward coast.

Mount Sinai and the Grand Soufriere hills in south-east Dominica, a Maroon stronghold

In his somewhat naive conception of the rebellion, Polinaire explained the objective thus: 'That since the arrival of Governor Orde, the Negroes had heard that he, Governor Orde, had given orders that the Planters should give their Negroes THREE DAYS in the WEEK, and that the Planters had refused to do it; but on the Contrary, were more strict upon them: And as the Planters had refused THAT to Governor Orde, they were all resolved to take that Time themselves, and that the Free People of Colour, who should refuse to assist them, should be put to Death, upon which their fight began.

'That all the Negroes of the Island were concerned in the Plot, even those of Roseau, who sent News to those of the Windward of the Island… That they had heard that Governor Orde was sending all the Guns from Roseau to Prince Rupert's Bay. That it was the project of the Negroes, to take the Windward part of the island for themselves, from Grand Bay to La Soye; except that Governor Bruce, and some other Gentlemen that were good to their Negroes, were to be permitted to remain on their Estates; and those of the Whites that were not killed, were to have the Leeward of the Island.'[9]

Reference to guns being moved from Morne Bruce to the Cabrits garrison at Prince Rupert's Bay was based on a fact but the reason was misunderstood. Military defences at the Cabrits were being extended at that time and the large cast-iron cannons taken from Morne Bruce were being shipped to the north of the island to be mounted on batteries atop the twin hills of that military post. It was planned that eventually Morne Bruce garrison would be replenished with new stock coming out from England.[10] But the slaves' interpretation of what they saw happening was that Orde was disarming Roseau.

The misunderstanding about Orde's role in this affair persisted throughout the revolt as rumour and misinformation made its way deep into the hinterland. The governor noted with some indignation that a soldier engaged against the Maroons reported that 'whilst his party occupied a post in the neighbourhood of the Runaways, the Runaway Chiefs called out to them and said If they came from the Governor they were welcome to come and breakfast with them but if they came from the People [the Assembly] they would fire on them.[11]

The uprising was somewhat unusual in the history of West Indian slave revolts for what the slaves under Polinaire's influence were demanding was freedom to work for themselves for more days in the week as well as the customary one and a half days on weekends. Historian Julien Scott has noted that such ideas bore a striking similarity to a proposed Spanish slave code of 1789, which received considerable attention in the Spanish colonies but never went into effect.[12] Discussion among sailors in Roseau taverns who had passed through Havana, Santo Domingo or San Juan could have been the spark that set off such rumours. But whatever the source, when the demand for extra days was denied, the slaves of south-eastern Dominica virtually went on strike on New Year's Day 1791 'without going off the estates or attempting any acts of violence'. Governor Orde even visited the affected estates to see the situation for himself and to tell the slaves that there was no truth in the rumour that he had returned from a visit to England with orders for the planters to allow their slaves three days in each week to work in their own gardens.

Nevertheless, at 10.00pm on 17 January the slaves changed their strategy and rose up in open revolt. Suddenly an area 'commonly called the French Quarter' in the south-east of the parish of St Patrick erupted into violence. A group of slaves 'headed by some Free Mulattoes' took up arms killing one white man and 'Threatening other acts of Violence and Hostility'.[13] Polinaire reported that 'the Slaves to the Windward of the Island, on the different Plantations, were all very willing and zealous to join the Revolt, as far even as Grand Bay.'[14] And that 'each Plantation was to have had its Chief; and that at the Hour of Supper, the Negroes were to put their Masters to Death, while they were at Table.' However, rebel slaves had expected reinforcements that never arrived: 'They had expected Pharseille with Three Hundred Muskets, and Pangalos with Two Hundred Muskets, which did not come.'[15] As Orde was to note later, these numbers appear to have been greatly exaggerated.

Mention of Pharcel here is significant as is the reference to a chief called Pangalos. In the context of French revolutionary ideas, a Doctor Pangloss is the main character in Voltaire's novel *Candide* (1769). His many hair-raising adventures include being enslaved by Barbary pirates and often being on the point of death; even so he responds to his misfortunes by saying, 'All is for the best in the best of all possible worlds.' In *Candide*, Voltaire mocks the view of the German mathematician and philosopher Gottfried Wilhelm Leibniz (1646-1716), who proclaimed that God chose to create the best possible world. It is a mystery as to how the name of a character in the writings of the French Enlightenment becomes the name of a Maroon chief in the forests of Dominica. Perhaps this was a nickname given to the chief who thought that the dangers which he encountered as a 'Neg Mawon' leader 'were all for the best'.

Whatever the reason, the name alludes to the far-reaching influence of French revolutionary ideas in the Caribbean at this time. Indeed, the effects of French Revolutionary ideas upon the enslaved were referred to in reports on the uprising. 'It was considered to be in consequence of French intrigues, and propagation of French principles in Dominica, [that] an alarming insurrection of the slaves took place in one quarter of that island, in which some lives were lost. By prompt and able measures of the Governor, however, the insurrection was happily quelled, and the leaders delivered over to condign punishment.'[16]

Polinaire, meanwhile, was busy visiting the Maroon camps and holding meetings with slaves on the outskirts of plantations in the east, keeping spirits up and campaigning for the intensification of the revolt. At the same time, Governor Orde was collecting every piece of printed revolutionary material that he could find to send on to his superiors in London as further proof of his precarious position. One four-page pamphlet, for instance, printed locally in French, was addressed to 'the People of Colour of the Antilles' exhorting them to overthrow the restrictions placed upon them while at the same time conjuring up a vision of a free society where they could take advantage of these bountiful islands and participate fully in commerce and agriculture and demonstrate to all the world their capabilities as free and independent people. It climaxed with a stirring call to action: 'My dear brothers, what are we waiting for? What reflections do we still have to make? Arise and abandon your chains; and this wretched state of slavery! And with our hands let us help one another create a new and agreeable chain of unity and brotherhood; and with united accord we repeat, arise, arise and grasp that liberty! At Dominica 1791.'[17]

While Polinaire was the key strategist of the revolt, the commander in chief was Jappa 'belonging to Anthony Bertrand', who said that he had consulted Pharcel in the heights above Morne Desmoulins on the upper slopes of Morne Anglais (chiefs were always consulting the mysterious Pharcel). Other sub-chiefs were Paul from Laronde's estate; Richard from Sorhaindo's estate; and a slave driver from Gally's estate 'who did not come when the time came, but stayed on his master's estate'.[18] Indeed, the revolt was disjointed and the small bands of slaves who had responded to the call from the various scattered estates were not a united force. However, it was clear that the attacks took the plantations by surprise: 'In one of these, the gentleman on the estate, assisted only by the overseers and house servants, and a lady, his sister-in-law, who loaded the musquets, resisted most heroically and successfully, until relieved by the military.'[19]

Over the next three days the governor, Council and House of Assembly in Roseau learned about what was going on in the parish of St Patrick. The 20 January 1791 was a whirlwind day of meetings, declarations, and movements of militias, rangers and troops. The fear that the rebels would be joined by sympathetic supporters from the French islands prompted Orde to issue the following proclamation:

'Whereas several Gangs of Slaves, within this Island, are in a State of Insurrection, and may receive great Succour or Assistance from an improper Communication of Foreign Vessels with the Outbays of this island. I have therefore thought fit by this my Proclamation, to call upon and require all Magistrates, and Other of his Majesty's faithful subjects within my Government to detain all Foreign Vessels that may be discovered landing or taking any Thing from any of the Outbays; and to deliver up such vessels to any Commander of his Majesty's Ships of War or to any Officer of his Majesty's Customs.

'Given under my Hand and Seal at Arms, in the Town of Roseau, this Twentieth Day of January, One Thousand Seven Hundred and Ninety One; and in the Thirty first Year of his Majesty's Reign.' J. ORDE.[20]

While Polinaire had admitted that 'he was not trusted by the Negroes until the last Extremity, when they were to March', he was soon a wanted man. On 21 January, the House of Assembly met to draw up a notice offering a reward for the apprehension of 'Paulinaire', dead or alive: 'Be it resolved that this House make good any sum not exceeding the sum of two hundred pounds currency to provide for the reward that may be offered by his Excellency the Governor to any white person or free person of colour or to purchase the freedom of any slave who may apprehend or kill the Mulattoe Man named Paulinaire, now at the head of a party of rebellious slaves.'[21]

Although the disturbances on estates in the south and east were causing considerable tension among the plantocracy, by 24 January the government forces, made up of members of two British regiments, planter militias and Black Rangers effectively overwhelmed the scattered bands of armed slaves. On 25 January 1791, Orde informed the House that strong detachments of 30th and 15th Regiments 'have forced the post occupied by the revolters without loss, have taken some of the insurgents in arms... Great numbers of negroes... have surrendered.'[22]

The soldiers and rangers required supplies of food, arms and ammunition while engaged in the forest, and porters were needed to carry these goods. Funds had to be voted for such an operation, particularly to pay the planters rent for hiring their slaves. And therefore it was resolved: '... that the Deputy treasurer be empowered to call in the different proprietors of estates for a portion of able Negroes not exceeding the rate of two per centum to be paid for at the expense of the Colony for the purpose of supplying a sufficiency of Negro labour to carry the provisions and other necessarys for such parts of his Majesty's forces or the similar parties employed in suppressing the present Rebellion amongst the slaves.'[23]

James Aytoun, a private in the light company of the 30th (Cambridgeshire) Regiment, was one of those soldiers called over to the windward coast to combat the sporadic outbreaks of Maroon activity. He recalled in his memoirs that in early 1791, after serving in Dominica for about three years, his company boarded a 44 gun warship called *Sheerness* in Roseau harbour bound for its home port of Portsmouth, England. However, they had hardly been a night on board when their ship was overtaken by a fast sloop carrying orders that they turn about and return to Roseau 'to chase some runaway negroes'.[24] 'We crossed the island being provided with a pound of flour and a gill of rum for our day's provisions. No horse, bullock, ass or mule could go on that road… covered with the finest natural timber I ever saw.' A section of his party was ambushed, 'three killed by stones that a party of runaway Negroes rolled down on them.'[25]

However, at Rosalie, on the east coast, no slaves came out to attack them. The Rosalie slaves had told Polinaire that they did not want to be the ones to start the armed revolt. As one of them, called Jack Sailor, explained to him, '… at the last Runaway War, when Rosaly was burnt, the Negroes of that Estate had got a bad Name, and that, therefore, this Time they would not begin.'[26]

So when the troops of the 30th and 15th regiments arrived at the banks of the Rosalie River, opposite the mill yard, having crossed the island via the Chemin L'Etang and Grand Fond track, the slaves were found crowded into a house on the estate where they were drinking while the manager, Orr, was away. He had left the estate in a panic having heard that Maroons were in the vicinity so the slaves were enjoying the contents of his liquor cabinet. The troops called to them from the other side of the river but no one came out except eventually 'a vagabond mulatto' waving a firebrand and shouting, 'We are all friends.' An estate attorney who was with the troops did not recognise the man and shouted, 'They are the runaways!' upon which the soldiers fired a volley and killed six slaves. (Months later, the colonial treasury compensated the owners of Rosalie Estate with £360 - £60 for each slave - for the loss of their 'property'.[27])

The absence of plantation owners and managers from the estates at this critical time angered Captain Combe, head of the Ranger Corps, who wrote Governor Orde a note from the area of Delices in the heat of the action to that effect: 'Mr Bertrand has been the most deceived man alive with regard to his own people in this late affair. Messrs Sorindo, Le Ronde, Gallée, Le Fevre and Roche are the gentlemen who, I believe are not now at their estates, and I am well persuaded that their returning immediately would be attended with infinite advantage.'[28]

In the mopping up operations, Rangers found a dead Maroon – in a case of presumed suicide or an accident – with a gun that had been stolen from the 30th Regiment. 'The gun laid at his side and the ball had entered under his chin and gone quite through the upper part of his Head. The deceased is supposed to be Ressauld, belonging to Mr. Anthony Bertrand. The gun is one of those that belonged to the 30th Regiment but its smell is so offensive that I have not forwarded it by this conveyance.'[29]

Meanwhile, the regular soldiers and the slave Ranger Corps were scouring the countryside for the mastermind of the revolt. Private Aytoun and his company continued north from Rosalie along the rugged coast past Petite Soufriere and Grand Marigot (now Saint Sauveur) to the broad river valley of Castle Bruce. 'When on our trip around the island we came to a plantation called Castle Bruce. Our deputy governor's name was Bruce... he had a considerable number of slaves armed with pikes... He had some small cannon mounted and cared not for the runaways.'[30]

At about noon on 1 February 1791 a Kalinago man came to Colonel James Bruce and informed him that he knew where Polinaire was hiding. Bruce offered him '5 Joes' if he would take him to the place, and the Kalinago agreed. Bruce was subsequently reimbursed by the colony for his on-the-spot reward to the Kalinago. Although by this time they were generally ignored, the Kalinagos were classified in the case of such eventualities as 'free people of colour'. The five Joes were valued at just under the equivalent of 'two hundred pounds currency' at the time, thereby fulfilling the terms of the 'wanted notice' issued by the legislature.[31]

Having settled with the Kalinago, Bruce immediately sent into the cane fields for slaves. 'I had twelve of my best people armed with every firelock that could fire.' They found Polinaire in a cave in the cliffs behind the plantation and brought him captive to Castle Bruce at about 7.00 pm and put him in chains. During the night he tried to persuade one of the Rangers guarding him to obtain poison but was refused and he was put on the next coastal sloop bound for Roseau to await trial.[32] It was deeply ironic that the very man whom the slaves had sought to exempt from attack during the revolt was the one who would ensure Polinaire's capture and death.

Polinaire was accused of leading the uprising on 17 January 1791 and that he '… unlawfully, maliciously and traitorously did compass, imagine and intend to raise and levy War, Insurrection and Rebellion… and in order to fulfil and bring to effect the said traitorous Compassings, Imaginations and Intentions he… with force and arms etc. at the Parish of St. Patrick… with great multitude of persons who names are at present unknown… to wit, to the Number of thirty and upwards armed and arrayed in a warlike manner, that is to say, with Colours flying and with Guns, swords, clubs, Bludgeons, Staves and other Weapons, as well offensive as defensive being then and there unlawfully, maliciously and traitorously assembled and gathered together… being moved and seduced by the instigation of the Devil… and wickedly devising and intending to disturb the Peace and Public Tranquility of this his Majesty's said Island of Dominica… and on divers other days and times between that day (17 January) and the twenty fourth day of the same month of January.'[33]

Wasting no time, the court tried Polinaire on 7 February 1791 with a jury made up of French and British residents. He was found guilty of treason, 'contrary to the duty of his allegiance', and was sentenced to be 'hanged, drawn and quartered' exactly one month later. As soon as the trial ended that same morning, he was brought before the Executive

Council to make 'a voluntary Declaration of the Truth of all he knows, concerning the late REVOLT, knowing he must die, and that he cannot commit his Conscience, by adding a new sin to it, in telling a lie.'[34]

Polinaire gave a detailed statement of events leading up to and during the revolt and provided the names of slaves and Maroons involved. His declaration was confirmed with the signatures of the President of Council, Thomas Daniell, along with members James Morson, John Matson, John Gillon, James Laing and William Lee, comprising together the most powerful men in Dominica at the time.[35]

Already since late January those slaves who were suspected of having been involved in the revolt were being rounded up, and trials commenced on 4 February. Now that the colonial authorities were armed with the names revealed by Polinaire in his 'examination', all hell broke loose in the forests and on the plantations of south-eastern Dominica. British troops and slave Rangers criss-crossed the forests to search for Maroon camps, to destroy them, and to apprehend anyone mentioned by Polinaire. As they were captured, so were they brought into Roseau, dragged before the court, tried and, in most cases, summarily executed.

Governor Orde directed that the trials and executions be conducted under martial law suspending the usual requirements of criminal court hearings and speeding up the process, thereby making sentences more arbitrary and brutal. 'The establishment of martial law is notified by the firing of two guns, and the hoisting of a red flag at the batteries; and is annulled by the same ceremony, substituting the British colours for the red flag.'[36] It was a process which would be repeated by Governor Ainslie in 1814 during the trials of Maroons that followed the Second Maroon War. But while Orde's method occasioned little comment in 1791, Ainslie was severely censored for his actions 23 years later, indicating the change in public opinion that took place as a result of the campaign waged by the anti-slavery and humanitarian movement in Britain during the intervening years.

The senior British military officers in the field kept Governor Orde abreast of events by sending almost daily reports to Roseau from their various locations in the mountains as they pursued the Maroons. Slave runners sprinted through the jungles or braved the ocean swells along the east coast in Kalinago canoes with these letters folded safely in rainproof Kalinago side baskets. Coming in from the remotest parts of the island the messengers were rewarded at the steps of Government House as they arrived at all times of day and night.

These dispatches are priceless for the information they provide on the life of the Maroons and conditions in the camps. For instance, a letter to Orde from an officer called James Gray, written at 'Point Mulatto, February 16. 1791'[37] gives an account of his exploits over two days in the heights of Myhambay, located behind Delices at the headwaters of what is called today Riviere Blanche or White River and its tributary, River Jack.[38] 'I followed… the bed of the Grand Soufriere River to where it became impracticable. I then steered to the height of Myhambay where I saw two large Runaway Camps… and I arrived at the place where they took their water from about sun set, where I halted until day break this morning, when I marched into their camp undiscovered, and upon calling on them to surrender they burst through all sides of their camp, threw themselves down a high Precipice which was within one jump of the camp.

'There was then a volley fired by the Rangers as they leaped out and am convinced that few if any escaped being either killed or wounded. We took three prisoners who informs me that it was Pangloss Camp which was composed of about twelve people. They had three firelocks…with Plenty of Powder and Ball and Six Cutlasses, as also a Parcel of Pots, Bowls, Knives, Spoons etc, etc, necessary for cooking, which I destroyed. I also set fire to their Camp which was consumed to the Ground in a few moments. I also found in the Camp a quantity of Salt Fish, Beef, Salmon, Loaf Bread, Farine etc, etc…The Villains Camp was so advantageously situated, that had we attacked them in clear daylight, I am convinced they would have kept us off, and very probably have killed a number of my Party, being so well supplied with ammunition... one of the prisoners taken has been twelve years in the Woods.'[39]

James Gray also observed the importance of a yam called wawa to the survival of the Maroons. A species of wild yam (*Rajania sintenisii*) found in the forests of Dominica at lower and middle elevations, it was called by the Kalinagos *bihi* and *kaiarali*. It was known from the 18th century by its African name *wawa* or *ouaoua* from the Twi language for 'large tree' as it is a tree-climbing yam with a widely spreading root system. An important food for the Maroons in their camps it was mentioned in the dispatches of British governors as being one of the main reasons for their survival in the forest. Although it was much used by the Kalinagos, they never cultivated it because of the belief that if they did so it would cause their family to die out.[40]

The reference made by officer Gray to 'Myhambay' is also of interest because the origin of the name is Mayombe, a Bantu-speaking tribe, part of a group referred to by the planters as Congos, many of whom were brought to Dominica. It may have gained its name as a hide-out of the Mayombe people.[41]

Meanwhile, executions were being carried out in Roseau. All of them are recorded in a document sent to London entitled: 'Lists of Persons of Colour tried at the Court of Special Sessions for being concerned in the Revolt among the Slaves, the trials commencing 4th February 1791.'[42] Executions were generally carried out within 24 hours of the sentencing. The first to face the gallows was Paul of Laronde's estate, known today as Mouca estate. He was hanged 'on Saturday the fifth day of February instant in the Public Market in the Town of Roseau, after which his Body to be hung in Chains over the River Roseau and near Woodbridge's Estate.'[43] Like the execution of Cicero at Fond Cole in 1786, this display of the body bound in chains was placed along the roadside on what is now Goodwill Road, leading to Roseau. It was aimed at striking fear into the minds of those slaves who, on the following day, would be walking to the main Sunday market from their various estates along the west coast.[44]

The executions and the display of bodies and severed heads sent out the message that any thought of resistance and revolt was futile and would result in similar punishment and death. On 8 February, Michael was hanged at an undisclosed place in the parish of St Patrick 'where he committed the Murder, after which his Body to be hung in Chains at the same place.'

And so it went on day after day during the month of February and early March: Jervier, hanged and displayed in chains at Rosalie; Antoine, hanged and displayed in chains at Colihaut; Jean Baptiste, hanged and displayed in chains at Grand Bay; Prosper, hanged and displayed in chains at Pointe Michel; Charlo, hanged and displayed in chains at Grande Savanna; Jappa, hanged and displayed in chains at Soufriere; Jinell, hanged and displayed in chains at the Old Battery, Loubiere; Renault, hanged and displayed in chains at Prince Rupert's.

Then there were those who were to be hanged and in addition it was ordered that 'their heads to be severed from their Bodies & stuck on Poles'. The executions of six such slaves were carried out on Friday and Saturday, 4 and 5 of March; three on one day, three on the next. Tom, Maya, Charles, Hypolite, Gregoire and Bart were hanged 'in the Public Market Place in the Town of Roseau, after which their heads to be severed from their Bodies & stuck on Poles on the Rosalie Road

beginning at the gate of the Estate of Charles Winston Esq. with one Head on each side of the Gate.'[45] Once again, the intention was to have the heads on display along the roadways leading to Roseau just prior to the Sunday main market day. Hannibal and Cyrus were similarly executed a couple of days later and their severed heads were displayed 'in the environs of Roseau'.

Some of those who faced trial and were not hanged, such as Jack Sailor and New Tim of Rosalie estate and Tombillo, Postillion, Louis, Bobadil and Giraud of Ouanary estate, were held in jail 'until security be given for their good behavior if kept on the Island or that they be Banished.'[46] Others such as Scion, Michel and Thomas of Belvedere, Charles of Rosalie and Alexander of Bagatelle were banished forthwith. This meant that they would be sold to new 'masters' outside of Dominica. Deportation was greatly feared because it tore the victim away from family and friends. In the case of those born in Africa, it forcibly removed them once again from a land to which they had got accustomed.[47]

A few captives, such as Jean Baptiste of Rosalie, were discharged due to lack of evidence as were some women and children such as those of Sorhaindo's estate at Belvedere listed as 'Gigi, Rachelle and child and infant Cypriene'. A 'free Mulatto', Monsieur Joseph Roseau, was also

Roseau market in the 1780s
(Agostino Brunias)

set free. One of the most intriguing entries on this list was the slave called Mahomet from the estate of Monsieur Gally. He was dismissed by order of the court, 'the Prisoner being a new Negro speaking neither English or French'. There is evidence elsewhere in the Caribbean that many enslaved Africans brought across the Atlantic were Muslims. This was in spite of Spanish directives in the early days of the slave trade that captives were to include 'no mulattoes, nor mestizos, nor Turks, nor Moors'. But as the trade intensified scant attention was paid to making exceptions of West African Muslims, and Mohamet, the Maroon, was probably one of these.[48]

As if designed to be a stage-managed drama of mass psychological warfare, the whole bloody business of public executions drew to a climax on 7 March 1791 with the execution of Jean Louis Polinaire himself. A platform had been constructed in the centre of a public space in Roseau, in the area now occupied by Peebles Park and the Cenotaph, where a crowd of hundreds could gather for the spectacle. Throughout a whole month of blood and death, the populace had waited, either in fear and trepidation, or in a spirit of satisfied retribution, for the carrying out of the sentence that had been handed down in court on 7 February:

'It is considered by the Court here that the said Jean Louis Pauliniere be taken from hence where he now stands to the Common Goal from whence he came, there to remain until Monday the seventh day of this instant Month of March, when between the hours of eight and twelve o'clock of the forenoon of that day, he is to be drawn to the place of Execution in the pasture or Savanne opposite to the store belonging to Samuel Chollet, and be there hanged by the Neck, and cut down alive, that his Entrails be taken out and burned before his Face, and that his head cut off and his Body divided into four Quarters and that his head and Quarters be disposed of at the King's pleasure.'[49]

That same week, in the city of Cap Français on the north coast of St Domingue,[50] the mulatto patriots Vincent Ogé and Jean-Baptiste Chavannes, who had visited France and England to gain support for their cause, were tried and punished with equal vengeance by the white plantocracy. It was specified that they must be publicly broken on the rack and wheel. The penalty was exacted on 12 March. The white mob 'howled gleefully over the tortures that were applied with medieval skill and callousness. The exhibition was supposed to be for the purpose of striking terror into the coloured people.'[51] Polinaire's execution in Roseau five days earlier had the same purpose in mind: to make it clear that the privileges and freedoms that such citizens possessed in Dominica had its limits. Free people of colour could go so far but no further. And much worse than fighting for their own rights was to inspire others – the enslaved – to revolt for their liberation as Polinaire had done.

The months of February and early March 1791 were the bloodiest since Britain had taken over Dominica in 1763, but it would be closely matched in brutality and numbers by the executions following the Second Maroon War of 1814. Addresses of gratitude from the House of Assembly and inhabitants would be presented to the governor, thanking him for saving the community from 'the Maroon menace' or for 'quelling the revolt'. On 21 March 1791 such a vote of gratitude was delivered to Orde bearing 230 signatures of all manner of free citizens, including two priests.[52] There was nothing like a Maroon threat to galvanise the warring British factions into a makeshift moment of unity.

It was unanimously agreed that the fortification of Dominica should be intensified with money voted for the improvement of all signal stations, coastal batteries and the main military installations particularly at the Cabrits Garrison in the north. A military force was also stationed in the south at Grand Bay 'to protect the estates to the windward; as attacks by these people [the Maroons] were not uncommon'. Stowe plantation house overlooking the main landing place for Grand Bay was requisitioned to accommodate the troops and a gun battery was constructed on the front lawn mounted with '24 pounder' cannons.

As a precaution against future revolt it also became the custom to proclaim martial law from 24 December through the holidays to New Year's Day and to put the different regiments and companies of militia on permanent duty 'attempts having, at times been made during this season to excite rebellion among the slave population'.[53]

The after-effects of the New Year's Day Revolt had serious repercussions for the efforts of British abolitionists. By coincidence and bad timing the events in Dominica derailed the passage of legislation that would have hastened the end of the Atlantic slave trade.

During the late 1780s, the abolitionist movement had grown in Britain. A handful of determined members of parliament and their supporters focused their efforts on the House of Commons with the aim of pressing for legislation which would outlaw the slave trade and, they hoped, lead to the collapse of slavery itself. Led by Wilberforce and Clarkson, they spent several years compiling a body of evidence on the horrors of the trade recording nearly 1,700 pages of testimony during parliamentary hearings from people at every level of the network. Their witnesses included former slaves, such as Olaudah Equiano (Gustavus Vassa) and Quobna Ottobah Cugoano. These men had emerged as vocal abolitionists, recording their experiences in the form of published memoirs recalling the conditions of enslavement from childhood capture in Africa to eventual freedom in England. The collected evidence revealed a sordid web of exchange among African middlemen that extended from the interior of Africa, down to the coast to the European traders, across the Atlantic to the Americas and into the British ports such as Bristol, London and Liverpool, which ultimately profited from the commerce in human beings.

Olaudah Equiano, whose memoir of 1789 is the most important slave narrative of the eighteenth century, succinctly outlined the conflict between master and slave which resulted in the permanent threat of insurrection within slave societies such as Dominica: 'When you make men slaves you deprive them of half their virtue, you set them in their own conduct an example of fraud, rapine, and cruelty, and compel them to live with you in a state of war; and yet you complain that they are not honest and faithful! You stupefy them with stripes, and think it necessary to keep them in a state of ignorance; and yet you assert that they are incapable of learning; That their minds are such a barren soil or more, that culture would be lost on them; and that they come from a climate …that has left man scant and unfinished… An assertion at once impious and absurd. Why do you use those instruments of torture? Are they fit to be applied by one rational being to another? And are ye not struck with shame and mortification, to see the partakers of your nature reduced so low? But, above all, are there no dangers attending this mode of treatment? Are you not hourly in dread of insurrection?'[54]

The abolitionists secured a date in April 1791 to table and debate the bill for the Abolition of the Slave Trade in the House of Commons. After years of hard work and lobbying, they were optimistic about their chances of success. However, in late March, the first sailing ships bearing news of the Dominica revolt started arriving from the Caribbean. As Adam Hochschild recorded in his book Bury the Chains: The British Struggle to Abolish Slavery, there had been many such uprisings on the Caribbean slave islands, but with this one, the planters could blame the abolitionists.[55]

The West India Committee, the planters' lobby in London, declared the rebellion 'to have been founded on no pretence of ill treatment, as to food, clothing or other particulars, but to have occurred in pursuit of what [the slaves] term their "rights". These doctrines, which are novel among the Negroes, have originated from the new language and proceedings in this country respecting the Slave Trade.' The abolitionists had done everything possible, said one pro-slavery writer, 'to excite a rebellion, except that of furnishing the objects of their solicitude with fire arms and ammunition.'[56]

The abolitionists fought a good fight on the floor of the House, but the powerful commercial lobby of West Indian planters had whipped up fear of further slave uprisings based on this concept of 'rights' and turned the tide against them. After two days of debate, the House voted 163 to 88 against abolishing the trade. Wilberforce and his colleagues would labour for another 16 years before the slave trade was eventually abolished by an act of parliament in 1807, and another 42 years until the first stage of full emancipation of British colonial slaves was granted in 1833, to become effective the following year.

Meanwhile, in Dominica in late March 1791, Governor John Orde reflected on 'our late disturbances' in a letter to his superior in London, Secretary of State William Grenville. He was 'happy in acquainting your Lordship… that quiet is perfectly restored and very likely long to continue.' He was clearly deluding his boss in this for everyone in Dominica was aware of the turbulence that continued in the neighbouring French colonies. However, with the planters still critical of Orde the governor had to give the impression that he was on top of the situation.

For all his efforts, Orde faced the wrath of the Privy Council even before the campaign was fully over. They accused him of procrastinating in taking action against the revolt: 'had not Your Excellency full information from several respectable Planters of the hostile intentions of the Negroes in different parts of the island as early as the 13th [January]. Did not the President of Council… advise your Excellency by letter to call the Assembly together? Did not those gallant Officers… offer the services of the Light Infantry… to go out against the Rebellious Slaves without pay or reward as early as the 14th?... If you cannot answer these [and other questions] you have not done your duty to the Public and the King.'[57]

Yet even Orde could not hide the fact that after the New Year's Day Revolt nothing would be the same again in Dominica. 'I think it right to mention my opinion, that notions and opinions have certainly got deep root in the minds of the slaves in general which I fear will be difficult to eradicate and which I much apprehend will militate against their ever again being such faithful, obedient and contented servants as they were formerly.'[58] In the decade ahead, the members of the Board of Trade who administered the colonies would discover to their growing alarm how accurate Orde had been.

11

An unstable decade: Maroons manipulate colonial conflict

I t would have been clear to the Maroon chiefs keeping track of what was going on in Roseau that there were serious divisions among the white people. As always, after a spate of executions and multiple floggings the planter class fell back into a false sense of security, confident that the message of punishments was sinking in and that fear of the gallows and the whip would tame the spirit of revolt, at least for a while. 'The late disturbances' had gone on against a background of personality conflicts within the British hierarchy of the colony.

Now, during this lull, when their unity was still vital for their security, the forced co-operation between Governor Orde, the Executive Council and the House of Assembly was swept aside. Feuds and personal ill-feelings were rampant, disagreement over the handling of the revolt and the French Republican threat raised tensions, and finally in a dispute over funds, the Assembly sent a petition to the Crown asking for Orde to be removed. In 1793 he was recalled to London to answer various accusations made against him by the inhabitants but was honourably cleared of all these charges which were dismissed as frivolous. After what he had been through, Orde had no interest in resuming duties in Dominica but rather opted to return to the navy and take up command on the high seas once more. He was promoted to the rank of rear admiral in 1795 and eventually left the navy to become a member of parliament. His replacement as governor of Dominica was George Hamilton, a spirited leader who gained the colonists' confidence and, in their view, guided them ably through difficult years.

World affairs were also shifting at a considerable pace. On 1 February 1793, the French Convention declared war against Britain and Holland. When the news reached Dominica on 19 March the tension of the past years turned to desperation. 'It induced many Merchants, Tradesmen and Manufacturers with Clerks, Servants and vessels employed in their affairs, to abandon this Country, by which, a very considerable body of land and seamen were withdrawn from its strength.'[1] Those who remained could only muster a militia force of 400 men scattered among the several parish companies. Military engineers with their bands of rented slaves worked feverishly on improving the line of defence at local forts especially on the Cabrits Garrison. In the same year, British forces captured Guadeloupe, Martinique and St Lucia but the occupation of these islands did not remain unchallenged for long.

As usual, the local Maroons took advantage of the colonial turmoil among the European powers to further exacerbate internal security. Whole groups of Maroons rather than individuals now took to the woods and established new bases. 'A number of of Negroes in Layou Valley have absconded from work; forming a camp at Mount George,' reported a representative for St Joseph in the House of Assembly.[2]

With their colonies in the Caribbean threatened, the French Jacobins

Victor Hugues planned invasion of Dominica with help of Maroons, 1795

who dominated the National Assembly in Paris sent out commissioners to spread the revolution to the Caribbean and ensure that their colonies were kept as part of the French Republic. The commissioners came out with troops to restore order and to defeat those planters loyal to the monarchy. Commissioner Sonthonax was sent to St Domingue, soon to be renamed Haiti, while Victor Hugues sailed further south to Guadeloupe. Hugues had formerly been a trader on that island and returned now with a guillotine lashed to the bow of his ship and sharpened in readiness for the Royalists of the colony. He landed and retook the island in June 1794, declared the abolition of slavery, and by that single act immediately gained thousands of men to join his forces. He mobilised the entire population of whatever ethnic origin to man the powerful coastal batteries and to commence offensives against the British-held colonies.

Royalist planters, most notably in Martinique turned to the British for help. To defeat them Hugues encouraged the slaves to revolt. He sent agents among the Maroons of St Lucia, Dominica and the Black Caribs (the Garifuna) of St Vincent. In Grenada, French whites, mulattos and their freed slaves under the leadership of Julian Fedon, a mulatto agent of the Republic, united to fight the British. Fedon had a marvellous repost to the British commander, Major General Oliver Nicholls, when he demanded that Fedon return all escaped slaves as a preliminary to negotiations. Writing from his Camp de L'Egalité in 1795, Fedon replied: 'As for those slaves of which you write us in your letter, allow me Sir to observe to you that we don't know of any slaves among our ranks. However if there is anyone of our people who wishes to return to you, we won't prevent them. They are free to go whenever they want.'[3]

Fedon's argument was based on his belief that the Africans should not perceive themselves as slaves but rather that they were free people upon whom others had imposed the concept and restrictions of being a 'slave'. It was a view that reflected the philosophy of Caribbean revolutionary leaders and Maroons across the region and it was a position which 'slave holders', furious at the loss of their 'property', refused to accept or understand.

Meanwhile in Dominica, on 30 May 1794, the House of Assembly expressed grave concern at the news that people of colour from Guadeloupe, with liberated Africans among them, were landing secretly along the north coast to join the Maroons. Members expressed their frustration at 'the painful state of the island, without funds to finance the mounting of an effective defence'.[4]

With Guadeloupe in the hands of Hugues the situation in Dominica became even more strained. Governor Hamilton called on the Assembly to provide parties of Black Rangers to search the heights and suspected parts of the island. He urged that ships patrol the Dominica-Guadeloupe channel and that 100 extra slaves be granted to work at the Cabrits Garrison. Martial law was declared in Roseau in March 1795 and the French inhabitants were directed to sign a declaration of loyalty to the British Crown. In spite of this the Assembly was still insecure. 'And people of colour are seen daily in the highroads of the island with arms... and numbers of slaves are secreted among them. As if carefully timed a party of armed people of colour... landed with arms at an outbay, and proceeded to the woods with intent to join the Runaways. So that a Proclamation had to be issued that magistrates, militiamen and every citizen was supposed to do his duty in this emergency.'[5] It was the alarm of 1791 all over again.

As French refugees continued to arrive, the British in Dominica were at a loss to know who to trust. 'The far greater part of these,' notes soldier Robert Browne in his diary, 'were Republicans professing themselves to be Royalists, many unquestionably Spies; a few, very few indeed, in whom confidence could be placed.'[6]

While the British were trying to make sense of all these unnerving events, Victor Hugues was hatching a plan for the invasion of Dominica with the co-operation of the Maroons, particularly those in the northern part of the island. He was also in touch with a hotbed of French Republican sympathisers gathered around the west coast village of Colihaut and surrounding communities in the parish of St Peter. This was the centre for the French coffee planters of the leeward valleys, a vibrant community with a Roman Catholic church, shops and a surprising number of taverns and billiard tables.

The message circulating Colihaut and the neighbouring communities of Dublanc, Bioche and Coulibistrie was that a force from Guadeloupe would land on the north-east coast in June of 1795. Hugues issued a proclamation calling on all true Frenchmen in Dominica to join the invading forces and many planned to do so. The Commissioner had added that those who did not assist would be punished by death along with their families. As far as the Maroons and many of the slaves were concerned, Victor Hugues and his revolutionary forces were to be welcomed and assisted so that the freedom granted to the slaves of Guadeloupe would be extended to Dominica as well.

Maroon tracks existed, as hunters' paths still do, from the Colihaut valley up and across the foothills of Morne Diablotin.[7] One set of tracks followed the south side of the mountain and then branched out to the north-east into the Melville Hall valley, while others kept due east into the Concorde valley and so on down to Pagua Bay.[8] On the northern flank of the mountain, forest trails passed across Fond Hunt, over Morne Turner ridge and along behind La Chaudière near Bense to link up with the more southern trails at the top of the Melville Hall[9] valley. Guided by the Maroons, most notably Pharcel, this latter path was the planned route to be taken by the invaders and local rebels. But as things turned out questions were later raised as to Pharcel's reliability given that he had secretly agreed a treaty of cooperation with the British some months before.

The north-coast invasion

The events of June 1795 were concentrated in three areas of the island: the north-eastern district in the parish of St Andrew; around Colihaut in the parish of St Peter; and at Roseau in the parish of St George. Each point of that triangle was so cut off from the others by mountains and an inaccessible coastline that communication between them was almost impossible. It was a perennial problem that further confused the whole episode. As with the Maroon uprisings in 1785-1786 and again in 1791, the appalling state of the public tracks was one of the greatest hazards to the security of the colony during any conflict.

Both parties, government and rebels, found themselves making grievous mistakes because they did not know or were misinformed about the state of their forces at the other ends of the island. Messengers moving across the forests with dispatches for their respective

IN THE FORESTS OF FREEDOM

commanders were ambushed; or events changed by the time their messages arrived. Under these circumstances rumour and misjudgment was rife.

The north-eastern coast of Dominica from Pagua to Anse Soldat is lined with sandy coves and jagged windswept headlands pointing towards the flat French coral island of Mariegalante. Most of these coves are inaccessible from the sea but about six of them can be entered by small sailing boats with captains experienced in dodging the several reefs and outcrops of volcanic rock which dot their entrances. At the time, these bays were used for shipping estate produce and most of them are still popular with fishermen and drug smugglers. The Atlantic breakers, coupled with the difficulty of landing, made this a low priority area for coastal defence, and only a few guns were mounted at Halifax Bay at Marigot, St Andrew's Bay at La Soye ('La Swa' now known as Woodford Hill Bay) and Batibou Bay, part of Hampstead estate, which at the time was one of the largest sugar plantations on the north coast.

British plantations dominated the north coast but the population was sparse and the district militias were very small. The higher ridges that rose behind the estates culminated in a knot of ravines and river sources around the summit of Morne Diablotin, the island's highest peak. The thick stands of rain forest remain today, protected within the Northern Forest Reserve and the Morne Diablotin National Park. Here, at a height of almost 2,000ft, was a semi-circle of Maroon camps occupied by escaped slaves from the plantations of the northern and eastern parishes of St John, St Andrew and St David.

In 1876, some 50 years after the Maroons had been active in the area, forest guides could still point out sites associated with their camps. In that year, the US ornithologist Frederick Ober was caught in a thunderstorm on the upper slopes of Morne Diablotin while searching for Sisserou parrots. At a place that Ober estimated to be over 4,000ft above the coast or about 700ft below the summit, his Kalinago guide led him to a shelter that, he said, was once a hideout for the Maroons:

'Just as we reached an angle of the rock he [the guide] turned abruptly from the trail and dived beneath another rock into a hole about breast high. Following him, I found myself in a spacious cavern hollowed out of the rock, with an entrance on the mountainside just large enough to admit a man conveniently… Meyong [the guide] drew out from a corner of the cave a manufactured flambeau and lighted it. By the glare it shed around I could see that I was in a smoke-blackened chamber large enough to contain fifty men with high vaulted roof and rude seats hollowed out of the rock near the floor which latter was covered with a thin coating of earth.'[10]

Elsewhere around the mountain, the bird hunter met an old man living in what the occupant told him was a repaired hut from the time of the Maroons: 'Returning to the cabin, my attention was called to the logs of which its walls were built. They were solid rosewood…The cabin was one of those built by some of the Maroons, or runaway slaves, some forty years ago, when they escaped to the mountains and formed so formidable a body that troops were required for several years to capture and subdue them. The space we were in was shaped like the bottom of a shallow bowl, surrounded by high hills, the dry crater, probably of an extinct volcano. There were many evidences of the residence of the runaways, in dismantled cabins, and gardens, and fruit trees. It is thought that the wild hogs roaming about the surrounding hills were from their stock.'[11]

From such locations on the upper flanks of Diablotin, there were lookout points on cliff tops and tall trees from where the Maroon scouts could clearly observe the north coast lying like an open fan extending from Vieille Case in the north to Pagua Bay in the east. The panoramic view extends across the sea channel to the islands of Deserade, Mariegalante, Guadeloupe and Les Isles des Saintes so that the movement of ships coming in from the Atlantic or sailing between the islands is plainly visible. It was for all of these reasons that Victor Hugues and his agents selected the north coast for landing their invasion forces. The invaders were a mixed bunch: a combination of freshly liberated slaves, passionate for success so as to maintain their state of freedom; white Creole middlemen and, lower down the social scale, there were the *petit blancs*; and lastly, trained regular troops of the French Revolutionary army. The plan was to take control of the windward side of the island and then swoop down on Roseau from the rear.

On the evening of 4 June, five boats containing about 50 men attempted to land at Woodford Hill but were repulsed by militiamen controlling the gun battery on La Swa Point. Four boats sailed west and landed at Anse de Mai but soon returned to Mariegalante. One report states that 800 men landed at Pagua that

Batibou beach, one north-coast site for the French invasion, 1795

day but other more reliable accounts indicate that they landed – after a journey of a few hours – in groups over the next four days at various points along the coast.[12]

On 6 June 1795, the invaders were back, landing at Batibou Bay with 200 men and moving cross-country to Pagua with no opposition. There they took control of Hatton Garden plantation house and sugar works, set up tents and established it as their main camp. News of the first attempt at landing had by now reached Roseau, where, in spite of the weak state of the British troops, Governor Hamilton was able to muster about 200 militiamen from the St George's regiment, the Point Michel regiment, the Coloured Fusiliers, the Coloured Artillery Company, the Black Rangers and members of the Light Infantry Company and Grenadiers. The St Mark's and St Patrick's militias were reserved as reinforcements. The combined force divided into two groups with orders to proceed around the island in opposite directions until they had the enemy between them. This tactic of approaching the enemy in pincer fashion is as old as warfare itself.

One detachment went up the west coast by sea to Prince Rupert's Bay where it was joined by 60 Regulars from the Cabrits Garrison as well as by detachments of the St John's and St Andrew's militias. The other group left Roseau for Laudat and Rosalie via the Lake Road (Chemin L'Etang) and then up the coast through the Carib Quarter. Slaves loyal to these government forces combed the woods ahead of the party to give warning of any approaching enemy. They spent the night at Richmond estate, just north of Castle Bruce. ' Here, at about 11 at night, they were alarmed by the bawling of Negroes in the Woods [but] the alarm appeared to be without foundation.'[13] On the 12 June, they reached Pagua and set up camp at Entwhistle (spelt and

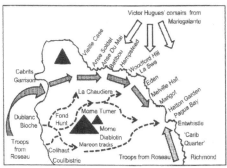

Map of French invasion and British response, 1795

pronounced as 'Antrizle' today). On the opposite side of the bay at North End, the other government forces had also set up an encampment. The revolutionaries' post at Hatton Garden lay between them.

On the same day another French force numbering about 400 in three schooners and smaller vessels landed at Batibou Bay and advanced towards Woodford Hill. From 12 to 17 June there were several skirmishes between the two opposing forces along the roadways, on the estates and in the forested hills between Woodford Hill and Pagua. Because of the failure of the groups from Colihaut and the Maroons from Morne Diablotin area to effectively link with the invaders, and because of dwindling supplies, the French suffered serious setbacks. Some escaped in canoes and others took to the hills.

On the afternoon of 16 June the main French group was surrounded by the British at Eden estate and surrendered. The Union Jack was hoisted above the Republican flag and the nine officers and 192 men assembled there were taken as prisoners of war. Two others, Norbert

Motard of Colihaut and Marie Petit of Pointe Michel, were seized as rebel British subjects. During the following days the militiamen combed the surrounding countryside for rebels; capturing some, killing others and repulsing various schooners and canoes from Mariegalante which arrived to rescue the remaining invaders still on the run. Prisoners taken during this action totalled more than 300 and were imprisoned at the Cabrits Garrison, pending their trials in Roseau.

The Colihaut revolt

There was one parish militia that was conspicuously absent in the action against the Republican invaders. The St Peter's militia of some 100 men with its base at Colihaut did not respond to Governor Hamilton's call for a volunteer force. Along with others, they planned to use the government arms to assist the invaders. Reports of suspicious conduct among them caused the governor to order troops to disarm the militia and burn every small boat and canoe on that part of the coast.

Colihaut had always been an area under suspicion for it was a channel through which the French had supplied arms and ammunition to the Maroons for years. From 14 June agents in the area were circulating false news that the British were being defeated at Pagua, ships were fleeing from Roseau and that the French inhabitants of Couliaboune (Giraudel), Pointe Michel and Grand Bay had taken up arms for the Republic and were in possession of the town.

This propaganda had the desired effect in most hamlets along the coast, spurring the people on to support their cause. On 16 June, the Coulibistrie division of the St Peter's militia took up arms against their British officer in charge and seized the keys of the arms and powder magazine. According to one officer's account, 'The Rebels marched off the ground huzzaing, Vive la Republique! Marchons! Marchons! They proceeded to join the Dublanc Company who were waiting for them, and together they advanced to Colihaut, where the Company of that place, joining, they formed a body of 150 men and commanded by three commissioned officers of the St Peter's Militia and J Meltze.'[14]

The band immediately set off through the forest to the north but because of the turn of events at Woodford Hill and Eden their departure was too late to be of any use. By the morning of 18 June when still on the foothills of Morne Diablotin overlooking Picard estate, they learned of the defeat and surrender at Eden. They had originally planned to go directly through the forest to Pagua. Instead they took the more dangerous route above Colihaut and Dublanc around the north face of Morne Diablotin. By 22 June they realised that the whole plan had been a failure. While about 16 of the ringleaders made their escape by sea, over the next three days 108 surrendered. Others took refuge in the mountains among the Maroons.

While all this was going on rumour was going wild in Roseau. 'On 18 June news was that the British had been overrun and the French were moving steadily for the capital. Before dark the bay was thronged with Ladies, Children, Female Domestics, Chests and Bedding, Chests of Linen, Books, China, Cash, Plate and other valuables of the generality, and the Boatmen attending to put them on board ships in the harbour.'[15] The scene was reversed 12 hours later when the correct information arrived in town.

With hostilities over, punishment and revenge fell heavy upon the captured rebels. Speedy trials in late June and early July sentenced 110 to be sent to England as prisoners of war. Others were banished from the island for life to places determined by the Crown while another group was simply sent away with orders never to return.

Norbert Motard and Marie Petit were sentenced 'to be hanged in the Market Place till dead and afterwards their bodies to be exposed in Chains the first at the River's Mouth Petit at Pointe Michel.'[16] Motard, a white man, was executed on 25 June while Petit, a mulatto, was executed two days later. Another two were hanged on 7 July. Two others were also sentenced to hang but had their sentences commuted to banishment almost as the ropes went around their necks. One agent was sentenced to be hanged but was banished instead. Three 'received

200 lashes each on their bare backs in the manner used in His Majesty's Armies'.

The strong links that were developing between free people and the Maroons caused serious concern to the British administration. The French invasion and the Colihaut Revolt, although ultimately unsuccessful, had been possible because of the co-operation of the Maroons. Slaves and French influenced free people, both white and coloured, were supplying Maroon camps with food and ammunition. Many slaves on the plantations had knowledge of this trade in supplies but existing laws across the British West Indies forbade the evidence of slaves to be accepted in court. The planter Assembly of Dominica decided to change this because of the island's special circumstances. The Dominica Act of 1798 'to make Testimony of Slaves admissible in certain cases and under certain restrictions for a limited time' was a notable exception in the region. Planters could now pressure or persuade their slaves to appear in court and expose anyone who they knew was assisting Maroons.

The volatile decade ended as it had begun with the relentless efforts to suppress what Orde had referred to in 1785 as the 'internal enemy of a most alarming kind'. As John Lucas, commanding the Loyal Dominica Corps, wrote to the retired General Melville in January 1798, 'The runaway negroes are beginning again to become formidable, in as much as the Governor judged it prudent to send out parties against them. One of our detachments fell in with a camp in the interior part of the island, consisting… of near two hundred of this Banditti, which they dispersed with loss of one of our men but were not able to take any of them. It has had however a very good effect as many of the Runaways have since surrendered to their owners and some stragglers have been killed and taken. The fugitives on quitting their camp set fire to it but left an astonishing quantity of provisions. Our party counted the foundations of upward eighty houses.'[17]

That a camp of such a size with its adjacent gardens to provide provisions for a couple of hundred persons could exist in spite of the forces continually waged against Maroon survival says something about the tenacity of its leadership. With French revolutionary support from across the channel dwindling as the decade made its close, marronage in Dominica had to develop its own internal strategies to face the challenges of the new century ahead.

By then the activities of Victor Hugues in the Antilles was even causing concern in Paris as he moved Guadeloupe towards virtual independence from France. In 1802, Bonaparte reimposed slavery in the French colonies and sought to reverse the revolution in Guadeloupe. Hugues was sent to French Guiana as an administrator where he served as governor and remained until his death.[18] Admiral Lacrosse who Napoleon sent out as the new governor of Guadeloupe found things so contentious there that arrangements had to be made with the British to allow him to govern Guadeloupe from Dominica until full control was secured. To reimpose slavery upon the labouring people of Guadeloupe after they had experienced six years of freedom would not be easily achieved and he administered the rebellious colony in absentia for a number of months until he felt it was safe enough to reinstall himself at the French headquarters in Basseterre.

Of all the Maroon engagements so far, the campaign by Victor Hugues to take over Dominica was the greatest threat faced by the British planters. A contemporary account says that on this occasion the Maroons 'shook the island to its foundations by their atrocities, but happily they were subdued.'[19] This term, 'happily they were subdued', had by now become the standard refrain voiced by the Roseau-based administration whenever there was a perceived victory. In fact, it always turned out to be only a lull in the action. Time and again it proved to be only a brief respite for the plantocracy while the liberation forces in the mountains regrouped and a new generation of leaders slipped in to the role of fallen chiefs.

Pharcel: the elusive Maroon

During the 1790s, a name which emerges again and again in the pages of the Assembly minutes, the letters of the governors, reports of regimental commanders and in the press is Pharcel. His name is sometimes written as Farsel, Farcell or Pharcelle, but, most commonly Pharcel. This is the same Pharcel who was of concern to Orde in 1786 – a man whose life is still buried in the archives in the same way that it was hidden to the British by the forests of central Dominica.

What we know of this Maroon chief is full of contradictions. He seems to have aided the French in their conquest of 1778. Other Maroon chiefs regularly consulted Pharcel on strategy. In 1786, after the attack on Balla's camp, the British forces found it increasingly difficult to penetrate far into Maroon territory in the vicinity of the stronghold controlled by Pharcel, who made good use of his excellent knowledge of the terrain and network of informants on the plantations and in Roseau.[20] In 1791 Orde offered 'a considerable additional reward to those who take the Rebel Pharcelle.' Yet, at the end of this 'New Year's Day Revolt', Orde hinted that he was beginning to doubt whether such a man existed. When he was 'examined' before his execution, Jean Louis Polinaire spoke of Pharcel commanding a force of 200 Maroons. Based on this information, the governor sent out 'a Party of Coloured People' against what was thought to be a formidable band of Maroons, but they were found to be only a dozen strong. The other band, he commented, 'commanded by Pharcelle (if any such there is) will I fancy, be found equally inconsequent.'[21]

However, as it became clearer that the influence of Pharcel was reaching far across Maroon Country, the governor and Assembly soon had no doubts that he was real. As Maroon activities intensified and as British efforts to suppress them became more ineffectual, the colonial leaders in Dominica opted for negotiation with certain leaders of the Maroon communities. They sought to win Pharcel over to their side, reputed to be the most influential of them all, with the hope that he would assist them in suppressing the movement.[22]

Accordingly, on 15 October 1794, the Assembly unanimously voted that the government should hold talks with Pharcel. Members proposed that he and other members of his party as he should name would be given their freedom and parcels of Crown land in return for a pledge of assistance in hunting and capturing Maroons. The Council concurred with this opinion and a special committee was appointed to begin negotiations with Pharcel, and on 9 December, an agreement was reached. The text of this agreement stated that Pharcel, his two wives – Martian and Angelique – and 12 of his men would be declared free and would be granted Crown lands adequate for their present and future subsistence. In return for this, Pharcel and his company were to hunt the woods for Maroons, receiving monetary compensation for each one brought in. It was further agreed that after passage of the act conferring their freedom that Pharcel and his company would be subjected to military discipline in the same manner as in the King's regiments. Pharcel would be under the jurisdiction of the governor who was authorised to appoint a chief or chiefs of the party in the event of his death, incapacitation or infirmity.[23]

This treaty had little effect on the intensity of Maroon activity during what remained of that decade. As the Jamaican historian Bernard Marshall stated, there are indications that either Pharcel was being deliberately deceptive when he put his mark to the text or that he subsequently changed his mind because he did not entirely carry out his side of the bargain. By 1795 he had been involved in French revolutionary activity in the heights of Colihaut,[24] guiding or mis-guiding French revolutionaries across the island to join invading forces. Then in 1798, he surrendered slaves to the governor, and in the church records, dated 14 January 1799, is the entry, 'Farsel, some 50 years old, born on the Guinea Coast' baptised a Roman Catholic in Roseau.

During 1799 Pharcel guided parties of Black Rangers against Maroons. Sometimes when he led Rangers to the camps they were deserted hinting that the occupants had got advanced notice of the intended raid. After one such expedition, the governor complained to the Council that 'the conduct of Pharcelle as a guide to one of the parties was such as to render it essentially necessary to confine him in gaol;

and, as his conduct was not only insolent and highly suspicious when employed, I recommend to you the propriety of Banishing him from the Colony.[25] On 15 December, martial law was proclaimed; done when the government wanted to carry out capital sentences after summary trials. During the same week a bill was passed into law, 'For banishment of sundry Runaway Slaves now in confinement.' Three days later the Assembly decided to banish Pharcel from the island. But as if hesitant to take action, the Assembly lingered until 16 December 1800 to introduce a bill 'to deliberate on the case of Pharcelle' with the details of his banishment to be decided. Finally he was shipped overseas, probably to the new British colony of Demerara that had recently been captured from the Dutch. And from then the records are silent.

12

The West Indies regiments: a challenge to Maroons

It was the middle of the rainy season of 1795. A square-rigged ship under full sail came in from the Atlantic Ocean and rounded Dominica's southernmost headland of Point Cashacrou, which the British had renamed Scott's Head after one of their early lieutenant governors. The fort on the point fired a signal to alert Roseau of the ship's arrival. As the dark brown vessel with its stained sails got closer to the capital it was seen to be a 'slaver', a slave ship, or as the French on the island called it *un negrier*, a 'transporter of Negroes'. There was nothing unusual about this; such ships were a common sight off Roseau at the time. But instead of sailing to anchor in front of the town or further north at Woodbridge Bay as usual, it dropped its sails and chain off Newtown, opposite to where the Savannah is today. Senior military officers from the garrison up the hill at Morne Bruce gathered on the shore. They stood in the shade of the large stone building that still stands there between Victoria Street and the sea. It has the date '1784' carved over the main door. It was the provision store, a warehouse belonging to the army for storing supplies offloaded for the garrison. On this day, it would become a barracks for African military recruits.[1]

Planters and merchants who began to converge at the landing place were told to stand back. This shipment was not for sale. Canoes and flat-bottomed lighters went out to ferry the occupants of the slaver ashore. As they shakily stepped through the surf and over the bouldered beach onto dry land, their naked bodies chained together, a certain puzzlement spread through the crowd. The new arrivals were all males in their late teens and early twenties, all well built and looking fit in spite of the long, slow passage from Africa. Usually a slave ship would have a mixed human cargo of women, men and children of various ages who by now would have been split up as various planters made their claims on board. However, this band of men were led to the large stone building and its surrounding wooden sheds behind its high wall to be housed and fed together for some time. By now it was clear to the crowd that these were not slaves for working fields or boiling houses and coffee pulping mills. Something else was going on.

By the end of the 18th century, military forces required in the Caribbean were causing a strain on the revenue of the islands and disease was taking its toll of the British soldiers stationed in the region. At the Cabrits, fever and other ill effects of the climate caused the loss of many members of British regiments stationed there. Added to this, by the 1790s, Britain found itself fighting wars in Europe, and the British army required as many of its soldiers as possible to be mobilised in that war zone. At the same time, the vast wealth in sugar and associated trades had to be protected in the West Indies. The army faced a dilemma: how would Britain be able to provide troops to man the forts to defend its 'sugar islands' from the French while at the same time have enough soldiers to fight wars in Europe? How could it

Enslaved soldiers were housed in this building in Newtown, Roseau, on their arrival in Dominica, 1795

continue to send out its British regiments to die of disease in the islands when they were needed nearer to home? Critics of the system of defence in the British West Indies, such as the army historian John Fortescue, comp- lained, 'Britain sacrificed the cream of British youth for the benefit of a handful of West Indian planters.'[2]

To solve the problem of manpower for defence, the British government, spurred on by the army, launched a plan to establish black West Indies regiments made up of West African men bought as slaves but to be trained as soldiers. The basis of this plan was that it was considered that Africans would better survive the tropical climate. The garrison on the twin hills at the Cabrits, close to the swamps surrounding Prince Rupert Bay, was notorious for its malaria and yellow fever. However, the local legislature was alarmed at the idea of having armed and trained black forces guarding the island. Maroon activity had escalated after 1791 and the colony had just survived the threat of a French invasion, but the British army and the Board of Trade, later to become the Colonial Office, was insistent.

The idea was influenced by the Black Carolina Corps, made up of African-American soldiers who had fought on the side of the British during the American War of Independence and who had to leave the United States after the British lost. The company was taken to the British West Indies and proved to be a successful addition to the regular British regiments stationed there. Since 1785, and more formally since legislation in 1788, the British in Dominica had raised a corps of rangers from among the enslaved to fight against the Maroons in the hills. This Black Ranger Corps, also known as Black Shots or *corps de chasseurs* by the French inhabitants, assisted in combat against the guerrilla warfare of the Maroons and with coastal defence in case of invasion.

During the French Republican uprising of the 1790s, the Roseau batteries were reinforced by the arrival from St Lucia of 40 members of the Carolina Corps, which was the first of its kind in these colonies. Blacks with arms training had already been attached to certain regiments as Pioneers, men responsible for setting up camps, heaving cannon, erecting palisades and other military preparations. The African contribution to colonial security was effective from the planters' point of view, but had been devastating for the Maroons due to the difficulty

Members of the West Indies regiment

of discerning in the depths of the forest who was friend or foe. Despite the planters' misgivings about formalising the engagement of black soldiers, establishing permanent regiments of armed Africans was the next logical step.

In early 1795, the military training of that first group of slaves, recently arrived from Africa and now housed in the former provision store in Newtown, began. The drill sergeants found the African names too confusing so they put large cardboard labels around the men's necks bearing such names as Congo Jack, Lightly and Cyrus. By repeatedly calling the men by the names labelled on them, the troops in training were forced to accept new self-identities.

The Anglican rector, Rev Charles Peters, visited the men often and noted from their arrival that things were not going smoothly among their ranks. 'They were lodged and fed in a spacious building not far from the Government House. And at one of their meals, I remember witnessing a scene which at first excited in our mind very serious apprehensions. Their provisions had scarcely been set before them when we perceived throughout the whole room the strongest indication of discontent and anger. The countenances of many became quite infuriated, and violent agitation of their minds expressed in their looks and gestures, seems to forebode some sudden and general commotion.'[3]

The men had been put together without any distinction as to their tribal origins and status in Africa. This was a revelation: in other situations, as soon as enslaved Africans arrived they were split up by purchasers and sent to the plantations or even to other islands. It was unusual for them to remain as one group or be administered together and therefore social differences were seldom observed in this way.

The new arrivals were grouped together as the 8th West Indies Regiment of Foot under a British commanding officer, Lieutenant

Colonel John Skerrett, on 15 September 1795. These 'slaves in redcoats' were to be under the command of white officers. Although still technically slaves pressed into service, they would receive the same allowances and be under similar regulations as other British troops. This peculiar arrangement would be the source of strained relations between the black troops and the regular European soldiers as well as with the plantation slaves, particularly those living around the respective garrisons on the islands.

Such divisions among the black population were actively encouraged by the colonial administration. Governor Cochrane, writing to the Secretary of State for War George Dundas in 1801 was anxious to move the West Indies regiments from island to island regularly 'every one in two years... as this would inevitably destroy any combinations or connections with the Negroes of the Country; whilst at the same time they would have the opportunity of acquiring the local knowledge of the interior of an intricate scenery, and be ready to act against the runaways.'[4]

In the Windward and Leeward Islands, Lieutenant General Sir Thomas Trigge, commander of British forces in the West Indies, had a policy to instil a sense of pride in the black West Indian soldier only in order to give him a feeling of superiority over the 'generality of Negroes'. He confessed that he sought 'to prevent the slaves and soldiers from making common cause which would endanger Britain's position in the Caribbean'.[5] Within seven years the side effects of this policy would impact the revolt of the 8th West Indies Regiment at the Cabrits Garrison's Fort Shirley and would further shape the soldiers' attitudes against the Maroons.

In 1797, a 29-year-old Scottish soldier called Andrew James Cochrane Johnstone was appointed governor of Dominica. He had served in the army since 1783 and after returning from deployment in India was elected to Parliament for Stirling Boroughs, a position he had to forfeit on his appointment as governor. Though he had assumed the title of Johnstone from his wife's surname, his real name, and the name by which he was best known in Dominica, was Cochrane. He bought Hope estate in the parish of St Paul and, as was the custom, the estate was popularly named after its master. (This is the origin of the present-day inland village of Cochrane where several of the governor's descendants still live today.) He served as governor until 1803 and during his tenure he behaved as a tyrannical dictator, supporting a flourishing trade in slaves and maintaining his own harem at Hope. As governor, he was colonel-in-chief of all British forces on the island including the 8th West Indies Regiment which, by then, was one of the 12 regiments serving in the West Indies.

In a letter to the new commander of the British forces in the West Indies, General Ralph Abercrombie, Cochrane expressed his total support for engaging African soldiers rather than British troops to defend the island both as regulars and as members of Ranger Corps for internal security against the Maroons. He argued his case by making comparisons based on economy and health: 'I am confident that hardly a British Soldier is landed in this country, including all expenses, under £70 Sterling; for which sum at this time, I could purchase a good Negroe in this Island. - A British Soldier's Services hardly upon an average exceed Two Years in this Country; lately not so much:- A Negroe would last many years.- The expenses attending a British Soldier, in the supplying of fresh meat, wine etc. and the Medical Department are very considerable to Government:- A Negroe is hardly ever sick, and he likes a salt ration better than any other.'[6]

By 1801, the 8th was stationed at the Cabrits Garrison and was well organised with some 500 men under the command of Major John Gordon who had replaced Lieutenant Colonel Skerrett. Captains Carr, Cummins, Casson, Cameron and Arbuthnot were at the head of 100 men each. By then, they had already distinguished themselves in action, notably at the capture of St Martin in that year. General Trigge, in his report on the fighting, wrote, 'I have particular satisfaction in being enabled to add that in the 8th West Indies Regiment, formed within the last three years, and composed almost entirely of new negroes, who never had before seen an enemy, engaged with a degree of gallantry, and behaved in a manner that would do honour to any troops.'[7]

Governor Cochrane's treatment of his men was, however, causing discontent. He set the soldiers to work for his private use. Someone who knew Cochrane Johnstone recalled years later that he was 'an able but most unscrupulous governor. He kept the pay of the black soldiers and made them work like slaves on his estate at Hope. Governor Johnson [sic] was a very polished gentleman, but at time could show himself in a very different character.'[8] They were put to dig fields, build the wall around Government House and work on his estate without pay. Food and clothing supplies were also becoming irregular and because of Cochrane's swindling, they failed to get the regular soldiers' allowance due to them. The soldiers' suspicions were further aroused when they were put to work clearing bush in the Cabrits swamp with cane bills, a tool that they associated with slave gangs in the field. The field slaves on the plantations around Prince Rupert's Bay taunted the men of the 'Black Regiment' that soon they would be taken away to be made plantation slaves like themselves and that the next tool that they would be ordered to use would be the dreaded hoe.

On 9 April 1802, having worked two days in the swamp, they could stand conditions no longer and the regiment revolted. Late that night they surrounded the Officers' Quarters in the centre of Fort Shirley and under the code word 'Black Man', they entered and seized the officers. They killed three of them, imprisoned the others, seized the keys of the powder magazine, ordnance store and artillery store and took over the entire garrison. A detachment of the Royal Artillery stationed there made their escape.

On the following day the men-of-war *HM Magnificent*, *HM Excellent*, *HMS Severn* and *HMS Gaiete*, a sloop of war, all with marines on board, anchored in the harbour. This arrival was pure coincidence as it was the dry season and the ships had come from Antigua to collect water. But it raised fears among the members of the 8th West Indies Regiment that the ships had come to take them away for sale to plantations. The mutineers were entirely made up of Africans. 'The "Creole slaves" had nothing to do with it and made their escape as soon as the mutiny broke out by swimming to the ships or taking such canoes as they could find.'[9] From the ramparts of Fort Shirley, the mutineers fired upon the *Magnificent* with no effect.

On 12 April, Colonel Cochrane arrived from Roseau and, after a truce was agreed, he entered the Cabrits Garrison with the Royal Scots Regiment, the 68th Regiment and some militia. Marines also landed from the men-of-war. Just as the slaves and Maroons had done during the New Year's Day Revolt in 1791, the rebel soldiers of the 8th West Indies Regiment declared their loyalty to the king even as they were in rebellion against the colony. As an English newspaper at the time reported, 'The King's Colours were kept flying the whole time the mutiny lasted – the mutineers constantly declared their readiness to fight for KING GEORGE and when General Johnstone and the Troops marched in the King's Colours were flying in Fort Shirley with the flag of truce over them.'[10]

The African troops of the 8th were drawn up on the parade ground in the valley between the East and West Cabrits to parley with the governor, their commander in chief. Here they held three of their officers as hostages and presented arms to the troops and island militias that had arrived from Roseau. Mounted on his horse, Governor Cochrane proceeded to admonish the members of the regiment for their actions. This caused much agitation among the men. When the governor ordered them to shoulder, order, and ground their arms, they obeyed. However, on being commanded to step three paces forward the cry was 'No!' and they resumed their arms and fired a volley. This was returned and followed by a charge of bayonets, which broke their ranks and a wild gun battle ensued on and around the field.[11]

The mutineers scattered in different directions. Some of them ran up to the summit of the Outer or West Cabrit in the hope of getting down to the sea. But those who tried to escape over the precipice were exposed to grapeshot and canister fire from *Magnificent*. Others went up the Inner or East Cabrit. They had previously turned the guns around to face into the valley and now they fired grapeshot onto the troops below, before dashing down the other side of the hill towards the swamp. A few who were able to get through the sedge and reeds of the marsh secreted themselves in the surrounding cane fields and then moved into the forest higher up the side of Morne Aux Diables. After this, they went across to the more secure massif of Morne Diablotin. 'A few are supposed to be still concealed in the bushes, and some are known to have got into the country,' wrote one eyewitness to the event 12 days after the revolt.[12] This was in spite of a line of militia which was posted across the isthmus to prevent the mutineers escaping from the garrison. Surviving mutineers trained in military skills added a new element to the camps.

When it was over, the bodies of 60 men of the 8th West Indies Regiment were found around the garrison. Others were left to rot on the inaccessible cliff face of the West Cabrit. The 60 were buried all together but this mass grave has not yet been located. The survivors buried their dead officers with full military honours. An estimate put the total dead at over 100 men while 130 prisoners were taken aboard the *Magnificent*.

The court martial that followed was held in British-occupied Martinique and it sentenced 34 of the rebels to hang. However, soon after, an investigation began in London into the conduct of Governor Cochrane. He tried to shift the blame to his subordinate John Gordon, but after hearing the evidence, the court acquitted Gordon and indicted the governor himself. In March 1804, Cochrane faced four charges before

'Pacification with Maroon Negroes' (*Agostino Brunias*). *The Garifuna of St Vincent and British troops were similar to the opposing forces active in Dominica*

another court martial, this time in London. To the disgust of King George III, the prosecution failed but the King ensured that Cochrane was never promoted and was made to resign his commission. The 8th West Indies Regiment was broken up and some of the men who were not implicated in the revolt were placed in other regiments.[13]

The revolt at the Cabrits did, however, have a long-term effect on the engagement of enslaved men by the army and navy. It raised serious questions for the British Army regarding the operation of non-European troops within its forces. Significant changes, including the liberty of black soldiers, were made as a result. It was the basis of new guidelines for 'native troops' in Africa, India and the Far East at a time when the British Empire was expanding its interests in those parts of the world. In 1807, the British Parliament made an amendment to the Mutiny Act and abolished the use of slaves in the armed forces. All members of the West Indies Regiments were henceforth free men. In commemoration of this, a plaque on the wall of the Officers' Quarters at Fort Shirley was unveiled in 2007 by the Prime Minister of Dominica, Roosevelt Skerrit, recording the event. The declaration reads: 'On this spot, the mutiny of the 8th West Indies Regiment broke out on 9th April 1802 and lasted for three days. This plaque is in memory of those members of the regiment who were killed or executed in their fight for freedom. As a result of their action here some 10,000 slave soldiers in the British army were freed in 1807. It was the first act of mass emancipation in the British Empire.'

Now that all men in the regiments had been emancipated this opened the way for any free man in the colonies to volunteer to join the regiments. All officers were European but after 1807, there were a few 'poor whites' among the rank and file. There was also at least one young Kalinago from what was then called the Carib Quarter who became a private in the 4th West Indies Regiment. From that time, until the garrison was shut down in 1854, the West Indies regiments formed the main body of troops manning the island's defences. They were also used against the Maroons and to deter slave revolts and unrest, as in the case when members of the regiments were called out to escort 11 slaves of Everton Hall estate (Tan Tan) to Roseau for trial after being accused of creating a disturbance.

The establishment of the West Indies regiments and their emancipation in 1807 heralded a new phase in the campaign to turn Africans against each other, and especially so in the case of Maroon conflicts. Various West Indies regiments, most notably the 3rd, 4th and 9th, would be active against the forest camps in the years ahead, seriously threatening the capacity of the Maroons to maintain their position of superiority in jungle warfare. White soldiers in red coats were easily discernible at a distance in the forest but now there were black soldiers supported with all of the fire power of the British Army pitted against them. It would now be more difficult to determine through the thick foliage in the shady depths of deep ravines who was friend or foe. What with the Slave Rangers, the Free Coloured militias and the West Indies regiments fighting for the colony against the Maroons it was now largely a war of blacks against blacks engineered by whites during what remained of the conflict. Several decades later, off and on from the 1820s to the 1870s, these descendants of enslaved Africans in the West Indies Regiments would even be transported across the Atlantic to fight on behalf of the British Empire against west African tribes, most notably in the Ashanti Wars.

Church and state

The Church of England was the church of the state and arrived as part of the colonial establishment when the British took over Dominica. At the end of the 18th and in the early years of the 19th centuries, the rectors of the church were deeply involved with the issues of slavery and marronage, most in very negative ways. The colony was officially Protestant and the rector was appointed through the government, worshipping for the government, controlled by the government and its buildings were repaired with government funds. The British planters were a very irreligious lot and soon the church, constructed in 1766, had collapsed and services were held in the Court House; it was not until 1820 that a permanent Anglican Church was built on its present site.

In any case rectors on the island were few and far between. Those who did not die 'a victim to the climate' left within a short time of their arrival. While Orde was governor in 1791, he wrote in despair to the secretary of state: 'The christenings and burials I cannot speak to there not being a Protestant clergyman in the island nor any provision likely to be made by the present House of Assembly for any. The state of religion is indeed truly deplorable and disgraceful considering the circumstances of the colony – the marriage ceremony is performed by a Justice of the Peace.'[14]

Eventually in 1795, Governor Hamilton was able to secure the services of an Anglican priest from England called Charles Peters. A dedicated and humanitarian cleric, he was appalled at what he saw as the den of iniquity in Roseau. He made observations on the terrible treatment of slaves and noted the arrival and progress of the African men brought to establish the West Indies regiments. He corresponded with the members of the Anti-Slavery Society, particularly William Wilberforce, about all manner of injustices, detailing the padlocked metal masks, heavy spiked iron collars and wood block weights chained to adults and child slaves as young as 12 years old.[15] These were aimed at restricting the enslaved labourer's ability to move quickly and were primarily used on those who had a tendency to run away. Similar observations to those made by Rev Peters had been noted

several years before by Dr Jonathan Troup when he inspected one of Dr Clarke's slaves at Clarke Hall plantation with 'a chain and collar of Iron round his Neck, the strong weight makes him bleed at Nose & Mouth.'[16] Rev Peters was of the view that the mulatto mistresses were particularly vengeful as if

Iron collars and masks used to punish and impede escaped slaves

they were endeavouring to make a distinction between themselves and their darker-skinned slaves.[17]

The planters hated Rev Peters. When it became known that he was going to preach a sermon against the harsh treatment of slaves at Good Friday and Easter Day services on 11 and 13 April 1800, his enemies surrounded the Court House and Assembly building where church was then held, shouting and booing him down. 'Sundry and respectable inhabitants in the island,' reported to Governor Cochrane Johnstone that the sermons were 'of a nature and tendency the most alarming and dangerous, and such as to threaten the subversion and destruction of the Colony.'[18] Within a few months, the members of the House of Assembly had drummed Peters out of the island. Their argument was that they paid the rector's wages and that they were damned if they would tolerate a priest who advocated against their interests. The planters had less power over the ministers of the Methodist Church who carried the Gospel among the enslaved but even so they harassed them whenever they could.

Rev Charles Peters' replacement as rector of the Anglican church was more to their liking: the notorious Rev John Audain was involved in trade and took to owning a schooner and privateering to supplement his income. Henry Nelson Coleridge recalled him once cutting short a sermon and dashing down to the Bay Front when he observed his vessel entering the port.[19] At the French attack on Dominica in 1805, Audain was wounded while handling cannon. Nursing his wound he departed to do business in the more prosperous Leeward Islands.

Rev Audain's replacement was perhaps the most extreme of all: he was the wheeling and dealing rector of Roseau, Rev Henry CC Newman. Even Council member William Bremner found him 'highly obnoxious'. Newman was elected to the House of Assembly, rising to the position of speaker despite several members arguing that he was not eligible to be a member of the House, much less be its speaker. During and after the Second Maroon War of 1814, Newman would play the role of propaganda agent for Governor Ainslie.

13

The prelude to mayhem: Maroons destabilise the system

Way up on the Chemin L'Etang, on the slopes of Morne Micotrin, above the small coffee estates of Byak, Spring Hill and Providence, slave porters 'heading' baggage over to Rosalie stopped to look down towards billowing pillars of smoke rising from Roseau. The entire town was in flames. It was February 1805 and a French invasion force was attacking the capital. The sound of cannon fire and the explosion of barrels of rum had been echoing up the valleys all afternoon. Refugees escaping the fighting were on the roads leading into the hills. Domestic slaves were assisting their white and free coloured mistresses and children who were followed by porters carrying their most valuable possessions. Among the stream of humanity heading for the interior were enslaved tradesmen, mill workers, fishermen, vendors and field hands. Most were in fear of being captured as prize booty and taken away to foreign lands should the town fall to the invading enemy. Others were taking advantage of the crisis to escape enslavement for good.

The year before, in 1804, the African slave army of Toussaint L'Ouverture had finally captured and taken possession of St Domingue after over a decade of fighting. Rechristened with its original Taino language name, Haiti, it was declared an independent republic. This achievement by a population of enslaved Africans sent a wave of fear throughout the white population of the West Indies that lingered well into the late 19th century. Stripped of the financial benefits of the massive income of Haiti's sugar and coffee plantations, Napoleon was desperate to recapture its former French West Indian colonies in the Lesser Antilles and to add some British ones to his possessions to make up for the loss.

Early in 1805 it became known that a French squadron had sailed from the port of Rochelle under the command of Rear-Admiral Edouard Thomas Burgues, Comte de Missiessy. The ships were loaded with arms and ammunition for Martinique and were cruising the Caribbean, making raids on British possessions and crippling British West Indian trade. The squadron had been joined in Martinique by more frigates and men. The forts and defences in Dominica were hurriedly put in some sort of order, the militia alerted and a close watch was kept for the French squadron.

At dawn on 20 February, the storm broke. Strange armed vessels flying the Union Jack were sighted from the signal station on Scott's Head. An alarm was fired and the news quickly spread through Roseau. Soon Fort Young was crowded with militiamen and a small body of regulars. The ships swept towards the town and when the harbour master boarded the foremost vessel he was immediately taken prisoner. The British flags on the ships were lowered and the French

tricolour hoisted in its place – it was indeed the enemy. It turned out to be a French squadron of nine ships, including four ships of the line, under the command of Missiessy, with 3,500 troops led by General Count Joseph Lagrange. Lagrange had served

Final French attack on Dominica, 1805

with Napoleon in Egypt; his fame had spread across the Atlantic, and for years, the invasion was spoken of in Dominica simply as 'Lagrange'.

The guns of Fort Young rang out and a steady fire was exchanged. Then from the leeward came more ships, including the *Majesteux*, several frigates amounting to 120 guns and 19 barges full of troops. They landed and marched on Roseau from the north and south. It was the 'pincer tactic' once again that the French had used to defeat Roseau in 1778. At one period in the fighting, 200 British were holding off 2,000 of the enemy.

Cannons on the northern ramparts of Fort Young were then shifted to aim towards the French troops at the Roseau River. But this meant that the cannon balls would pass perilously low over the centre of the town. Unsurprisingly, the houses were accidentally set on fire. Flaming cotton wads, used for padding the space between the gunpowder and the cannon balls, were scattered by the cannon fire and were blown onto the rooftops by the wind. The dry wooden shingled roofs caught fire easily. Barrels of rum awaiting shipment in the basements of the houses exploded and, to add to the destruction, the French aimed their cannon fire into the conflagration. All this sealed the fate of Roseau and with the British governor's permission, the Council surrendered the town.

Although Roseau had fallen, Governor George Prevost was determined to hold the north of Dominica. He did not want a repeat of what had happened in 1778 when the French had occupied the whole of the island simply because they had taken the capital. He ordered his troops, the 46th Regiment and the 1st West Indies Regiment to make forced marches across the island via Rosalie, then along the east coast and through the 'Carib Quarter', to join him at the Cabrits. With a few of his staff, and with help from the Kalinago, and a certain Pascal Laudat, Prevost made a dramatic 24-hour dash to Portsmouth. 'I lost sight of the town about sunset, but during my progress in the night, I repeatedly heard the explosions of the rum stores.'[1] On his way, Prevost passed the slaves along the track. 'The Negroes very early of the day abandoned the town,' he recalled, 'and those I overtook on the road did not appear to me loaded with plunder.' The troops made the difficult journey in four days. At the Cabrits, Prevost hastily put the garrison in order. When the French squadron turned up there, its ships surrounded the Cabrits headland and Lagrange demanded that Prevost surrender but the governor refused.

Noting the formidable appearance of the garrison and the danger of trying to land any troops beneath the array of guns, the French returned to Roseau. There, Lagrange demanded a ransom of £12,000 or he would take the members of the legislature as hostages to Guadeloupe. The full ransom was not forthcoming so he settled for just over half the amount, about £8,000, but not before seizing everything of value he could lay his hands on including a number of slaves. After hanging about the island for some days, the squadron sailed north towards Guadeloupe and St Kitts and the last French attack on Dominica was over.

By going into the hills the slaves had escaped capture by the French. Many were tradesmen and domestics who preferred to return to the security of their tasks in Roseau and surrounding districts. Others, however, took the opportunity of the six days of chaos to join the Maroons as was common practice during previous periods of upheaval between the colonial rivals on Dominica. Those slaves who had been held and transported off the island by the French took the first possible opportunity to escape back to Dominica from Guadeloupe after the fleet stopped in Basseterre to sell their captives to raise prize money for the ships officers and crews.[2]

The destruction of Roseau was yet another severe blow to the British. When Prevost returned to the gutted town after a week's absence he despaired at the sight of it, 'The condition of it then was a heap of ruins.' With every rum barrel exploded and every hogshead of sugar or sack of coffee burned to ashes went the loss of thousands of pounds sterling. The Committee that was set up to compile a petition from Dominica, 'respecting loss by the fire at Roseau', estimated the damage to be valued at £203,349 not including the estimated £14,268 in loose currency which was burnt in the fire.[3] The petition was sent to London in the hope of obtaining some relief, but by the time it had been drawn up, the island was lashed by a hurricane on 9 September 1806. The Roseau River burst its banks and flooded the town sweeping 131 people to their deaths. A report on that additional damage and loss of life had to be added in the appeal for relief from the 1805 destruction of Roseau by fire. The complete report only reached London in 1807. 'A very severe gale of wind and a large quantity of rain fell during the night of the 9th of September [1806], which blew down many of the houses and others were carried away by the overflowing of the river, and others much injured; that a great deal of merchandise was destroyed at the time, and a great many lives lost, both whites and negroes by the same cause.'[4]

Tactics for survival

A weak colony meant Maroon strength. This is a significant thread that runs through Dominica's history. Marronage existed parallel to the colonial course of events. In spite of the upheavals among the Europeans, Maroon society had its own tactics for survival. It has been observed that 'also conducive to rebellion was the high proportion of African-born to Creole slaves; for many revolts were tribally exclusive, and most were African led. Only after the slave trade ended and Africans ceased to enter the Caribbean did Creoles, seeking more to ameliorate than to escape the plantation system, dominate slave uprisings.'[5] For those who had been born in Africa it was easier to attempt to recreate an alternative to the plantation system than for those who were second or third generation islanders with no experience of west Africa.

Morne Gros Bois named after the Maroon chief of that name

It could be said that Maroon society at this time was a combination of farmers, philosophers and radicals. The 'farming Maroons' with their slash-and-burn gardens on isolated plateaus were active from the earliest years of interaction with the Kalinagos, in the 1550s up to the First Maroon War in 1786. The many years of 'neutrality' of Dominica enabled them to pursue their livelihoods for some 220 years when Africans were first observed among the Kalinagos. These farming strongholds were disrupted after 1786 when bloody conflict commenced as the British renewed their grip on Dominica. This was followed by a period of 'radicals' when concerted attacks were waged against the system merging with the leadership of 'philosophers' after 1789 when the new revolutionary ideas from France spread through the island via Guadeloupe, Martinique and Haiti. All converged after 1800 as enslaved labourers walked off estates in significant numbers to develop alternative agricultural livelihoods in the forest.

This 'freedom of the garden', whether on the edge of the plantation or in the forest, was probably the most important focus of slave life in Dominica. The size and produce of their hidden garden/farms amazed those who came upon them. 'In 1785 the Mountainous interior which the Maroons inhabited abounded with… rivulets of water on almost every acre and great plenty of ground provisions in all parts. In 1800 when three detachments of the 9th West India Regiment penetrated a part of this country they discovered 300 acres of cleared land fully stocked with all kinds of provisions'. Previous to that, officers reported having seen… 'as fine sugar canes as on any estate in the country with all articles necessary for their subsistence.'[6]

Before, during and after slavery, the mass of the people on the ground had more freedom when chaos gripped the governing elite. Periods of a weak economy, a depopulated upper and middle class, abandoned plantations and little or no restrictions to use of land may appear to be chaotic when judged from the point of view of traditional western economics. But for a people who had nothing, it was a period of opportunity. For subsistence farmers and food gatherers in a fertile tropical setting, such conditions allowed communities of this nature the freedom to thrive. Hurricanes and fires contributed to the instability. When such chaos did not happen naturally, the Maroon tactic was to add to the crisis in the hope that a total collapse of the plantation society would occur. So it was for the Maroons of Dominica in the early years of the 19th century.

The intensification of Maroon activity began roughly in 1802 and climaxed with a guerrilla war between 1812 and 1815. Visitors to Castle Bruce estate in 1802 'found the manager by no means at ease. The ground provisions had been more than once dug up; the plantain trees robbed, and stock carried away. Not unfrequently, the insurgents carried off, as prisoners, those whom they met with unarmed, and could not be induced to join them by fair means; and it was, consequently, judged necessary to write to the commanding officer in Grand Bay, for a party of military.'[7]

At the outset of the war in 1812, the slave population had reached its peak. There were 24,000 enslaved people on Dominica as against 1,500 free people of colour and only 800 white persons. In the Windward and Leeward islands, only Grenada had more free people of colour at this time and all the other islands with the exception of the smaller islands of Nevis, Montserrat and the Virgin Islands, had more slaves.

Nonetheless, slave numbers at the time were the highest since Dominica had become involved in the trade a century before. There had been a sudden surge in the purchasing of slaves during the first years of the 19th century when it was apparent that the British Parliament was moving swiftly to make the trading and transportation of slaves from Africa to the Caribbean illegal. In anticipation of this, the planters made a rush on the slave markets to stock up on slaves before the trade closed.

In England, Wilberforce, Clarkson and their group of abolitionists doggedly pursued their goal. The information accumulated in the previous decades on the coast of west Africa, on the slave ships, in the Caribbean and in the port cities of Britain itself, had helped to turn the tide of public opinion. Miniature wooden models of slave ships; the display of heavy locks, chains and fetters; the publication of diagrams and engravings of scenes of brutality associated with the trade were all part of a wider campaign of speeches and popular performances driving home the message of abolition. But even public support and attempts at garnering enough votes in the House of Commons was not enough. Wilberforce needed the support of the government. At first, his friend, Prime Minister William Pitt, supported him, but he could not muster the majority of his ministers of government to do the same. Because of divided opinion within his Cabinet, Pitt dropped the subject altogether. However, there was another reason for Pitt's sudden lack of interest. As we have seen, the army had convinced the government that it needed to replace white soldiers serving in the Caribbean with slave soldiers brought in from Africa. Army agents were buying slaves quietly, in small groups, to conceal what it was doing and to avoid making Prime Minister Pitt, who still gave lip service to abolition, look like a hypocrite.[8]

There were also powerful people against abolition. Sir William Young, son of the first British governor of Dominica (also Sir William) argued on the floor of the House that abolishing the slave trade would be disastrous for the British manufacturing industry. Among other things, he said that the sale of coloured cloth produced by the cotton mills of England, 'which is so loved by the slaves in their Sunday markets', would collapse.[9]

Prince William Henry, Duke of Clarence, later King William IV, defended the slave trade in the House of Lords. He knew the system first hand having spent some time in the West Indies. He called himself 'an attentive observer of the state of the negroes' and he declared that he found them well cared for and 'in a state of humble happiness'.[10] The site of 'Clarence House' where he lodged while in Roseau in 1784 is still marked with a small gateway on Victoria Street between Roseau and Newtown. Here he stayed with his mulatto mistress, who was chosen for him by members of the island's Council. She henceforth called herself 'Princess Clarencia' and, if as is rumoured, she had royal offspring, his descendants may well be somewhere around Dominica today.

Prime Minister William Pitt died in 1806 and another attempt was made to get the bill for the Abolition of the Slave Trade accepted. This time Wilberforce got the support of the government and the bill was passed in both the House of Commons and the House of Lords in early 1807. A few weeks later, on March 25, George III officially gave his assent and the bill became law. It came into operation on 1 January 1808 and all trading in enslaved Africans was 'utterly abolished, prohibited and declared to be unlawful.' The last slave ship to arrive in Roseau under the legally constituted terms of the slave trade landed the final cargo of enslaved Africans on 29 February 1808. In all, since 1764, it has been estimated that about 100,000 Africans were transported to Dominica during those 44 years of the trade.[11] However, as already mentioned, this included several thousands who were trans-shipped on their arrival to other destinations and never stayed in Dominica.

Although the trade across the Atlantic was outlawed, the use of slave labour in the colony itself continued. The abolitionists had the rather naive belief that once the trade was stopped, slavery would eventually just wither away. The Abolition Act enforced a fine of £100 for every slave purchased, sold or transported. Any British ship engaged in the trade would be seized. The planters of Dominica, like their colleagues across the British West Indies, felt furious and betrayed. In 1811, another act was passed to punish any British subject who traded in slaves by having the offender forcefully transported to a colony in need of labour such as Australia.

Back in Dominica, the government grappled with a failing economy and a rise in Maroon activity without having a sufficient budget to finance an effective military response. The value of Dominica's exports was equivalent to that of the smaller islands. Estimated at a value of £258,858, only Nevis, Montserrat and the Virgin Islands had smaller incomes. For all of its estimated 186,000 acres and the capital invested and the physical effort put into it by the new wave of British planters since 1763, Dominica had not fared too well in comparison to the other Ceded Islands.

The activity of the Maroons had certainly had an effect on this. The poor economic showing was a triumph of sorts for chiefs such as Jacko, Pharcel, Sandy and others still alive, whose aim had been to retard the success of the plantocracy. The Maroons had forced the colonial power to spend tens of thousands of pounds to raise the Legions and to feed and clothe and arm the slave Rangers as well as to pay compensation for the regular troops. This had been a tremendous drain on the economy at a time when they also had the French to worry about and coastal defences to construct. In the ten years since the New Year's Day revolt of 1791 the awareness of *egalité, fraternité et liberté* had increased and many of the enslaved understood that slavery was now regarded with some disfavour in Britain.

The instability that the Maroons had created struck fear into the white population; they had retreated from plantations and, in many cases, had given up their enterprises and left the island completely thus reducing their numbers. A glance at the minutes of the House of Assembly of this period tells the story. There are repeated requests to hold new elections for certain parish constituencies because the incumbents had left the island. Finding white men, as stipulated by the racist laws, to fill any position of public trust, became increasingly difficult. This strengthened the hand of the free people of colour but they would still have to wait until 1832 to get the right to hold public office of any sort. Yet, even as they continued in their quest to create a new indigenous elite, the free coloured plantocracy understood what the Maroon leaders and slave rebels had achieved. They had ensured that no authority, of whatever skin shade, would henceforth take the enslaved blacks for granted.

As the new century dawned, the Maroons kept up the pressure. Building upon the instability of the previous decade, their chiefs took total advantage of the collapse of internal security and control. Their destabilising activities had run parallel with the side effects of the French Revolution and the news of the first black republic of Haiti that was carried to them by sailors arriving on merchant ships and naval frigates. Slaves came and went from plantations to forest, absenting themselves on *petit marronage* despite the continued threats of punishment. The increasing 'boldness of the negroes' was repeatedly commented on.

The intensity of confrontation on both sides was also increasing. A typical account of one altercation with Maroons gives an idea of how such battles took place and shows that British forces were now adopting more appropriate guerrilla tactics rather than their traditional method of attack: 'satisfied that this was a runaway encampment, the exploring party immediately retraced their steps; but they had not marched halfway back, when they were attacked, flank and rear, by the enemy, who being excellent marksmen, kept the woods ablaze. Scarcely a man was to be seen, all were so concealed by the luxuriant foliage. The commanding officer directed the soldiers to keep to themselves as much as possible under cover, and to retreat from tree to tree, firing at the spot whence they perceived the fire of the enemy, who followed with great perseverance, to proceed. In this manner they retired, until they got clear of the woods; but their retreat was considerably impeded by the difficulty of assisting the wounded; several men of the detachment, as well as their commander, having been hit by this invisible enemy.'[12]

The number of Maroons at this time was estimated to be 800 strong and camps had been established behind Woodford Hill, Hampstead, Rosalie, Pointe Mulatre, River Claire, Morne Anglais and in the upper Layou area as well as the other earlier sites behind Colihaut and Dublanc. 'Neg Mawon' leaders at this period were Elephant, Soleil, Gros Bois, Battre Bois, Hill, Nicholas, Diano, Noel, Robin, Quashie, Apollo, Jean Zombie, Lewis, Moco, Nico and Jacko. This latter chief had, by the time of his death in 1814, been in the forest for over 40 years.

There were violent clashes with Maroons in 1808 and again in 1810.

In response to the 1808 assault by Maroons on a couple of west coast plantations, the affected planters sent out a party of armed slaves to attack a camp near Morne Diablotin. They succeeded in killing its chief and taking six prisoners. In 1809, the legislature was again requesting the governor to take measures to break up encampments. On 15 August, Rangers in the parish of St Patrick attacked a large camp of 20 huts overlooking Grand Bay, but the escaping Maroons burned it down. News of the increasing threats from the Assembly and Ranger forces reached the Maroon leaders and they followed it up with another strike upon coastal plantations the following year. In response to this, renewed rewards were offered in 1810 to parties capturing Maroons.

Freedom would be granted to those slaves who killed or captured chiefs. Officers in charge of Rangers and of companies of the West Indies Regiments who succeeded in capturing Maroon camps were rewarded with grants of Crown land upon which these camps stood. This at the same time restricted its continued occupation by Maroons and extended plantation lands

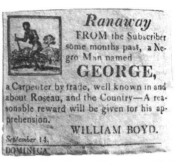

Advertisement for runaway slave

further into the forest. In one such case 'an officer of one of the regiments... a Creole, as well as a proprietor in the colony had received a grant of this tract of land, which he had now converted into a fine coffee plantation, and been appointed captain in the militia, a justice of the peace, and a member of the assembly.'[13]

In 1811, the camp of the 'notorious' Chief Elephant was taken and a number of other camps destroyed. The legislature noted Maroons increasing in the parishes of St Joseph and St Peter. It was becoming clear that Maroon raids were not merely arbitrary attacks but that news reaching the camps from Roseau was being analysed and acted upon. Verbal reports giving the general outline of deliberations and decisions made by the House of Assembly and Council were finding their way into the mountains. Any deliberations on an increase of forces against the Maroons seem to have been met by preemptive strikes from the hills. Sometimes they simply abandoned the camps to the invading forces so that all their exertions were in vain. After a long and tiring march of six hours duration, one Ranger captain found that the Maroons had deserted their camp. 'Indeed', he wrote, 'we have reason to suspect that they have too many friends in every direction along the shore to leave them ignorant of any step taken against them.'[14]

In another instance, this lack of success was attributed to the suspicion that the Maroons 'were perfectly acquainted with our expedition, and were prepared for us'.[15] All the following year, 1812, the state of things in Dominica was unnerving even senior members of the legislature. In the view of Dr William Bremner, a Scottish medical doctor, slave owner, planter, estate attorney and member of Council, the island was 'torn by divisions in her internal politics, and... threatened by a growing enemy in her vitals: the daily accumulating hordes of runaway negroes.'[16]

As the tension mounted, the lieutenant-governor, Colonel Barnes, decided to make use of the Regular troops stationed in Dominica, as part of the offensive against the Maroons. The regional commander of the British forces in the West Indies based in Barbados, General George Beckwith, objected on the grounds that it was against universal practice to use such Regulars to quell internal disturbances. When the matter was referred to London, the authorities were astonished that the system of internal security which worked elsewhere seemed to have failed in Dominica. Despite the colony's anxiety, Beckwith, acting on their orders, declined to give any immediate permission for the Regulars to be used. Barnes was caught between a rock and a hard place. His numerous local critics accused him of not being able to take control of the crisis. According to Bremner, Barnes' policies appeared 'to augment the numbers [of Maroons], inspirit the insolence, and increase the outrages of these Banditti'. For all his criticism, Bremner must have known only too well that the lieutenant-governor's power to act was severely limited without the support of Regular troops from England.

General Beckwith in Barbados was simply reflecting the concerns of his army chiefs in London. The British army had already lost thousands of its men fighting against the forces of Toussaint L'Ouverture in Haiti. In 1795 alone, hundreds more had lost their lives in campaigns against the liberated slaves of Guadeloupe; against the Black Caribs (Garifunas) in St Vincent; and against the French influenced mulattos and slaves in Grenada, as well as similar forces whom they described as 'brigands' in St Lucia. Many more British youth lost their lives without ever tasting battle. They succumbed to deaths from malaria and yellow fever in the crowded, ill-equipped and understaffed hospitals and camps that dotted the hilltops of military garrisons across the islands and in the transport ships where disease swept easily through troops packed in the confined spaces below decks. The army had had enough of waging war against black guerrilla fighters in the West Indies. Their young soldiers from the English shires were desperately needed to defend their own 'green and pleasant land' in the wars against the French on European soil. Their troops were overstretched at home as it was, and the planters of Dominica would simply have to understand that they must pay up or piece together what forces they could in their campaign against the Maroons in the colonies.

The next 'outrage', to use Bremner's word, came in July 1812 when over 75 slaves of Castle Bruce estate packed what little they had and took to the woods. If this sort of mass exodus caught on elsewhere, plantation production would be crippled while Maroon forces were further strengthened. By now, new developments had added to the complexity of the situation. Scattered among the Maroons were a few deserters from the 'Black Regiments' as well as some white soldiers who had deserted from their regular regiments, men well trained in British warfare.

Towards the end of 1812 the United States declared war against Britain. The conflict lasted until December 1814 and is known as 'The War of 1812'. It resulted from US anger over trade issues, the capture and impressments of its sailors, and British support of Native American attacks on the US western frontier. The conflict saw the US Army attempt to invade Canada while British forces attacked the south including the nation's capitol at Washington DC, which they burned to the ground. The war affected Dominica and other British West Indian islands because shipping was disrupted and food supplies from the United States became scantier every week and soon ceased completely. Even when Britain and America signed a peace treaty, the Treaty of Ghent, in December 1814, it was some time before trading was back to normal. 'Not a single hogshead of salt fish or pickled pork was for sale, nor lumber of any description,'[17] wrote one planter. In desperation, some of them made a few unsuccessful attempts to establish a trade link with Canada.[18] The problems that had been faced during the American War of Independence (1775-1783) cropped up once more. The slaves were not getting their imported supplies of dried peas, beans and corn, nor the salt cod (*lamowi*) and salt pork (*gel cochon*) that formed an important part of the rations given to them.[19] This caused further suffering and many argued that they ran away simply to find food to survive.

While the British government was distracted by the Napoleonic Wars in Europe and the War of 1812 with the United States in North America, news was coming from Dominica of the intensification of Maroon activity and the brutal manner in which the colonial administration on the island was trying to suppress it.

14

The Second Maroon War: an eradication policy

I n 1813, George Robert Ainslie (1776-1839) was appointed governor of Dominica and was immediately faced with the challenge of the Maroons' increased ferocity and boldness. He was a Scotsman, born in Edinburgh.[1] He entered the army in 1793 and served in Europe fighting the French. Though he had no administrative experience, he used family influence in 1812 to obtain the governorship of St Eustatius, then part of the British Leeward islands. Two months after his appointment he became lieutenant-governor of Grenada. There he had a confrontation with the free people of colour over their rights as free citizens of the colony. He was made brigadier-general in early 1813 and was named governor of Dominica in April of that year.

Sir George Ainslie

The appointment to Dominica proved most unfortunate as he was totally unsuitable for the challenges he had to face on the island. Ainslie had an excitable temperament, which did not fit him for civil administration, and he was at one point reprimanded for suspending the secretary and registrar of the colony. More serious, he reacted with undue violence towards the Maroon presence. He issued proclamations offering a free pardon to those who would surrender but this was in vain for no Maroon would dare take the risk of being tricked by an amnesty, given what had happened in previous years. He then sent messengers to offer terms to them but, still suspicious of treaties, they murdered the couriers.

In one case, the messenger was a slave who had turned himself in to the authorities and had offered his services to locate Maroon hideouts. When he appeared before Chief Quashee with Ainslie's offer of an amnesty, he was seized and tried by the chief and his elders, and then executed by gunshot. William Bremner, a member of Council, recalled the event in his memoirs. 'The spirit of the banditti now appeared in a very conspicuous light. For after the Governor's messenger had delivered the object of his mission at the first camp he visited, so far were they from expressing any inclination to return to their duty, that the chief immediately ordered him to be shot on the spot; an order which was immediately carried into execution! After such an act of atrocity, all further parley was of course at an end.'[2]

The House of Assembly deliberated on another 'atrocity' that was committed on messengers bearing the offer of an amnesty whereby 'A poor harmless Carib, a soldier of the 4th West India Regiment, and a white man named McFarlane they actually did murder in a most wonton and cruel manner'.[3] Such executions galvanised Ainslie into action and for most members of the legislature it marked the point of no return in the offensive against the Maroons. The Kalinago private and the Scotsman, McFarlane, were shot and had their hearts ripped out of their chests and placed on poles at the entrance of the camp. The site of this camp, in the heights of the Macoucherie valley in the hills behind the present day village of Salisbury, is still called McFarlane. It sent a clear message to Ainslie that negotiations and treaties were not on the Maroon agenda. They were not going to get involved in treaties as Pharcel had done in the previous decade. News may well have reached the camps about the deceptive treaties arranged between the British forces and the Black Carib Garifunas under Chief Chatoyer in St Vincent in 1773 and 1795. These wars had climaxed with the British exterminating some 2,000 Garifunas by starvation on the barren Grenadine islets of Balliceaux and Battowia and by transporting and banishing the 2,500 survivors to the island of Roatan in the western Caribbean. From there they made their way to Honduras and Belize. The Maroons of Dominica were not going to risk such deception on their home ground.

Almost two years later, in June 1815, Sir Robert Heron, a British Member of Parliament and defender of Ainslie's action, informed the House of Commons about the incident: 'All the efforts of the former governors had been ineffectual, and attended with great loss, and to such a degree had the daring boldness of the Maroons increased, that they had murdered the messengers Governor Ainslie sent to them with the offer of pardon.'[4]

In response to the Maroon action in murdering his emissaries, Governor Ainslie issued a reward for the head of Quashee. An amazing sum of 1,000 dollars was offered. Such a sum was especially remarkable when in the 1780s and 1790s the rewards offered for the capture or death of Maroon chiefs were generally in the region of £150. In the case that a slave fulfilled this service, freedom was guaranteed. In a totally unexpected reaction, a counter offer by Quashee was proclaimed in Roseau trouncing Ainslie's offer, with a reward of 2,000 dollars for the head of the governor himself. If it was in the

The House of Assembly, Dominica, early 20th century

form of a printed notice, some have suggested that there must have been the connivance of an educated free person of colour in this action. Others have pointed fingers at the eccentric planter and printer John Lowndes, but this may be unlikely since he later signed a petition in support of Ainslie.

A former resident also recalled that 'the insurgents became even more daring, and carried their incursions into the town of Roseau itself; where a proclamation from them was found one morning, offering a reward for the capture of the governor! By some, however, this was believed to have been a waggish trick of a certain white inhabitant, a member of the Assembly, and no admirer of his excellency.'[5] However, the same writer also reported that the offer of a reward for the governor's head was conveyed verbally in chants by bold Maroons who ventured as close as the outskirts of Roseau to deliver their message.[6] Whoever it was, and however it was done, it roused Ainslie into action with a vengeance.

Soon it seemed that the successes of the Maroons were encouraging the slaves on the plantations to consider revolt. It was Ainslie's view that things were rapidly getting out of hand and that if firm action was not taken immediately the situation would escalate to the point where the plantocracy would be powerless to hold their ground and the system would be overthrown. A situation which the planters' rector, Rev HCC Newman, would describe as 'This dangerous intestine enemy.'

In June and July 1813 there was renewed squabbling between General George Beckwith in Barbados and the authorities in Dominica over the use of regular troops in the internal business of the 'Suppression of the Runaways'. By the tone of Beckwith's letters it is clear that the commander was getting increasingly irritated with the requests coming from Dominica. The Council members appealed to Barbados for arms and provisions for the black slave Rangers. They sought permission 'to employ a certain number of the 4th West Indies Regiment on a similar service'.

In reply, Beckwith reminded them that he had already granted them use of two companies of the 3rd West Indies Regiment. He pointed out his responsibility for the well-being of his troops and demanded that the House of Assembly vote money for their support. He was also concerned about injuries received by his men in action, one case being Lieutenant Butler 'who is a cripple for life'.[7]

On 14 July 1813, in response to Beckwith, the House of Assembly in Dominica offered 'one shilling [per day] be paid to every private and non commissioned officer of His Majesties troops and one pair of shoes and repair of clothing and other accoutrements be paid for by the colony'. The money was to come out of funds already voted under the Rangers Act and eventually the House granted Lieut Butler £200 in compensation for his injuries.[8] The following day the legislature argued over how they were going to pay the outstanding amount due to the detachments of the 3rd West Indies Regiment. It amounted to only £153 13s 6d but such was the paucity of the colony's finances that it had to be scraped together from various sources under other heads.

Hurricane havoc

When the Speaker of the House of Assembly adjourned the meeting of the legislature on 14 July with the intention of reconvening at the end of the month, little did the members know that a few hundred miles out in the Atlantic Ocean one of the decade's most destructive hurricanes was plowing its way towards Dominica. This was the great hurricane of 23 July 1813 and it laid waste the island. In Roseau, all the major buildings were destroyed: the House of Assembly, the Governor's House, the main warehouses, particularly those along the Bay Front, and the colony's jail that had been constructed more than 30 years before following another devastating hurricane in 1780. When the House met on 3 August for the first time since the hurricane, all discussion shifted from the subject of suppressing the Maroons to the urgency of rehabilitating the public buildings and commerce of the island.

There was particular concern over the state of the prison. Forty-eight prisoners were confined there, many of them being Maroons who had been brought in from the camps in the months before the storm. 'Damage to the jail is such that we request to remove the prisoners and confine them into the Engine Room under the Town Hall until the Gaol can be roofed over and repaired.' The engine room was where the hand-operated fire engine was stored. But there were too many prisoners for this small place and it was decided to 'limit the number' by separating Maroons from 'common criminals' and hold the 'Runaways' in the more secure building.[9] At the same time, it was obvious that looters were taking advantage of the confusion caused by the hurricane. An act was passed to punish persons receiving stolen goods and 'regulating the shipping of old metals etc' with the penalty of 'imprisonment, Pillory or both'. In the circumstances, with the prison destroyed, it was the pillory that was the favoured punishment.

On 4 August, Governor Ainslie informed the House of Assembly of the action he had taken: 'in response to the unprecedented calamity which has befallen the island from the hurricane of 23rd July... By the

last convoy, I wrote to the Colonial minister urging in strong terms the claim, which Dominica has on the sympathy and protection of His Majesty's Government for pecuniary assistance. I am happy to co-operate with the House and sanction any measure of immediate relief.'[10]

Destruction of vegetation, Hurricane David, 1979

While the powers in Roseau assessed the effects of the catastrophe and were busy trying to restore the business of government and internal security, reports were coming in from the country plantations about the devastation there. The attorney on Grand Marigot estate (today's Saint Sauveur) writing to a friend, described the destruction on the estate after the hurricane of July: 'The shingles were stripped off the east of the dwelling house and part of the east end of the boiling house roof fell in. The hospital, horse stable, wood and timber house blown down as well as several of the Negro houses. Others were unroofed and otherwise injured. Canes twisted and twirled about and most of them laid flat. And an almost entire destruction of the provision grounds... At present the island is destitute of rice flour biscuits corn meal or in fact any sort of eatables. We shall be obliged to feed the

Negroes three or four months, regardless of the expense or inconvenience as they may be driven to use improper food which might bring disease or other serious ills... I have never witnessed such havoc and destruction in so small a compass and how to convey the sad intelligence I am really at a loss.'[11]

The land that had been loosened by the hurricane of 23 July was hit again by another storm on 25 August. This second hurricane was notable for its rainfall in the way that the previous one was distinguished by the force of its wind. Torrential rains swept through the debris of the previous disaster bringing down landslides, blocking rivers and causing widespread flooding. As the natural dams broke, walls of water raged down the valleys. Fallen trees were torn from the hillsides and rode on the powerful waters like battering rams clearing everything in their path. As had happened in 1806, and in July 1813, people living in several river valleys were swept away in their houses to their deaths. The forests were stripped of what foliage remained and the trees were tossed across the landscape so that everything was exposed to view.

This was catastrophic for the Maroons. Not only were many killed in the storms but their flimsy ajoupas had also been blown away and any defence systems such as traps and palisades were destroyed. Following this second hurricane the plantation slaves became dispirited. Deaths of friends and families and the destruction of their houses and food crops made many give up resolve to start again, to build or to replant, much less to resume the miserable regimen in the plantation fields and mills and boiling houses. Many refused to cultivate crops in their food gardens but turned to trying to subsist on what they could scrounge from the land. It was reported that many malnourished and diseased slaves escaped for days to forage for food.[12] In October 1813, there was concern about the lack of provisions in the ground available for the 'sustenance of the slaves and the poorer classes of inhabitants' and a committee was appointed 'to take measures to avert an expected famine.'[13]

Protests and proclamations

In the aftermath of the disaster, Ainslie saw a perfect opportunity. It was as if fate had erased the forest and dispirited the enslaved in his favour. Now was the opportunity for his forces to deliver a coup de grace.

In these circumstances, Ainslie gave orders to renew and intensify the ruthless extermination of the Maroons, which he had ordered in his proclamation of 10 May 1813, a couple of months before the hurricanes. The widespread action against them was stepped up in late 1813. Even so the walkouts and the acts of protest on the estates continued in defiance of official policy. On 5 January 1814, 20 slaves marched off Hillsborough estate and walked to Roseau to complain that the manager had murdered a slave on the estate by flogging him to death. This practice of walking off the plantation to seek a hearing from the governor about grievances was something new. It would happen again later that year when 11 slaves on Everton Hall estate at Douglas Bay, led by one, Thornton, protested about being sold to the black slave owner and medical doctor, John Baptiste Birmingham.

At Birmingham's request, the group was rounded up and marched to Roseau by members of the West Indies Regiment. When they reached Canefield estate, Thornton left the group and diverted up to Hope estate, where the former governor Cochrane Johnstone had his plantation. Thornton wanted to inform him of their unfair treatment. He then continued on to Roseau only to find that his colleagues were in jail and that they were all destined to work in the chain gang at Dr Birmingham's demand. By taking it upon himself to protest at who would own him and how his fellow slaves would be treated, the doctor dragged Thornton to court to be tried for his life for insubordination. Birmingham lost the case, but was waiting for Thornton outside the court and directed that he be flogged in the public market place and return to the chain gang repairing the streets. A report of this incident was sent to London and the case was taken up by the Anti-Slavery members of the House of Commons. In conclusion, it declared:

'It is here necessary to state that Dr Birmingham, although a member of the Honourable College of Physicians of the City of Edinburgh, is a black man, of the same colour as poor Thornton, who is the subject of this Statement; and that the cause of the disturbance on the estate was, their having expressed to the Doctor their regret at his having privately purchased them from Mr. Matthews without acquaint-

Hillsborough estate, site of the revolt of January 1814

ing them; and that they did not wish to work for him, knowing him to be cruel in his treatment towards negroes. Thornton was a carpenter on the estate, a negro of an excellent character, who had never been punished.'[14]

Meanwhile at Hillsborough estate, the dissatisfaction over the dead slave erupted into protest action as several of his fellow enslaved took to the woods absenting themselves at one of the busiest times of year when the sugar crop was starting to be harvested. One of the most prominent slaves on the estate, Peter, was directed to lead an armed group into the hills to locate his absconded colleagues. But it eventually became clear that he was leading them astray; he was tried and executed for being an accomplice in what was argued to be an uprising.[15] It was all fuel to the flame of wide-scale resistance that was spreading across the island. Ainslie decided to act.

On 25 February 1814 he issued an official proclamation in which he announced that a punitive expedition would be launched by the Rangers to deal with the problem once and for all: 'I hereby declare to the Maroons who are still in the woods that the Rangers have orders to take no prisoners, but to put to death men, women and children.' In the preamble justifying the harsh measures to be taken, the governor declared: 'These sable hands were property – they were rebel slaves from sugar and coffee plantations who commenced savage hostilities against the white inhabitants, and being well acquainted with the secret avenues of a woody and mountainous country, skilled in forming ambuscades and concealing themselves from pursuit, shifted their ravages and depredation from place to place as circumstances required, and became so formidable at last that the alarm was given that the town of Roseau itself was an object of attack.'[16]

Governor Ainslie sent out Rangers, principally in three directions: to the windward from Rosalie and Tabery to Pointe Mulatre in the south east; above the Layou valley in the centre of the island ; and in the heights of Colihaut around the slopes of Morne Diablotin. The governor sought approval of the House of Assembly to vote more money for '400 stands of arms for the Militia.'[17] As many free people who could do so got involved in the action against the Maroons and apprehended any slaves found to be off work away from the plantations. To assist in this, Ainslie had let it be known since the previous year that free people of colour from the French islands would be welcomed to Dominica to participate, and 1,015 of them swore allegiance to the British Crown in May 1813.[18] In essence it was like an invitation to a lottery: come Maroon hunting, with the chance of picking up a reward. Besides, the administering of every oath of allegiance brought some much-needed foreign money into the struggling economy. It was also an insurance against any transgressors at a time of crisis. Anyone who swore allegiance to the Prince Regent of the United Kingdom could be charged with treason if they changed sides and, as Jean Louis Polinaire had discovered in 1791, the punishment for treason was a miserable death.[19] The final list recording the names of Maroons killed, surrendered or captured includes a column showing the names of those who apprehended them.[20]

Among the captured groups of runaway slaves were a few white deserters from the army, soldiers who had escaped the rigours of life in the military garrisons either at the Cabrits or at Morne Bruce overlooking Roseau. Their presence among the Maroons further heightened tensions within the white community, for not only did it indicate that in some cases, at least, soldiers and Maroons were making common cause, but that they were adding their military knowledge to the skills of the Maroons as guerrilla fighters. The Dominica Journal (or Weekly Intelligencer) of 19 March 1814 informed its readers that a deserter 'who was long absent with the Runaways' had surrendered, and a few days earlier the same newspaper reported that another 'White Man' who had associated with the Maroons for about two years had been captured by loyal troops. The 'Planters, merchants and Inhabitants' did not fail to make a point of the presence of troops among the Maroons when they wrote their petition in support of Ainslie: 'The Maroons have made their camp an asylum for deserters from His Majesty's Troops three of which were lately tried by Court Marshal… and sentenced one to receive 1000 lashes and to be branded on the arm with the letter D and two others to be shot.'[21]

It was less common to find a member of the West Indies regiments deserting to the Maroons because their status as soldiers provided them with the most secure position in the black social hierarchy of the time. However, there was one deserter, Private Hypolite of the 4th West Indies Regiment, who was captured and subsequently executed by firing squad. Other surprises turned up as the Rangers and militiamen scoured the shredded forest. One member of the St George's Militia, John Fatheringham, operating in the south east, came upon five American prisoners who had escaped jail in Bridgetown, Barbados, and had quit that island in a small boat to land on the east coast of Dominica and secreted themselves among the Maroons. The governor awarded Fatheringham £16 10s for capturing them and escorting them to Roseau.[22] In this way the cost of the operation increased as such awards were handed out. In the case of killed or executed slaves, there were the planters to pay for loss of their 'property'. On 18 April, a chief called Clemence was captured and brought in from the Colihaut area. In May, Hill from Woodford Hill and Robin from Hampstead were taken. Fifteen Maroons were brought to Roseau by sloop from Rosalie.

In June 1814, at the height of the action, Governor Ainslie was recalled to England to answer to the Secretary of State for the Colonies for the severe measures he had taken. The anti-slavery lobby in London and other major British cities was growing ever stronger and its members were closely monitoring any transgressions in the West Indian colonies and pressing parliament for justice. The recall of Governor Ainslie was a cause célèbre. However, fate would give the governor many months' grace. In spite of the order to return to answer charges, Ainslie could not get a passage home. Such was the state of shipping at the time, because of the brief war between Britain and the United States, that Ainslie's departure was delayed for five months as no vessel called in to sail him to London. He hung around the island in a peculiar bureaucratic limbo until he eventually embarked on 23 November 1814.

All the while, the President of Council, Benjamin Lucas, acted in his place as head of government. Before leaving, Ainslie received addresses from the inhabitants, both coloured and white, and from both of the main religious denominations, thanking him for saving them from the 'Maroon menace'. They were all couched in the same terms, probably because the same individual had composed them: for example, 'We the Free People of Colour, Planters of the Island of Dominica most humbly beg leave to express… as an act of strict justice to our best friend, Major General Ainslie, the concern we feel to learn the injurious prejudices which are entertained and misrepresentations which have been circulated about your actions.'[23]

The Roman Catholic planters of the parish of St George's as well as 'the planters, merchants and Inhabitants' (apparently made up of 162 whites) also presented him with a statement of gratitude and condemnation of the Maroons. Not to be outdone, the numerous absentee planters in England followed suit, painting an even more alarming picture of the situation to the point of stating that there was much cause to apprehend a general massacre of all the white inhabitants and free people of colour. 'Such a plan was certainly formed. This dreadful catastrophe we believe was averted by the measures adopted by Governor Ainslie.'[24]

All of these expressions of thanks were engineered by the rector of the St George's Anglican church in Roseau, Rev Newman, who amassed these tokens of gratitude from as diverse a collection of inhabitants as possible. He organised the publication of a booklet in London containing all of the petitions in support of Ainslie and recounting the 'atrocities' of the Maroons. The booklet, he stated, was a 'short and unexaggerated recital of their crimes'.[25] His intention was that the British government would be swayed by a show of numbers representing a wide cross-section of the population who approved of the governor's actions and would be suitably shocked by what they claimed that the Maroons had done.

Although Ainslie was technically no longer in charge as commander in chief his plans were still followed through and the most decisive blows on the Maroons fell after his suspension from office. The Assembly had guaranteed him 'that we will ensure a continuation of your actions and maintenance of Rangers, until the nature of the circumstances will permit.'[26] The war reached its climax in July and August when Ainslie was still on island to observe it all and no doubt to give unofficial advice behind the scenes.

The aging Jacko was shot on 12 July after a valiant defence and later, dispirited by the loss of their respected leader, five men from his camp surrendered. A report of his final moments recalls that 'the camp of Jacko, one of the chiefs of the maroons at Dominica, was surprised by a party of rangers. Jacko made a desperate resistance; he killed two rangers, wounded a third, and was shot through the head while levelling a musket at the fourth. He has resided in the woods upwards of forty years and was considered chief of all the runaways.'[27] The man who killed him was a slave in the Ranger Corps called John Le Villoux and the officer in command of the Rangers, Captain Stephan Savarin, sent a memorandum to the legislature requesting that Le Villoux be rewarded by granting him his freedom: 'In the month of July last John Le Villoux, Private or Corporal in the Ranger Corps, killed Jacko, the

Principal or Head of the Maroons whilst this Jacko was in the act of firing at him. I beg leave to request his Excellency's recommendation to the House of Assembly for the Freedom of the said John Le Villoux.'[28]

It took almost a year of negotiation to agree on this manumission and to find funds to compensate both the 'owners' of Jacko and of John for the loss of their 'property', but eventually on 6 June 1815, John Le Villoux was granted his freedom. In the meantime, he had gained yet more kudos among the plantocracy for killing the chief, Louis Moco. Another slave to gain freedom by killing a chief was Joe Gibbon who killed the important northern chief, Noel. As members of the slave Ranger Corps, the arrangement was that the treasury would compensate their 'masters'. 'The treasury is directed to pay the owners of the said slaves [John Le Villoux and Joe Gibbon] their estimated value on their joining the Ranger Corps. A paper to this effect to be lodged with the treasurer which will be deemed sufficient proof of freedom.'[29]

Among the chiefs killed in the forests were Elephant (also known as Policy) who was one of the first to fall when the assault began in February 1814; on 20 April, Chief Moco George was shot by Rangers,

followed by Chief Gabriel on 30 April. As already noted, Chief Jacko, listed as 'the oldest Chief', fell to Rangers on 12 July.

Quashie (also Quashee) described as 'Old Chief', who was captured by members of the Loyal Dominica Rangers, was banished from the island. In the case of some females

Visitors at Jacko Flats, site of Jacko's camp

with children, there was the double punishment of being banished from the island, while their former 'owners' held their children in Dominica, separating mother and child forever. This happened in the cases of 'Flore mulattress' and her child, and Jenny and her child, while Clementine was banished but her child died in jail. Some of those who were captured were later pardoned for having assisted the Rangers in some way. An example of this was the slave Dorinda, alias Belinda, of Permansio estate and her two children who were taken. But Dorinda was pardoned for 'killing a runaway and delivering the same to the owner's attorney'. Two others were sentenced to hang but died in jail. Fourteen received whippings ranging from 100 to 30 lashes each. Of these, one Pierre of Mount Eolus estate died following his punishment. Several others were sentenced to work in chains for three months.[30]

Jacko Steps lead to his camp

The trials followed the method of speedy judgments instituted by John Orde in February 1791 when he was faced with a large number of accused associated with the New Year's Day Revolt. It was a convenient solution for dealing with mass trials while keeping up the appearance that British rule of law was being upheld. However, justice in these cases was not the issue but rather the imposition of an arbitrary regime of intimidation, a charade of judgment by jury combined with court martial. It was aimed at striking terror into the minds of the accused and the slaves at large by the speed and callousness of the process from the point of arraignment and cross examination to the gallows and execution.

Using this as a precedent, Ainslie declared martial law. Adding to the terror of the trials was the close proximity of the court and the place of execution. Both locations still exist: the trials were held in the upper floor of the Market House, now a small museum, overlooking the cobbled old market place in Roseau. In the centre of this historic space, less than 50 meters away, stood the gallows and whipping platform. Trials were in progress while punishments were being inflicted, all clearly seen and heard from the windows of the temporary courtroom. As with the prosecution of the women from Balla's camp and that of Chief Cicero in 1786 and the Maroon trials of 1791 as well as the courts martial of the soldiers of the 8th West Indies Regiment in 1802, special dispensations had been passed to permit the evidence of slaves. The recorded testimonies of the accused ring clear down the centuries giving a voice to a people so seldom heard. In 2015 a verbatim account of the trials relating to Ainslie's war of extermination was published to commemorate the 200th anniversary of the event.[31]

Those who were hanged had their heads cut off and exposed on poles at various places around the island. As with the method of executions after the New Year's Day Revolt in 1791, the beheaded bodies were displayed in public places elsewhere on the island. Guillaume, a slave of M. Moreau, was hanged in the market place and his head was cut off and sent to his 'owner', while his body was burned on the Roseau seashore. Similarly, Buoy, also known as Caliste, was hanged; his head

was cut off and sent to his 'owner' Miss Foye, of the parish of St Peter. John Pierre of Grano estate was hanged, had his head cut off and put on a pole along the public road while his body was hanged in the metal frame of a gibbet. Peter of Hillsborough suffered the same fate as John Pierre, on 22 May 1814, with his head displayed at Hillsborough. Another slave

Bodies exposed along the track to Roseau

from that district was Michel, who had been in the camps for seven years. After being hanged, his head was cut off and displayed on a pole at Hertford Estate, now known as Jimmit on the west coast.

Among the women, there was Hester who had been taken in a camp and sentenced to hang, but died in jail before the sentence could be carried out. Nevertheless, her head was cut off and her body was suspended for two hours in the market place and then burnt on the seashore. Two other women, Vieille Ebo (alias Marie Claire) and Zabet were condemned for 'practising witchcraft' (obeah), in addition to running away, and for remaining in the camps for over 10 years. Like the others, they were hanged and had their body parts distributed to their former 'owners' and burned. The day of 3 April 1814 was probably the most bloody in the Roseau market place as several executions took place in quick succession. One woman lined up on death row that day was Rebecca, a slave of M. Marceau, who had been captured in a camp by Rangers. She was pardoned as she stood at the gallows.

Some of those captured were the enslaved on the estates charged with supplying the Maroons with gunpowder, salt fish, tobacco, and salt and of breaking open storerooms to get provisions. Others were found guilty of selling gunpowder and provisions to the Maroons. From the outset of the British period in the 1760s, the relationship between the enslaved labourers on the plantations and the liberation forces in the mountains consumed the attention of the planters. Trying to cut the network of supply between the coast and the interior was the reason behind the harsh punishments contained in the earliest legislation dealing with 'the runaways'. Although the forest may have provided basic foodstuffs, these were seasonal and widely scattered and as profuse as their 'slash and burn' gardens may have been these were at the mercy of natural disasters as well as being destroyed by the military forces ranged against them. Also lacking was food seasoning, particularly salt, and the occasional plantation rations such as beef, fresh sea fish and imported salt cod and herring which were popular additions to the mainly starch diet of yams. Such comforts as blankets and forks, knives, spoons and iron cooking pots were also in demand in the camps. Arms and ammunition, most notably a regular supply of gunpowder, which did not last well in the damp jungle, were crucial for their defence. Throughout the Maroon era, court records show that numerous plantation slaves were apprehended and punished for supplying these and other commodities or for participating in a two-way trade of *wawa* yams and other forest produce in return for useful subsistence goods.

One may question why after such a formidable resistance in the years before 1813 the whole Maroon force collapsed so quickly and why so many surrendered. In most cases it appears that it was hunger. With the forests destroyed and the pressure on to prevent any supplies coming to them from the plantations, starvation, particularly of those with children, was too much to take. In spite of the fact that some pockets of Maroons remained, their forces never recovered from the events of 1814. Their camps had been broken and their respected leaders were dead. The forest cover, which had been devastated by the hurricanes of July and August 1813, would take 20 years or more to recover to the point where the foliage began to thicken again.[32]

It was also the Rangers – fellow slaves who knew the forests as well as the Maroons – who were a leading cause of the downfall of the Maroons at this time. To be a Ranger was a position of privilege in the slave hierarchy, with bonuses of clothes, blankets and food. To be a Ranger, one was free, for a while at least, from the mind-numbing duties of fieldwork or factory labour. There was the added possibility of freedom for killing a chief. However, the 110 Rangers had cost the colony dear. When accounts were reviewed in 1815, the expenses for maintaining the Corps during the Maroon War totalled £10,504 12s 11d. Looking at the campaign against the Maroons over a longer time span, the cost over 20 years between 1795 and 1815 was in the region of £50,000. The diversion of such an amount of funds from the everyday business of government was a serious drain on the struggling economy of the colony. When the war was over, the Assembly reduced the number of Rangers to 50, including officers, privates, pioneers and guides. Land was set aside for them near St Joseph as a small military base.[33]

There were other demands on the treasury. Once the executions and deaths in captivity were over, the planters were quick to demand their compensation for their dead slaves. Members of the House of Assembly pressured the Council 'to ensure the valuation of the slaves executed in 1814 under sentence from Court Marshal, so that owners can get their compensation' and requested that the treasury release the respective funds.[34]

In August 1815, the President of Council, Benjamin Lucas, admitted to Lord Bathurst, Secretary of State for the Colonies, that the trials had been illegally contrived. Instead of trying slaves by a Court of Special Sessions composed of three justices and a jury of six men, these slaves had been tried by a court martial trumped up by Ainslie at the Roseau Market House on any designated day, by raising a red flag at Fort Young, declaring 'an alarm' lasting 24 hours and trying the slaves by military court during that time. According to Lucas 'the Prisoners brought before them; tried; the sentence frequently carried into immediate execution and the Court discharged by one or two o'clock all on the same day.'[35]

For all the condemnation of the events of 1814, these had been matched, if not exceeded in brutality, by those inflicted by Governor Orde in 1791. Eleven persons had been executed in 1814 compared to 19 in 1791. In both periods there were speedy trials carried out under a dubious system of states of emergency and courts martial. What was different was the historical periods in which they had been carried out. During the 23 years that separated them important changes had taken place, particularly in respect to the altered views on slavery in Britain. What could be dismissed as a necessity of the system in 1791 was not going to stand unchallenged in 1814.

For decades afterwards, people continued to talk of Ainslie's War. Someone who was there at the time recalled those events many years later to Dr John Imray (1811-1880): 'The Runaway negroes in the time of Governor Ainslie became so bold and fearless that they offered a reward for the Governor's head. Then it was decided to adopt measures to subdue the Maroons and accordingly the government sent against them the militia and the garrison of the island. The woods were thoroughly scoured and the strongholds of the runaways captured. The General in charge of the regular troops was afterwards censured for allowing the soldiers to be employed in such service.'[36]

In 1837, Joseph Sturge and Thomas Harvey, two Quakers who were investigating the state of the plantation labourers after the first phase of emancipation, were told of the conflict and the terrible executions. 'Many parts of the island have never been explored, except by the Maroons or runaway negroes, and the rangers who were employed about twenty years ago, in the war of extermination against them. They were at the time about one thousand five hundred in number but were entirely destroyed. Many were brought to Roseau and butchered in cold blood; and there is a well there, which though of sweet water, and in the centre of the marketplace, remains unused to this day from the belief that it is defiled with the blood of these unfortunate people. The governor who sanctioned these atrocities was recalled.'[37]

As for Ainslie, he eventually appeared before the Secretary of State to answer for his 'war of extermination'. On 15 August 1815, the House of Assembly formed a committee 'to draw up a statement of facts in order to counteract certain mis-statements of the administration about His

Excellency Governor Ainslie.' The committee 'perceived with astonishment that the subject appears to have been entirely misunderstood in England.' As already noted, to clear Ainslie's name, the Dominica planters and the proprietors and agents in London printed a booklet with all of the statements of gratitude presented to him so as

Roseau market, 1870s, site of executions

to persuade the British government of the support that he had among the free people of Dominica.

However, this had little effect. Ainslie was censured for his extreme actions and demoted in the colonial service by being transferred to the governorship of the relatively insignificant colony of Cape Breton, Canada. Later, back in England in retirement, he pursued his real passion which was coin collecting and he published a book on the subject. As souvenirs of his time in Dominica, he had the letters of gratitude from the white, free coloured and Roman Catholic planters thanking him for saving them from 'the Maroon menace'. But perhaps most significant of all, he had his 'sword of honour' granted to him by the joint houses of the Dominican legislature inscribed with the words 'To His Excellency Major General Ainslie, Governor of Dominica etc.etc. This sword is presented by the Two Branches of the Legislature in Testimony of His Meritorious conduct in the Reduction of the Maroons in the year 1814.' There had been some heated debate over the wording of this engraving. In the original version the term 'Suppression of the Maroons' had been used. But influential members of the Council objected to this. They pointed out that despite the action that had been taken, it was mainly women and children who had been captured and that there were numbers of men still at large and therefore the Maroons had not actually been totally suppressed. As a compromise, the term eventually used was 'Reduction of the Maroons'.

The official list[38] giving the final account of the climax of the Maroon conflict between February and November 1814 is as follows:

Maroons executed: 11[39]

Maroons killed in the forest: 15 men and 3 women

Those captured in the forest and jailed: 109 men, 11 women and 68 children

Maroons who surrendered: 6 men and 1 woman

Slaves taken and jailed for 'loitering off the plantations to which they belong without passes': 100 men, 48 women, 5 children

Those who surrendered and were pardoned and returned to their owners: 75 men, 31 women, 5 children

Slaves who surrendered direct to their owners: 100

The total directly involved: 577

15

The road to emancipation: halfway to freedom

In the years following the Second Maroon War, the colony struggled through a period of grievous depression. Debts were high, credit to reinvest into agricultural enterprise was non-existent, supplies of imported food and building materials were short and British import duties, which had to be paid on sugar entering the 'mother country' rose sharply between 1810 and 1820.

Those free citizens who could emigrate were moving to the new and promising British colonies of Trinidad and Demerara and they were taking their slaves with them wherever loopholes in the laws governing their transportation allowed. A special provision of the law allowed an owner going from one British colony to another to take with him four slaves as personal attendants. The Dominica and Grenada planters, especially, abused this section in order to supply slaves to Trinidad and other colonies which were prepared to pay high prices for them.

James Corlet of the Dominica Treasury Office reflected in 1816 that, apart from Ainslie's action, 'the decrease of negroes between 1813 and 1816 was mainly occasioned by the hurricane of 23 July 1813 and the flood on the 25 August following which destroyed the provision grounds and great mortality followed'. Another reduction of the enslaved population between January 1815 and 1816, he said, was due to emigration to other colonies, particularly to Trinidad and Demerara and Berbice, which had been added to Britain's empire in 1814. As early as 1783, free people of colour from the French Antilles had been welcomed to settle in Trinidad as a result of the Cedula of Population granted by the King of Spain, and promulgated by the last Spanish governor of Trinidad, Don Jose Maria Chacon. It decreed and granted 'free negroes and mulattoes who shall come to settle in the said island a quantity of land for them and their slaves.' By the time the British took over the colony there was still a need for new settlers and labour and many of those Dominica Maroons 'banished' abroad in 1815 were sent to Trinidad as slaves.

By 1817, supplies of imported food and goods from North America were trickling into Dominica but prices were very high and the discontented legislature was pressing the British Crown to remove trade restrictions in its dealings with foreign countries, particularly with the Dutch, French and Americans. Another hurricane struck that year, but Britain rejected the legislature's plea for relief aid adding to the mass of ill-feeling already evident in the planter-merchant community.

In 1815 Napoleon Bonaparte had been finally overthrown and the threat of French attack on Dominica was over for good. For almost a hundred years the inhabitants had lived in constant fear of invasion and yet now they were faced with problems no less important than war. The most insistent was slavery.

After about a quarter of a century of agitation the British humanitarian movement had secured the passing of the Act for the Abolition of the Slave Trade in 1807. In the West Indies this caused considerable discontent among the planters, and in the assemblies they at once voiced their dissatisfaction. Parliament, they claimed, had no power to make laws concerning local affairs. In 1815, the Imperial government urged the assemblies to promote the physical, religious and moral improvement of the labour force. A few minor changes in the slave codes were made but generally made little difference to the lives of the slaves.

When Henry Nelson Coleridge visited Dominica early in 1825 he found the capital of the island virtually abandoned. 'All was silent and soft and lifeless like a city in the Arabian Nights. Roseau is now in a most singular state of existence... the dirty row of storehouses gave me an impression of want and depopulation...the grass grows lush and verdantly between the stones... But I am afraid, the spirit which should undertake... obvious and easy improvements is at present something drowsy in Dominica... the community is first divided by language then by religion and the inconsiderable residue, which is supposed to represent the whole, is so torn to pieces by squabbles as bitter as contemptible, that the mere routine of government was at a dead stand while I was on the island.'[1]

Later that year, another severe hurricane hit the island, as reported in the Roseau Chronicle of 3 August. 'We have received distressing accounts from the northern parts of this Island particularly in and about Prince Rupert and La Soye. Mills, works and dwellings are destroyed; canes lodged or torn up, Coffee Estates almost deprived both of their old and young plants, some pieces completely washed away, and their buildings blown down are among the heavy calamities occasioned by this afflicting visitation of Providence. Negro houses and grounds laid waste, plantain walks ruined, fruit and other trees destroyed, and the Country round those parts looking as if a fire had gone through and blasted it, makes a finale of this devastating gale. Indeed we may also add that there is not an Estate in the whole Island but what has had their Plantain trees blown down.'

Although the Ranger Corps had been much reduced since 1815, a small number was maintained throughout the 1820s. Maroon activity had declined to the point whereby only a few minor incidents of escape and refuge in the forest were reported. Occasionally individual cases were mentioned in the press, most commonly as paid notices placed in newspapers by owners appealing for information on the whereabouts of their escaped slave, and offering rewards for their apprehension. As late as 1817, one sergeant and three privates of the Loyal West Indies Rangers were shot by firing squad at Morne Bruce and one private received 1,000 lashes for the crime of desertion and escaping into the mountains.

Rather than allow the Rangers to sit idle their members were put to work on government projects and they were placed under the charge of the Board of Public Works. In 1827, for instance, the Ranger Corps was set to work opening up the bridle track across the island from Canefield to Castle Bruce. The most difficult part of this project was in the middle of the island from Brigantine, near today's Sylvania, and down into the Castle Bruce valley past the Emerald Pool.[2]

An alarm was raised during the construction of this trace that Maroons from Martinique had landed in an isolated part of the southeast coast and were moving through the woods. As a report at the time put it, 'At the end of November last year (1827) the rangers were called off for the purpose of scouring the country in search of the Martinique runaways, and since that period the weather has been such as to render the working of the road impracticable.'[3]

This is an indication that there was continued cross-channel marronage from the French islands to Dominica. This would intensify after 1834, when the first phase of slave emancipation in the British colonies took place. The news spread among the enslaved people in the neighbouring French colonies that once they set foot on British soil they would be free people and many risked the sea crossing in rafts and canoes to reach freedom. This *'marronage la mer'* 'marronage by sea' continued until slavery was abolished in the French colonies in May 1848.

In 1817 a law had been passed demanding that all slave owners register their slaves, giving details of sex, age, health and type of employment so that the government could keep an eye on working conditions on the plantations and other places of commerce and trade. The first triennial registration of slaves was carried out that year. Efforts by governors to ensure the better treatment of the enslaved were hotly opposed by the plantocracy. The Grand Jury, the highest court in the colony, censured Governor Charles W. Maxwell 'for his efforts to protect the slaves from oppression and ensure their humane treatment'.[4] By directions from England, certain slave owners, guilty of cruelty, were prosecuted by 'exofficio information provided to Parliament' instead of by indictment before the Grand Jury. Such ill-treatment of slaves in Dominica was brought before the House of Commons by the anti-slavery MP Sir Samuel Romilly in 1818. However, advocates of emancipation who actually visited the island were in for a harder time. One of these, Timothy John Kelly, was imprisoned and heavily fined by Judge Archibald Gloster for speaking out in favour of freedom.

The planters of Dominica were a deeply conservative and belligerent group, desperate to hang on to the institution of forced labour for as long as they could despite the obvious changes taking place in the society and economy. Emotions were running high. In 1823, a circular was issued by the Assembly protesting against the move towards full emancipation. 'Sir: The House of Assembly of this Island appalled at the Enormity of the proposition lately introduced into the House of Commons relative to the Emancipation of the Slave Population of these colonies, have seized the earliest opportunity... to bring the same under their most serious consideration, fully aware from sad Experience that even the slightest discussion on that fatal project places in jeopardy the Lives and fortunes of all the White Population of these Colonies, and that should such a Measure be carried into Effect it will sweep the whole of us into a Vortex of indiscriminate Ruin such as has overwhelmed the unfortunate island of St Domingo some Years ago, from precisely the same cause…'[5]

The letter also called on the other assemblies to join efforts to condemn the action being taken by the Anti-Slavery Society, the Methodists and other bodies striving for abolition. At this period the planters were even talking recklessly of declaring the island independent.

During 1825 the Crown government pressured the reluctant local assembly to enact legislation for 'the Encouragement, Protection and better Government of Slaves and for general amelioration of their condition.'[6] Details on such matters as the provision of clothes, the granting of plantation land for gardens and subjects of marriage, holidays, music making, markets and religious instruction were dealt with. A repeal of tax on the manumission of slaves made its slow progress through the legislature finally being passed in November. Formerly the tax was used to retard the process of gaining freedom by payment of fees sometimes at the slaves' own expense. In one case, of a skilled slave who was assessed at a higher value than normal, the

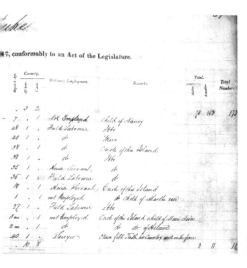

Extract from slave register for Dr Birmingham's estate, 1817

applicant paid £136 plus tax of £16.10s and a 'recording fee' of £1.7s. Once manumission had been made cheaper and easier to obtain there was a run on the registry office indicated by the tight columns in the thick ledgers containing the names of the freed. Mainly they were women manumitted for 'faithful service' or 'services rendered', most in the prime of life and many in their mid to late teens. In several cases this was as a result of free men marrying enslaved women, permitted by legislation passed earlier that year.

By the end of the 1820s it was clear that the tide was turning in Dominica despite the rearguard action by the local planter-legislators who did everything that they could to obstruct emancipation up to the very end. Using their control over the island's budget and voicing their concern for the economy as a motive, they slashed the salaries of pro-abolitionist governors such as Charles Maxwell in a reaction to the British government's slavery policy.[7] The Colonial Office responded in 1832 by placing Dominica under the governor of the Leeward Islands based in Antigua and putting a lieutenant governor in Roseau to administer local affairs so as to smooth the way towards enforcing emancipation on the belligerent colony by order in council in the British parliament the following year.[8]

Political agitation and social change in Britain was transforming the parliament there. The economic importance of sugar and slavery was not what it had been in the previous century and the once powerful West Indies lobby was losing its influence in London as the industrial revolution at home and the move to develop colonies in Africa, the Far East and Pacific focused British interests elsewhere. Although the events of 1814 and 1815 in Dominica had stunned the Maroon and slave populations into retreat, the issues that it raised fed into the continued pressure for emancipation that came from the slaves themselves.

Three major uprisings in Britain's most prized colonies of Barbados, Demerara and Jamaica gave the closing salvo to the slave era in the region. The Barbados 'Bussa Rebellion' of April 1816, the Demerara Revolt of August 1823 and the Samuel Sharp uprising in Jamaica in

December 1831 sent a concerted message to Britain that its time was up. Each of these revolts was triggered by the mistaken belief that the local authorities were withholding freedom that had been granted by the British Crown. The Great Reform bill which transformed the British parliament in 1832 swept new men and new ideas into the House of Commons in a general election dominated by the issue of emancipation and support for its enactment.

Meanwhile the Dominica House of Assembly was going through a transformation of its own. The Roman Catholic Emancipation Act passed by the British Parliament in 1829 gave the right to Roman Catholics in Britain and her colonies to serve in public office and participate in the business of government for the first time since the 16th century. In Dominica, this enabled an important sector of society to contribute to the governance of the colony and to challenge the old Protestant dominated Assembly. In 1830 the legislature was again being petitioned to further revise its slave codes and it was obvious that the Colonial Office was determined to liberate the slaves in spite of local opposition.

The following year all legal discrimination on the grounds of colour was abolished in Dominica. The 'Brown Privilege bill' allowed equal political and social rights to free non-whites and it came into effect the following year. Since many of the free coloured were Roman Catholics, these two pieces of legislation combined to catapult a whole new sector into positions of power and influence. By the general elections of 1836 a non white majority swept into the House, making the Dominica House of Assembly the first British colonial legislature to be controlled by a majority of African descent. It has been noted that in the British Caribbean 'white rule was successfully challenged only in Dominica, where a group of coloured families, known as the 'Mulatto Ascendency', kept control of the legislature for two generations after emancipation.'[9]

On the 29 August 1833 the Abolition of Slavery Act received Royal assent and became law. It would take effect on 1 August the following year. Ironically, the signature that made the bill into law was that of King William IV. As Duke of Clarence, he had been one of the most vocal pro-slavery members of the House of Lords but whatever his personal views on the matter, the power of Parliament prevailed.

When the sun set on the 31 July 1834, there were some 668,000 enslaved labourers in the British West Indies – in Dominica there were 14,175 – and at midnight they were free from slavery as they had known it although they were still beholden to their former masters and mistresses under a system of 'apprenticeship'. It was initially reported that the drunkenness and disorder which planters had expected on emancipation eve did not occur, many going to religious services in thanksgiving. But within a few days the recently emancipated labourers became apprehensive about the nature of their new condition as they observed that it was little changed from what had existed previously. This was not the 'freedom' that they had been led to believe would take place. On 15 August, Lieutenant Governor Charles Schomberg reported curtly that 'some insubordination has occurred on the French estates. The Negroes are hostile to the system of apprenticeship but order has been restored.'[10]

Worse was to come in the following month when the most powerful hurricane to hit Dominica during the 19th century tore across the island on the night of 20 September. Among many other aspects of devastation noted by Schomberg was that 'the whole Negro population is unhutted, the provision grounds and gardens destroyed... the planters of Dominica are without the means of feeding a starving and dissatisfied population.'[11] As the young Dr John Imray picked his way through the devastation in Roseau and toured the country districts he too observed that 'The negro houses almost all blown down and their provision grounds utterly ruined... The negroes will be starving in a few months. Since the hurricane they have been doing just as they please.'[12] Without relief, the labourers had no alternative but to piece together their trash huts and to replant gardens where they could. Those few Maroons who remained scattered in the forest began to drift down to the coast although many maintained their gardens in the mountains and commuted back and forth to maintain their cultivations.

On emancipation the former slave owners were to receive monetary compensation for the loss of their 'property' as well as being assured that their former slaves would continue to work at their various tasks without pay for 40 and a half hours a week as a form of additional compensation in kind. It was designed to ensure a continued supply of labour for four more years in the case of domestics and six more years in the case of field workers, at the end of which time all would gain 'full free'. Children under six years old were granted total freedom in 1834. Seventeen special magistrates were appointed to oversee the system island wide. As it turned out this cumbersome regime was scrapped in 1838 after four years of operating in a manner that was inefficient and unsatisfactory.

Monetary compensation was given to the former slave holders according to the age, health and status of each enslaved labourer based on evaluations made by a team of assessors. The slave owners of Dominica received a total of £275,547; the beneficiaries varied from huckster women controlling a couple of slaves, to householders with cooks and chambermaids, shipwrights and house builders with skilled carpenters and joiners, boat owners with mariners and stevedores as well as the plantation owners, both local residents and absentees, with field labourers and factory hands ranging in number from half a dozen to a couple of hundred. The money granted them was put to a variety of uses: to pay off debts such as those on their encumbered estates or to reinvest in their plantations with improved machinery and to effect repairs to their homes and businesses as a result of the damage inflicted by the hurricane of 20 September. In the case of many absentees, they arranged for the transfer of funds from sugar and coffee production in the colony so as to invest in railways, insurance companies and industrial ventures in Britain and elsewhere in her expanding empire. Dominica, like the rest of the British West Indies, was thus stripped of much of its capital and in effect the region and its workforce once used were seen to have served their purpose and were abandoned.

In a prophetic farewell address to a joint meeting of the House of Assembly and Executive Council as he departed Dominica for a promotion to Demerara in early July 1838, Lieutenant Governor Henry Light exhorted the members to conceive of a new society based on mass education: 'So long as Slavery or distinction of class existed, it was sufficient that European intellect directed the energies of the island. That time is passed. There will daily be an augmentation of native energy. It ought to be the first object of legislation to give it a solid foundation and that can only be ensured by liberal education.' He had helped guide Dominica through 'apprenticeship' to 'full free' and he, more than most, realised that although the abolition of slavery had been achieved, the challenge of securing investment and commitment for the transformation of that society lay ahead but that resources were limited on both fronts to accomplish significant change.[13]

16

The aftermath: Zion, Babylon and the globalised colony

When the liberated labourers of Dominica pushed open the rough wooden window shutters and doors of their huts to let in the sunlight of the new day of 1 August 1838 they possessed nothing. Not even the huts were their own much less for the land on which they stood. The new lieutenant governor of Dominica, John Longley, had made this clear some days before when he read out the declaration of emancipation on the steps of the Court House and House of Assembly in Roseau: 'Now let me tell you what the law has ordered for you; now you are to be free men, – You may remain in the Houses, and on the Estates where you are until the 1st of October, if you wish to do so: The Houses in which you live and the Grounds which you have planted, are not yours; but if you continue to work by agreements with your Master, and work as the Labourers work in England, and all other free Countries cheerfully and diligently for your Employer he will let you live in his House, and plant your Provisions on his Ground. This is what I advise you to do; what I know the Queen, would wish you to do.'[1]

Freedom had been granted in principle but the former slaves now had to begin another struggle to free themselves from the hold of the plantations and that would take another century to achieve. 'A race has been freed, but a society has not been formed,' a colonial official informed Britain in 1848.[2]

Emancipation in the British colonies came 14 years before abolition was declared by the government of France on behalf of her colonies in the Antilles. The US abolitionist Joseph J Gurney writing to Henry Clay of Kentucky reported on conditions under the first years of freedom in the British West Indies and noted that during his visit to Dominica in 1840 several hundred slaves, mainly from Guadeloupe, were making their way across the channel to liberty. 'The poor creatures run prodigious risks in their attempts to cross the water, in small open boats; and we were well informed that at least one-third

A treadmill was introduced to Dominica's prison, 1836

of them perish before they reach the land. One hardy fellow arrived on the shore of Dominica, after extreme peril, on the remains of a small craft which he had constructed of the pithy stems of the great aloe, or century plant. When at Dominica we heard excellent accounts of the behaviour and industry of these runaway slaves. About two hundred of them remain on the island – the rest have migrated, in pursuit of higher wages to Trinidad'.[3]

Following abolition in the French territories in 1848 most of the cross-channel Maroons returned to their home islands. It was estimated by Alexandre Gatine, the Commissioner for the Republic responsible for Guadeloupe, that some 800 Maroons who had escaped to Dominica returned to the east coast commune of Moule alone, not counting those from plantations along the south coast or on Mariegalante, all within clear sight of the British island.[4]

With emancipation, Dominica's colonial government took over the business of law enforcement, punishment for criminal offences and the imposition of law and order that had been formerly administered by the individual plantation and slave owners. Punishment in the Roseau prison was reinforced with the introduction of a treadmill in 1836[5] and the following year a police force was established with constables under the direction of district magistrates.[6] With a police force in place, slavery abolished and France no longer an enemy there was no reason to maintain fortifications or station troops. In July 1854 the garrisons at Morne Bruce and the Cabrits were shut down and the last of the British regiments sailed away. Fort Young was converted into the police headquarters, and the soldiers' barracks on Morne Bruce were turned into an infirmary for the aged and destitute. The Cabrits, Fort Cashacrou and all of the coastal batteries and signal stations were abandoned to forest and coastal scrub woodland. In the decades following emancipation starting in 1840, a raft of laws, such as the wide-ranging vagrancy acts, were passed to keep control of the masses. Their aim was rigid regulation of all aspects of social behaviour, to limit the right to vote and to determine everything in the lives of the labourers from the rates of their labour to the nature of their sexual activity.

Legislation criminalising homosexual acts, for instance, was introduced in the 1860s and 1870s in all of the British West Indies colonies, whereas no such laws were enacted in the neighbouring French, Dutch, Danish or Spanish dependencies. Therefore, today, the only nations in the whole of the hemisphere of the Americas which still have such legislation on their books are 10 members of CARICOM, all former British colonies.

While slavery and the slave trade had been abolished in Dominica and other British colonies, certain African traders on the coast of West Africa resented its demise and conspired, mainly with Portuguese shippers, to maintain the supply of slaves to places such as Brazil, Cuba and the United States. The Royal Navy was detailed to scour the Atlantic and Indian Oceans to apprehend slave ships and free their human cargoes. In 1837 Dominica received an unexpected influx of new Africans in this way. A Portuguese vessel, the brig *Don Francisco*, was bound illegally from Ouidah (in what is today Benin) for Cuba, with 437 enslaved Africans aboard. It was sighted and captured by the

Royal Navy frigate *HMS Griffin* some miles off Dominica and the ship was brought into Roseau.[7] The slaves were immediately set free and settled in areas such as Portsmouth, Woodford Hill, Castle Bruce and Soufriere although a number of men were pressed into service in the West Indies regiments and taken to Trinidad. Many of those refugees in Dominica maintained their African surnames such as Mingo, Akie, Cuffy, Firmin and Sango, while others, gathered around Woodford Hill, adopted the surname, Africa.

A surviving workers' barracks, River estate

The islands were still dominated by labour-intensive plantation agriculture and social and economic structures changed little in the years ahead. As early as 1836, two years before full emancipation of all the 'apprentices' had been granted, Lord Glenelg, then Secretary of State for the Colonies, explained his policy to the West Indies governors. If stable economies were to prosper, he said, they would have to make it 'the immediate and apparent interest of the Negro population to employ their labour in raising them'. This could be done by 'impeding' their acquisition of land and forcing them into estate labour for their survival.[8]

Crown Land sales were to be carefully priced out of reach of persons without capital and always sold to the highest bidder above a set minimum. 'The object is not to force the cultivation of the present staples by depriving the Negroes of every other resource for their subsistence, but merely to condense and keep together the population in such a manner that will always contain a due proportion of labourers.'[9] This policy was intended to limit access to land even where it was plentiful, as it was in Dominica and Demerara for instance.[10]

In Dominica, Crown Land was to be priced high enough to keep most people as landless labourers, but not too high to discourage the most industrious workers from saving out of their wages in the hope of purchase.[11] But even for the industrious, only private lands held by those either willing to sell or forced to do so by economic circumstances, were generally available to the newly emancipated. Most large estates lay overgrown and abandoned to bush while several were heavily encumbered. Absentee landlords held others as collateral for interests elsewhere.

As late as 1945, an acre of Crown Land only cost ten shillings but the regulations ensured that a purchaser was not permitted to buy less than 40 acres at a time thereby effectively cutting the prospective smallholder out of the market. The low wages in Dominica during the latter half of the nineteenth century made the purchasing of such land by estate labourers virtually impossible.

Workers at Clarke Hall estate, 1890s

Landless black labourers were caught in a vicious circle. This was a colony where ironically, in the 1850s, the very fertility of the soil was used as an argument for keeping a labourer's wages low. 'Six pence a day for field labourers is adequate remuneration in a colony where ground provisions are so easily cultivated and to be obtained at a very reasonable rate, an advantage not possessed by the labouring population of most of the other West India islands.'[12]

In 1882, the acting President John Spencer Churchill declared that 'peasant proprietorship is no doubt rather to be deprecated than encouraged in the case of the Negroes, who are apt in that state, to lapse into barbarous idleness.'[13] Political upheaval and economic decline on the island at the end of the century eventually goaded the Colonial Office into taking action to ameliorate such policy.

The labourers were wary of anything that hinted a return to slave conditions. In 1844, there was an uprising in the southern half of the island when officers commenced to take the first census since emancipation. Violence broke out during these Census Riots when the labourers misunderstood what was happening as enumerators appeared outside their huts to compile lists of their occupants without previous explanation or warning. In Creole it was called '*Ladje Neg*', the Blacks' War. The rumour spread that the enumerators were taking their

names and the numbers of persons in each household so as to make lists to reintroduce slavery.[14] In the 1850s there were disturbances at Batalie Bay due to the armed eviction of squatters along the west coast. All along the west coast, squatters who chose to leave the estates took the pieces of their

Huts were packed along the coast within the dotted line of the 66 yards of the Queen's Three Chains

huts and re-erected them within the 66 yards of the 'Queen's Three Chains' that had been surveyed by John Byres for government use back in the 1760s. Some estates made arrangements to take over this government land, but others such as Belfast, Wallhouse, Check Hall, Soufriere and Castile took no action; this mass squatting is the origin of the crowded beachfront communities of Dublanc, Colihaut, St Joseph, Layou, Mahaut, Massacre, Loubiere, Pointe Michel, Soufriere and Scott's Head.

As one senior colonial official commented: 'The abolition of slavery in 1834 and of apprenticeship in 1838, caused a large number of labourers who were unwilling to reside upon the places where they had been slaves… to rush like a torrent down upon the vale, and carrying posts and boards to the bays at nights, houses were seen weekly rearing their trashy heads clandestinely. Indeed some people believed that the boon of freedom was incomplete, if not insecure, without a small piece of land being attached to it.'[15]

Along the east coast the squatters crowded around the rugged borders of estates such as Castle Bruce, Wesley and Marigot. Large portions of land held by the Roman Catholic church at La Plaine and Saint Sauveur were parcelled out by church authorities to create free villages. In an unusual case at the northern village of Clifton, the owner, Elizabeth Wallace, a devout Methodist, divided up her estate for her 44 ex-slaves. Here and there, in various ways, other free villages emerged but it was a tug of war between the plantation interests and the people struggling to become free independent small farmers.

Land taxes, first imposed in 1886 and increased in 1888, were other ways the colony sought to stem the possibilities for independent landholding. By raising a tax, they hoped that the smallholder would have to work on the plantation to get cash to pay these fees. It was a way to force dependency on plantation wages among the labour force. This action resulted in protest by villagers of La Plaine on the south-east coast in 1893. It erupted into a violent confrontation between the smallholders and marines of the Royal Navy vessel HMS *Mohawk*, backed up by the local colonial police force. Property was seized and four villagers were shot dead by the police.[16]

It was as a result of this climactic confrontation that the Colonial Office, exasperated by decades of unrest on the island, appointed a one-man commission of inquiry to assess the grievances. The commissioner, Sir Robert Hamilton, a former governor of Tasmania, was sent out in late 1893 with orders 'to make a diligent and full enquiry into the state of affairs existing in Our Island of Dominica. To investigate why the colony was: more backward and less developed than any other of the islands and why its people were less prosperous and contented than Her Majesty's other West Indian subjects.'[17] Hamilton's report made recommendations for pro-moting small farmers and encouraging peasant industry, but many of his proposals were never carried out.

Four died in the La Plaine tax revolt, 1893

Fifty years later yet another commission of

inquiry had to deal with the same issues. This was the West Indian Commission headed by Lord Moyne, which visited Dominica in 1938, and reported in 1945. 'Of all of the British West Indian islands,' it stated, 'Dominica presents the most striking contrast between the great poverty of a large proportion of the population, particularly in Roseau, the capital, and the beauty and fertility of the island.'[18] The report called for the distribution of land for more peasant holdings, improved housing and better communications, particularly a road across the island.

At last, from the late 1940s, more than 100 years since full emancipation, the status of the independent smallholder was assured. The results of these proposals were seen in the land settlement schemes of the 1950s and 1960s whereby former estate workers became landholders in their own right for the first time. In the hilly Crown Lands behind the crowded coastal 'plantation villages' and beyond the boundaries of 18th-century plantations, the government surveyed and sold plots at an affordable price to independent farmers. In the years that followed, 'feeder roads' for farm access were constructed to link the cultivations to the main highways. Backed by the rise of the banana industry from 1954 a new generation of small farmers began securing an economic base enabling them to build better houses, educate their children and develop a level of security to match the older established class of 'peasant proprietors'.

Plantations that had featured during the Maroon era were taken over and occupied by the descendants of those who had participated in the struggle. Around the capital and other urban areas, government purchased, subdivided and redistributed the former sugar and lime estates of Goodwill (1950s), Canefield (1960s), Bath and Elmshall (1970s) to provide for slum clearance in central Roseau and housing for the surge of workers coming in from the country areas and for the expanding middle class. Private housing areas took over Belfast, Check Hall, River, Copt Hall, Wallhouse, Grand Savannah, Castle Comfort, Shawford and Warner estates, heralding a surge of urban expansion along the west coast corridor and Roseau Valley. The takeover and redistribution of Castle Bruce and Melville Hall estates in the 1970s from the British Commonwealth Development Corporation (CDC) was in response to demands by the populace for farmland and village expansion while the government's acquisition of Geneva in 1974 was as a result of political upheaval involving violence and arson on the scale of the 18th-century Maroon revolts. All this caused a rapid transformation of demographics, settlement and social change within a space of two decades.

Political change came along with the other recommendations of the Moyne Commission. Universal Adult Suffrage became law in 1951. The establishment of the first political party, the Dominica Labour Party, came soon afterwards in 1955. During the next decade, gradual constitutional changes gave Dominicans increasing control over their own affairs. In 1967, internal self-government was granted, when Dominica became an 'Associated State' of the United Kingdom. Under this arrangement, all internal affairs were the responsibility of Dominicans while Britain only maintained responsibility for defence and external affairs. Then, on 3 November 1978, that umbilical cord was cut, and the island gained full political independence.

Along with the nationalist symbols of flag, anthem and coat of arms there came the legends of nationhood. There developed a narrative of heroes and nation builders among which the exploits of the Maroons and their leaders played a prominent part. Balla, Pharcel, Congo Ray, Cicero, Jacko and Quashee were lauded for their roles as resistance fighters and architects of eventual freedom. This came at a time in the 1960s and 1970s, when a radicalisation of thought was sweeping the Caribbean. In Dominica, an increasing number of young people adopted the lifestyle of the Rastafari. This had its roots in 1930s Jamaica and was inspired by the coronation of Haile Selassie of Ethiopia which was merged with the resurrected teachings of Marcus Garvey and his united African movement UNIA. It was joined by the civil rights and Black Power messages from the United States and local concerns over what kind of society was best suited for Dominica. All this converged in the mid-1970s at a time of great local political upheaval. After initial reservations by the traditionally conservative sectors of the local community, Rastafarians were accepted as peaceful members of a back-to-the-land movement who occupied small farms in the hills, referred to as Zion. They saw redemption in following a lifestyle marked by self-sufficiency and a composite of selective African traditions that rejected the colonial-based society.

That other 'colonial imperialist dominated path' was Babylon. Babylon was the urban, coastal world of capitalist 'mafia exploiters', the 'Grand Mulatre Gwo Boug' (the powerful mulatto class), and the police. Tensions rose with the emergence of a violent wing referred to as 'the Dreads'. As in the days of the Maroons the urban and coastal communities reacted fearfully to the news coming from the hills of attacks on farmers and stealing of crops, the burning of property and isolated murders. Similarly, names were given to the most daring characters of this period: Tumba, Mal and Pokosion were some of them. How much of this fear was encouraged for political purposes in the run up to a forthcoming general election so that a new political leader could be seen as the saviour of a nation in turmoil is debatable but it certainly was a time of heightened anxiety.

In November 1974, legislation was enacted to outlaw the Dreads but details of the act soon proved to be unconstitutional although at the time it gave many citizens a feeling of security. As Mary Eugenia Charles, then leader of the opposition, put it during the debate, 'I rise to support this Bill. I do so reluctantly. It is regrettable that the day should have arrived when we ourselves must take away one of our human rights enshrined in our constitution…However, it becomes necessary because a greater majority of peoples' freedom is being eroded and that is freedom from fear.'[19]

To add to this, serious social and political upheavals took place including numerous strikes and protest demonstrations particularly in 1973, 1977 and 1979. The creation of a politically directed Defence Force and offensives against 'the Dreads' from 1974 created a mood of fear and tension. It all began to resemble the Maroon era of the late 18th century, with the forested mountains of Dominica once again the scene of conflict. This period climaxed in March and December 1981, with two attempts to overthrow a duly elected government, and the kidnap and murder of this author's father as mentioned in the dedication of this book.

However, during the 1980s, the positive and constructive elements of the Rasta lifestyle came to the fore and had a major influence on society. Although Dominica entered independence under a veil of austerity disguised by nationalism, there was an upsurge of creative talent in the arts inspired by this new identity. The creation and exportation of zouk and cadance music and the formation of bands which gained a regional and international following lifted spirits and gained positive publicity for the island. The Rastas' advocacy of healthy living, vegetarianism and respect for the natural environment as well as the encouragement of creativity in dance, music and art spread. Their long-standing support for the growing and use of marijuana, and the decriminalisation of the use of the plant, continues to be an area of dispute. It could be said that in the quest to create an alternative society the Rastafari have become the inheritors of the spirit of the Maroons in all of its most positive aspects.

Remembering the Maroons, carnival band, 2017

As the 21st century dawned, Dominica, like other small island nation states, was increasingly sucked into the globalised economy. Debate intensified over what kind of society its people should seek to develop. For some, the answer is to create an oasis from the mainstream globalised world in the spirit of the agricultural Maroons of the early 18th century, before the colonial colossus took over and distorted the nature of development. For others, this utopian view is unrealistic. For them, they seek the materialistic trappings of a metropolitan lifestyle that they experience in exile, mainly in North America, and argue that this should be imposed upon the island's fragile landscape regardless of the long-term consequences. In their eyes, this route will lead to 'development' whereas the more ecologically sound and socially secure path is regarded as 'backward underdevelopment'.

These two opposing views emerge regularly in debates in Dominica on major national projects, foreign investment or international agreements, particularly those involving the sale of citizenship and relations with countries such as China, Russia and certain Gulf states. A collective memory with reference to the exploitation of the island and its people during the time of slavery is never far from the surface. Understanding the role of the Maroons, who built on the foundations laid by the Kalinagos, is a significant place from which to start that quest.

Endnotes

1 A LASTING MEMORIAL: THE LEADERS OF LIBERTY

1. Jean Casimir, 'Social structural changes in Dominica', prepared by the Social Development Unit of the Economic Commission for Latin America, ECLAC, 1984
2. Orde to Grenville, 7 February 1786 - 20 July 1786 (dispatches) CO 71/10
3. Scottish planter and member of Council William Bremner compiled a collection of pro-slavery quotes from the Bible, including a few absolving the owner if he fornicated with, or had children by his 'bondsmaid'. Memoir of William Bremner, National Library of Scotland

2 AN ISLAND CITADEL: THE MAROON LANDSCAPE

1. James Anthony Froude, The English in the West Indies or the Bow of Ulysses, Longmans Green and Co, London, 1888, p141
2. John Matson, letter 30 March 1803 in CARIBBEANA, miscellaneous papers relating to the history etc of the British West Indies, Vere Langford Oliver (ed), 1910-1919
3. Raymond Breton, Dictionnaire Caraibe Français, Auxerre, 1665, p45
4. John Eaden, The Memoirs of Père Labat 1693-1705, Constable, 1931, p94
5. Michael Zamore in The Wildlife of Dominica quotes Swank and Julien (1975) who say that the manicou was only introduced in 'the 1800s', but the fact that it has a Kalinago name, recorded by Raymond Breton in 1665, suggests an earlier introduction.
6. Captain Combe to Orde, 3 February - 15 June 1791, CO 71/20

3 THE FIRST MAROONS: THE KALINAGO FOUNDATION

1. Letter written by Dr Chanca to the city of Seville, in Christopher Columbus: The Four Voyages, JM Cohen (ed), Penguin Books, London, 1969, p132
2. Text of the *requerimiento* issued to Pedro Arias de Avila by King Ferdinand in 1514 at the commencement of his voyage to Darien during which he briefly visited Dominica.
3. John Eaden, The Memoirs of Père Labat 1693-1705, Constable, 1931, p112
4. Chief Anthony in southern St Lucia is a case in point. He had been enslaved by the Spanish to dive for pearls and was wary of English castaways landing upon his territory at what is today Vieux Fort, in 1605.
5. Eaden, p107
6. ibid, p104
7. ibid, p101
8. John Esquemeling, The Buccaneers of America, George Routledge & Sons, London, 1926, p235
9. Peter Hulme and Neil Whitehead (eds), Wild Majesty, Encounters with Caribs from Columbus to the present day. An anthology. Clarendon Press, Oxford, 1992, pp38-42
10. John Davies, The History of the Caribby Islands, London, 1666, p295
11. Lennox Honychurch, Carib to Creole, a history of contact and culture exchange. Unpublished doctoral thesis, 1997, Bodleian Library, Oxford University
12. The main informant on the 'Carib language', Father Raymond Breton, lived among the Kalinago in Dominica 1642 to 1653. By that time several Spanish words had been adopted and adapted by the Kalinagos.

13. Basil Davidson, The Story of Africa, Mitchell Beazley Publishers, 1984, p113. An account is given by Mansa Musa of Mali in 1324 of 200 canoes with one year's rations sent west into the Atlantic. Another larger fleet was sent some time later but neither returned. However, it has been shown that due to contrary currents and winds it was unlikely that Africans who made it across the Atlantic to the Americas were ever able to return home.
14. Raymond Breton, Dictionnaire Caraibe Français, Auxerre, 1665, p52
15. The work of linguist and anthropologist Douglas Taylor, who was resident in Dominica 1929-1978, is important in this regard: see 'Outline of Dominican Creole' in his Language of the West Indies, Johns Hopkins University Press, Baltimore and London 1977, pp198-211
16. What is commonly called the 'Carib language' is in fact a branch of Arawakan which was widely spoken in lowland South America and up the islands.
17. Anthony Trollope, The West Indies and The Spanish Main, Harper and Brothers, New York, 1860, p157
18. Marina Besada Paisa (ed), Dictionnaire Caraïbe-Français, Révérend Père Raymond Breton 1665, nouvelle édition, Karthala Editions, Paris, 1999, pp274-275
19. Pierre Pelleprat, Relations des missions des Pierre Pelleprat de la Compagnie de Ièsus dans les Isles, et dans la terre ferme del'Amerique Meridioniale. Paris, 1665, pp53-54
20. Lennox Honychurch, 'An introduction to the African Heritage of the Caribbean', in The African Heritage in Brazil and the Caribbean, Carlos Henrique Cardim and Rubens Gama Dias Filho (eds), Fundação Alexandre de Gusmäo, Ministry of External Affairs, Brazilia, 2011, chap 6, p117

4 THE NEUTRAL ISLAND: CREATING A MAROON BASE

1. Jean Jacques Rousseau, A Discourse on Inequality, Penguin Classics, London, 1984, p145
2. Nellis M Crouse, The French Struggle for the West Indies, 1665-1713, Columbia University Press, New York, 1943, p54
3. From the notebook of Dr HAA Nicholls (Phyllis Allfrey collection), p87
4. William Stapleton in Calendar of State Papers (America) 5: no 1152, p499
5. Jean Baptiste Du Tertre, Histoire General des Antilles habitées par les Francois, vol 2 (1667-1671), p536

5 THE FIRST PLANTATIONS: JEANNOT ROLLE AT GRAND BAY

1. Léo Elisabeth, 'The French Antilles' in Neither Slave nor Free: The Freedman of African Descent in the Slave Societies of the New World, David Cohen and Jack P Greene (eds), Johns Hopkins University Press, Baltimore, 1972, pp134-171
2. Robert Harms, The Diligent: A Voyage Through the Worlds of the Slave Trade, Perseus Press, Oxford, 2002, pp341-375
3. Jean Baptiste Du Tertre, Histoire General des Antilles habitées par les Francois. vol I, 1667-1671, p503
4. Gordon K. Lewis, Main Currents in Caribbean Thought, Heinemann Educational Books (Caribbean), 1983, p232
5. This account, copied down in French by one of the Jesuit priests, was rewritten in its original form in the notebook of Dr HAA Nicholls (Phyllis Allfrey Collection) from which it is taken, pp13-20
6. Arlington James, Cabrits plants and their uses, Forestry and Wildlife Division, Dominica, 1986, p39
7. The original site of this stone cross was on a ridge overlooking the sea on Geneva Estate. In the late 19th century there was a dispute between the Church and the Lockhart family, owners of Geneva, over title of the land, and in the 1920s the cross was dragged onto

clearly defined Roman Catholic land overlooking their new church.

8. Young Papers, Rhodes House Library, Oxford University

9. Manuscripts of Lord North, Reflections on the true interest of Great Britain with respect to the Caribbee Islands, ff181-189(5). Written as 'Anonymous, by a Planter of Barbados 1762' but with a note that it was probably the hand of William Patterson, surveyor general of the Leeward Islands and also a Barbados planter, who, between 1759-1762 wrote six lengthy advices from Barbados to John Stuart, Earl of Bute, then Secretary of State for Trade. Lord North Papers, Rhodes House Library, Oxford University

10. Thomas Atwood, The History of the Island of Dominica, J. Johnson, London, 1791, pp226-227

6 THE BRITISH TAKE OVER: MAROONS CONSOLIDATE

1. Sir Alan Burns, The British West Indies, Alan & Unwin, London, 1954, p94

2. For a full account of these land sales see DC Murdoch, Land policy in the eighteenth-century British Empire: The sale of Crown Lands in the Ceded islands, 1763-1783, The Historical Journal, vol 27, no3, 1984, pp549-574

3. Like many British officials at the time, Governor General Robert Melville purchased one of the best pieces of land in Dominica, which he named Melville Hall after himself. Here he raised a plantation that was operated by his descendants into the middle of the 19th century. It is the site of the present Douglas-Charles Airport and surrounding valley.

4. Young Papers, vol 1, 1789-1814, p20, Rhodes House Library, Oxford University. Besides musicians, Sir William brought out his own artist, Agostino Brunias, to paint the people and scenes of the islands that he administered.

5. Melville to the Earl of Hillsborough, CO 71/3

6. Minutes of Council, Dominica, CO 74/4

7. Minutes of House of Assembly, Dominica, CO 74/4

8. The sales of His Majesty's Land in the Island of Dominica, 1772, CO 71/76, and Acts of the Privy Council, Colonial Service, CO 101/9, pp113-114

9. Thomas Atwood, The History of the Island of Dominica, J Johnson, London, 1791, p202

10. CO 101/1

11. Joseph Boromé, 'The French in Dominica 1699-1763', in Aspects of Dominica History, Roseau: Government Printery, 1972, p54

12. 'Observations on the Slave Trade, and a Description of some part of the Coast of Guinea', London, 1789, in James Pope-Hennessy, The Sins of the Fathers, Weidenfeld & Nicolson, 1967, p122

13. In spite of the large areas taken up for housing today, there is more forested land in Dominica in the 21st century than there was in the late 18th century because of widespread clearing of forests for sugar in the 1760s. Most of those estates have long since been abandoned and are back in forest today.

14. The ruins of 61 water mills survive around the island.

15. An account of the value of produce of Dominica from the year 1767 to 1778, Inspector General's Office, Custom House, London, 26 March, 1806

16. Sir William Young, Considerations which may tend to promote the Settlement of our New West India Colonies by Encouraging Individuals to embark in the undertaking', London, 1764

17. Awéte neg (*Mimosa ceratonia*), mountain l'epine, is a trailing shrub covered in fine curved and flattened prickles.

18. Carey Robinson, 'Maroons and Rebels (a Dilemma)' in Maroon Heritage: Archaeological, Ethnographic and Historical Perspectives, E Kofi Agorsah (ed) , Canoe Press, Kingston, 1994, p90

19. Directory of land sales, 1777, accompanying the 'Byres Map' of Dominica detailing land lots published 1776. Personal collection
20. Certificates appearing in 'A Report of the Committee of the Legislature appointed to enquire into the condition of the Negro Population of this Island' 12 June 1823 (misc. papers on slavery and abolition), Dominica National Archives
21. Will of John Simpson. Personal collection
22. John Davies, The History of the Caribby Islands (translation of Charles de Rochfort, 1658), London, 1666, p202
23. After the hurricane of 1780, money sent from England for public relief was diverted to build a larger, more secure jail. This was also levelled in a hurricane, in 1813, and replaced.
24. Loftus Roberts, The Negres Marons of Dominica, notes, Roseau Public Library, Dominica, p2
25. Charles Winstone Letter Book, 1777-1786, manuscripts division, William L. Clements Library, University of Michigan
26. Examples can be found in The Dominica Chronicle, 14 September 1825, and earlier newspapers.
27. For more information on this, see Lennox Honychurch, Dominica's Cabrits and Prince Rupert's Bay, 2013, and A History of Fort Young, 2010
28. Orde to Grenville, 17 May-15 June 1791, CO 71/20
29. Anon. Sketches and Recollections of the West Indies by a Resident dedicated to James Laing, formerly of Dominica, Smith, Elder & Co, Cornhill, London, 1828, p84
30. Today the sound of the kon lambi carries only one message: there is fresh fish for sale.
31. Atwood, p223
32. The examination of Polinaire, A Free Mulatto Man, CO 71/20, p2
33. Diary of Joseph Senhouse, 1776, in The Journal of the Barbados Museum and Historical Society, vol 37, no3, 1985, p283
34. Minutes of the House of Assembly, Dominica, 1814
35. Anon, Sketches, p148

7 THE FRENCH RETURN: MAROONS GAIN STRENGTH

1. Thomas Atwood, The History of the Island of Dominica, J Johnson, London, 1791, p114. Atwood is the main source for much of this chapter along with colonial papers from the National Archives of Dominica and the UK.
2. ibid, p109-110
3. ibid, p114
4. Susan Campbell, 'Africans to Dominica: 100,000 Middle Passages from 'Guinea' to the Eastern Caribbean, 1764 to 1808 http://da-academy.org/AfricanstoDominica.pdf
5. Atwood, p227
6. Raymond Proesmans, unpublished manuscript, in Arnold Bogaert Centre, Roseau. From documents formerly held in the registry building destroyed by fire in June 1979
7. Atwood, p132
8. ibid, pp236-237
9. Joseph Boromé, 'Dominica during French occupation 1778-1784', in Aspects of Dominica History, Government Printery, Roseau, 1972, p112
10. Atwood, p229
11. Boromé, p112
12. Atwood, pp235-236
13. Mair's account of the Battle of the Saintes in a letter to a friend in Jamaica is now in the National Archives of Jamaica, Spanish Town.

14. John Spencer Churchill, booklet, The Leeward islands, London, 1898, p12
15. Atwood, pp112-113

8 THE FIRST MAROON WAR: THE BALLA UPRISING

1. Thomas Atwood, The History of the Island of Dominica, J Johnson, London, 1791, p168
2. ibid, p169
3. The petition of His Majesty's faithful American subjects who have taken refuge in this island. Signed 3 April 1786 by 29 heads of households.
4. In official documents Cicero's name is followed by the words 'also known as Sussex' in brackets. There is a possibility that his followers had given him the name 'Sisserou' after Dominica's Imperial Parrot and that he was not named after the Roman consul Cicero; in the same way Jacko could be named after the smaller red-necked parrot. No evidence exists for either possibility.
5. Observation by Bernard Marshall in 'Maronage in Slave Plantation societies: A case study of Dominica, 1785-1815', Caribbean Quarterly, University of the West Indies, Mona, vol 22, Nos 2&3, June - September, 1976
6. Speech by Sir Robert Heron, in Defence of Major General Ainslie, Governor of Dominica in the House of Commons 2 June, 1815 in 'A collection of Plain Authentic Documents in Justification of the Conduct of Governor Ainslie: In the reduction of a Most Formidable Rebellion among the Negro Slaves in the Island of Dominica, at a Crisis of the Most Imminent Danger to the lives and Properties of the Inhabitants'. C. Lowndes, London
7. Orde to Sydney, 15 December 1785, CO 71/9
8. Atwood, pp237-240
9. Raymond Proesmans, unpublished manuscript on Maroon cases, p54. The records of these cases are based on notes made by Father Proesmans in the 1960s. On visiting the building that housed the High Court, Registry and House of Assembly one day, he saw a roll of papers on the floor upstairs and when he opened it, discovered them to be the Maroon trials of 1786. He made some notes and put the papers back in a nearby cupboard. On 16 June 1979, the building was destroyed by fire and all historic court records went with it.
10. Raymond Proesmans, transcribed speech on the History of Dominica, 1969
11. Atwood, p246; and Anon, Sketches and Recollections of the West Indies by a Resident to James Laing, formerly of Dominica, Smith, Elder & Co, London, 1828, p77
12. Proesmans, speech
13. Loftus A Roberts used Fr. Proesmans' notes in a pamphlet, The Negres Maroons of Dominica, on the Maroons and thus they survive in this form. Roseau public library, p4
14. Court of Special Sessions, Roseau, 27 February 1786
15. Proesmans, speech
16. Roberts, p4
17. ibid, p5
18. ibid, p62
19. Proesmans, speech
20. Minutes of the House of Assembly, Dominica, 1786, CO 71/10
21. Orde to Grenville CO 71/10
22. The Cashibona River was the Kalinago name for what is called today the Melville Hall River.
23. Garrett to Orde, CO 71/20
24. Proesmans, manuscript, p54
25. Jerome Handler, 'Anti-Obeah Laws of the Anglophone Caribbean, 1760s to 2010', Virginia Foundation for the Humanities, Charlottesville, Virginia, 35th Annual Conference, Society for Caribbean Studies, Liverpool, 29 June - 1 July 2011

26. Gordon K Lewis, Main Currents in Caribbean Thought, Heinemann, 1983, pp188-189
27. Acts of the Dominica House of Assembly 1788, Dominica National Archives and Professor Jerome Handler, personal communication. Amazingly, in the legislation currently on the books in the 21st century (Laws of Dominica 1991) writing the above paragraphs could be construed as an offence since there is still a $3000 fine or six months in jail 'for writing or publishing literature on the subject.'
28. For references to obeah in Dominica see: Hesketh Bell's books: Obeah: Witchcraft in the West Indies, S Low, Marston Ltd, 1893 and Glimpses of a Governor's Life, S Low, Marston & Co Ltd 1946; also Jeffrey W Mantz, Lost in the Fire, gained in the Ash: Moral economies of exchange in Dominica, unpublished doctoral thesis, University of Chicago, June 2003, pp184-200

9 A NEW CHALLENGE: THE FRENCH ASCENDANCY

1. Address and petition from the Council and Assembly of Dominica to His Britannic Majesty requesting relief for the island after a series of calamities 17 April 1786, CO 71/10
2. Mulatto, a term originally used to identify the first shade on the broad genetic spectrum between black and white, was by then applied loosely to all 'high coloured' people.
3. Copies of broadsheets from January 1791 headlined 'L'Ami de la Liberté, et L'Ennemi de la Licence' with articles giving a review of the political turmoil in Martinique and Guadeloupe and making pointed references to the decline of the Roman Empire with quotes in Latin. In CO 71/20 Orde to Grenville, 3 February 1791, no 14
4. John Lowndes, planter, printer, charged and found guilty of libel, paid fees. Minutes of Court and King's Bench and Session, 1791-1806, Dominica National Archives, p3

10 THE NEW YEAR'S DAY REVOLT: MAROONS AND 'THE RIGHTS OF MAN'

1. Jean Louis Polinaire could only affix 'his mark' of a cross at the bottom of the 'Examination' which he made before his execution in 1791. Alternatively he could have been suffering the effects of torture and was in no condition to sign his name. The examination of Polinaire, A Free Mulatto Man (dispatches), 3 Feb - 15 June 1791, CO 71/20
2. Anne Pérotin-Dumon, 'Free Coloreds and Slaves in Revolutionary Guadeloupe – Politics and Political Conciousness' in The Lesser Antilles in the Age of European Expansion, Robert L Paquette and Stanley L Engerman (eds), University Press of Florida, 1996, p269
3. Minutes of the House of Assembly, Dominica, February 1789, Dominica National Archives, p106
4. On the Gold Coast, now Ghana
5. Horace Walpole quoted in Basil Davidson, The African Slave Trade, James Currey, 2004, p270
6. Adam Hochschild, Bury the Chains: the British struggle to Abolish Slavery, Pan Macmillan, 2006, p265
7. W Adolphe Roberts, The French in the West Indies, Cooper Square Publishers, Inc. New York, 1971, p199
8. Examination of Polinaire, CO 71/20
9. ibid
10. Expenses of the Armament in the Engineer Department in the Island of Dominica, 1790, CO 71/20
11. Orde to Grenville, Dominica, 13 February 1791, CO 71/20
12. Julien S Scott, 'Crossing Empires' in The Lesser Antilles in the Age of European Expansion, Robert L Paquette and Stanley L Engerman (eds), University Press of Florida, 1996, p140
13. ibid, quoting Minutes of the Privy Council, 20 January 1791, Orde to Laforcy, 20, 28 January

1791, CO 71/19 and CO 71/20

14. Examination of Polinaire, CO 71/20

15. ibid

16. The Naval Chronicle, vol 11, p189

17. Orde to Grenville, 3 March 1791, CO 71/20

18. Examination of Polinaire, CO 71/20

19. Anon, Sketches and Recollections of the West Indies by a Resident to James Laing, formerly of Dominica, Smith, Elder & Co, London, 1828, pp74-75

20. Contained in correspondence from Orde to Melville, CO 71/19

21. Minutes of the House of Assembly, Dominica, 20 January 1791, Dominica National Archives

22. ibid

23. ibid

24. Private Aytoun was very lucky to have survived three years without death by disease as a soldier in the West Indies.

25. James Aytoun, Redcoats in the Caribbean, East Lancashire Regiment Museum, Blackburn Recreation Services Department, 1984, p16

26. Examination of Polinaire, CO 71/20

27. Private Aytoun gives an account of this incident in his memoirs and Polinaire also mentions it in his 'Examination', CO 71/20

28. Combe to Orde, 3 February 1791, CO 71/20

29. ibid

30. Aytoun, p16

31. In 2004, a Kalinago youth from Gaulette River in the Kalinago Territory brought me a coin that he had found while digging a yam 'fosse' in his family garden. It was a perfectly unblemished gold 'Joe' dated 1742. I explained how valuable it was, and that he should keep it safely and I wondered whether it was one of the '5 Joes' given by Colonel Bruce to one of his ancestors. A search on the internet revealed that its value in 2004 was US $400.

32. Bruce to Orde, 1 February 1791, CO 71/20

33. Minutes of Court of Kings Bench and Session, 1791-1806, Dominica National Archives, p1

34. Examination of Polinaire, CO 71/20

35. ibid

36. Anon, Sketches, p83

37. Known today in its French form as Pointe Mulatre.

38. Myhambay is now spelt as Mayambe on the official maps. It was a centre for the 'Dreads' in the 20th century when it featured in the conflicts between this group and Defence Force police in the 1970s.

39. Gray to Orde, February 16 1791, CO 71/20

40. WH Hodge & D Taylor, The Ethnobotany of the Island Caribs of Dominica.Webbia, vol 7, no 2, p542

41. Robin Blackburn, The Making of New World Slavery, Verso, 1997, London, p442

42. 4 February 1791, CO 71/20

43. The plantation, owned by William Woodbridge, now called Goodwill.

44. In 1990, when the offices of the Dominica Banana Growers Association (Vanoulst House) was being constructed I was called to the site on the corner of Goodwill Road and Charles Avenue and shown a hole where a skeleton had just been found. It had already been taken to the pathologist who declared that 'it was not recent' and it was thrown away. I thought that it may have been the body of Paul, buried at the site of his exposure.

45. Charles Winston's estate was Bath estate.

46. 4 February 1791, CO 71/20

47. RC Dallas, writing about Jamaica, describes how the Jamaican Maroon prisoners in 1796 feared deportation even more than death itself, because of their love of Jamaica.
48. Such Spanish directives were part of the assientos or licences granted by the Spanish crown to other European traders to supply slaves to Spanish colonies in the Americas. Basil Davidson, The African Slave Trade, James Currey, 2004, p66
49. Minutes of Court of Kings Bench and Session, 1791-1806, Dominica National Archives
50. Cap Francais was renamed Cap Haitian later in the Revolution.
51. Roberts, The French in the West Indies, p190
52. Orde to Grenville CO 71/20. Many of the descendants of those signatories are citizens of Dominica today.
53. Anon. Sketches, ibid, p82
54. Olaudah Equiano, The Life of Olaudah Equiano, or Gustavus Vassa the African, Paul Edwards (ed), Longman African Classics, 1989, p75
55. Hochschild, Bury the Chains, p189
56. ibid
57. Minutes of the Privy Council, Dominica, 5 February 1791, Dominica National Archives
58. Orde to Grenville, 1791, CO 71/20

11 AN UNSTABLE DECADE: MAROONS MANIPULATE COLONIAL CONFLICT

1. Letter of Robert Browne, a resident of Dominica during the 1790s, published in the Bermuda Gazette, Hamilton, Bermuda, 1795. The activities of Governor Hamilton were followed closely in Bermuda where he had previously served as governor.
2. House of Assembly minutes, Dominica, 20 April 1793
3. Fedon to Nicholls, 1795, Melville Mss, Rhodes House Library, Oxford
4. Bermuda Gazette, ibid
5. House of Assembly minutes, ibid
6. Bermuda Gazette, ibid
7. In 2010, some of them were incorporated into the Waitukubuli National Trail, a hiking trail covering 115 miles from one end of Dominica to the other.
8. This route forms Segments 8 and 9 of the Waitukubuli National Trail
9. This route forms Segments 10 of the Waitukubuli National Trail
10. Frederick Ober, Camps in the Caribbees, Lee & Shepard, New York, 1880, p143-144
11. Ibid, p153. Ober is rather loose with his estimate of the time span since the Maroons were active. His 1876 estimate of 'some 40 years ago' would take him back to 1836, at which time slavery had been partially abolished
12. The author has done this journey in open fishing boats with outboard motors from Anse de Mai in Dominica, to Gros Bourg, the main town of Mariegalante in 45 minutes.
13. Bermuda Gazette, ibid
14. ibid
15. ibid
16. ibid
17. Lucas to Melville, 20 January 1798, Melville Mss. f105, Rhodes House Library, Oxford
18. Account from Roseau, Dominica, 7 May 1795, the Bermuda Gazette, 6 June 1795
19. Minutes of the House of Assembly, 27 August 1795
20. Orde to Sydney, 16 April 1786, CO 71/10
21. Orde to Grenville, 3 March 1791, CO 71/20
22. Much of this is also covered by Bernard Marshall in 'Maronage in Slave Plantation societies: A case study of Dominica, 1785-1815, Caribbean Quarterly, University of the West Indies, Mona, vol 22, nos 2&3, June-September 1976

23. Minutes of meetings of the Dominica Council, 15 October and 9 December 1794, CO71/27
24. Marshall, p28
25. Cochrane Johnstone to Council, 10 August 1799

12 THE WEST INDIES REGIMENTS: A CHALLENGE TO MAROONS

1. Besides serving as a warehouse during its long history it was at other times a temporary House of Assembly, a barracks for freed slaves in 1837, the site of the Roseau Boys School, and is now a community centre.
2. John Fortescue, History of the British Army, 1899-1930, vol 11, reprint Macmillan, London, 1935, pp10-27
3. Father Raymond Proesmans' notes and typed manuscript, Book 9, p23, Roman Catholic Church archives, Roseau
4. Cochrane Johnstone to Dundas, 30 November 1801, Melville Mss f 116 (3), Rhodes House Library, Oxford
5. Trigge to Hobart, 2 April 1802. Quoted in Buckley 'Slaves in Redcoats' p124, CO 318/19
6. Cochrane Johnstone to Sir Ralph Abercrombie, Commander in Chief of His Majesty's Forces, West Indies, 14 April 1797, CO 70/10
7. Trigge to Hobart
8. Dr HAA Nicholls notebook (Phyllis Allfrey collection), p1. Dr Nicholls took notes of conversations that he had with his mentor Dr John Imray, who had arrived in Dominica in 1821. Imray himself had known and had conversations with people who had experienced events at the end of the 18th and early 19th centuries. These he passed on to Nicholls. This conversation was with President Lockhart, a former president of the Executive Council.
9. Insurrection at Dominica. Report from St John's, Antigua, April 22 1802, published in The Evening Mail, London, Monday, June 14 ,1802, p1
10. ibid
11. In 2010, when the Parade Ground was being graded to level out the field, more than 200 spent lead shot were found scattered over the area indicating action at close range.
12. The Evening Mail, Wednesday 9 June, 1802, London, p3. This report was written in Roseau on 14 April 1802 and indicates the time a letter took to cross the Atlantic and reach its destination.
13. Defence of the Honourable Andrew Cochrane Johnstone, including a view of the evidence produced on his trial etc, PJ Barfield, Wardour Street, London, 1805
14. Orde to Grenville, 14 February 1791, CO 71/20
15. Parliamentary papers 1817, dispatch from Government House, Dominica, 30 September 1817 and reported in Bell's Weekly Messenger, London, 24 May 1818, p166. Also: further papers relating to the treatment of slaves in the colonies ordered by The House of Commons to be printed, Colonial Department 1 May 1818, p7. Personal collection.
16. The Diary of Jonathan Troup 1788-1790, ff11-14, University of Aberdeen, Scotland (MS 2070)
17. Rev Charles Peters, Two Sermons Preached at Dominica on the 11th and 13th April, 1800, John Hatchard, London, no date. In this he mentions the iron collars and brutality of the mulatto mistresses emphasising that the white slave owners were not alone in their cruelty.
18. Concerning two sermons preached at Dominica by the Rev Charles Peters, Nicholls and Son, London, 1802
19. Henry Nelson Coleridge, Six Months in the West Indies in 1825, John Murray, London, 1832, pp138-139

13 THE PRELUDE TO MAYHEM: MAROONS DESTABLISE THE SYSTEM

1. All quotes from Prevost are in the 'Report from the Committee on the petition from Dominica, respecting losses by the fire at Roseau etc', mainly p4-5. Parliamentary paper printed 27 July 1807, reprinted 11 May 1808, London
2. Anon. Sketches and Recollections of the West Indies by a Resident to James Laing, formerly of Dominica, Smith, Elder & Co, London, 1828, p181
3. Report from the Committee, p19
4. ibid, p6
5. David Lowenthal, West Indian Societies, Oxford University Press, 1972, p44
6. Bernard Marshall, Society and Economy in the British Windward Islands, 1763-1823, University of the West Indies, Mona, Jamaica, 1972, pp506-507
7. Anon. Sketches, p75
8. Adam Hochschild, Bury the Chains: the British struggle to Abolish Slavery, Pan Macmillan 2006, p275
9. Young Papers, Rhodes House Library, Oxford
10. Hochschild, p187
11. Susan Campbell, Africans to Dominica: 100,000 Middle Passages to the Eastern Caribbean, 1764-1808. http://da-academy.org/AfricanstoDominica.pdf, 2007. Almost 30 years later, in 1837, an illegal slave ship, the Don Fernando, was captured by the Royal Navy, which landed more than 400 slaves at Roseau as free people.
12. Anon, Sketches, pp146-147
13. ibid, p148
14. Governor Johnstone to the Duke of Portland, 16 December 1797, CO 71/30
15. ibid
16. William Bremner covered this period in his Memoirs, the National Library of Scotland.
17. Anon, Account of the effects of the Anglo-American War of 1812 and Hurricane of 1813, Roseau public library, 1818
18. ibid
19. During the years of the national heritage movement in the late 20th century and beyond, this "slave food" would be celebrated as part of Dominica's 'national Kweyole cuisine'; Caribbean states remain the largest importers of dried salted cod in the world.

14 THE SECOND MAROON WAR: AN ERADICATION POLICY

1. RJ Morgan, "AINSLIE, GEORGE ROBERT," in Dictionary of Canadian Biography, vol. 7, University of Toronto/Universite Laval, 2003-, accessed March 22, 2014, http://www.biographi.ca/en/bio/ainslie_george_robert_7E.html; also Gentleman's Magazine, January-June 1814, p509
2. Memoirs of William Bremner, National Library of Scotland, p142
3. Minutes of the House of Assembly, Dominica, 1814, Dominica National Archives
4. Speech by Sir Robert Heron in Defence of Major General Ainslie, Governor of Dominica, in the House of Commons, Hansard, London, 2 June, 1815
5. Anon. Sketches and Recollections of the West Indies by a Resident to James Laing, formerly of Dominica, Smith, Elder & Co, London, 1828, p87
6. ibid, pp86-89
7. Letter from Beckwith, minutes of the House of Assembly, Dominica, 9 July 1813, Dominica National Archives, p73
8. Minutes of House of Assembly, Dominica, 17 April 1813 - 28 November 1815, Dominica National Archives, p74
9. ibid, 4 August 1813, p56

10. ibid, 17 April 1813 - 28 November 1815, p82
11. Anon, Account of the effects of the Anglo-American War of 1812 and Hurricane of 1813, Roseau public library, 1818
12. Bremner, p139
13. Minutes of the House of Assembly, Dominica, 5 October 1813, Dominica National Archives, p132
14. Further papers relating to the treatment of slaves in the colonies, ordered by The House of Commons, to be printed, 1 May 1818, p 4-6, Parliamentary papers 1818; also printed in Bell's Weekly Messenger, London, 24 May 1818, p166 (Both personal collection)
15. Bremner, p144
16. Minutes of the House of Assembly, March 1814, Dominica National Archives, p112
17. ibid, May 1813, p116
18. ibid
19. The oaths were sworn to the Prince Regent, George, Prince of Wales, because the King, George III, was mentally ill.
20. An Account of Runaway Slaves, Killed, Taken, and Surrendered, Colonial Department, printed by House of Commons, 9 February 1816
21. A collection of Plain Authentic Documents in Justification of the Conduct of Governor Ainslie: In the reduction of a Most Formidable Rebellion among the Negro Slaves in the Island of Dominica, at a Crisis of the Most Imminent Danger to the lives and Properties of the Inhabitants', C Lowndes, London, 1815
22. Minutes of the House of Assembly, Dominica, November 1814, Dominica National Archives, p309
23. A collection of Plain Authentic Documents
24. ibid
25. ibid
26. Minutes of the House of Assembly, Dominica, 14 October 1814, Dominica National Archives, pp265-266
27. Notes compiled by British administrator Hesketh Bell, from The Journal of Occurrences at Dominica, the Royal Military Chronicle 1814, vol 4, p559
28. Minutes of the House of Assembly, Dominica, 8 May 1815, Dominica National Archives, p431
29. ibid, p432
30. ibid
31. Your Time Is Done Now. Slavery, Resistance, and Defeat. The Maroon Trials of Dominica (1813–1814), Polly Pattullo (ed), Papillote Press, 2015
32. This was the experience in the two decades following Hurricane David, which hit Dominica on 29 August 1979
33. Minutes of the House of Assembly, 10 January 1815, Dominica National Archives, p333
34. ibid, 9 May 1814, p469-474
35. Lucas to Earl Bathurst, letter 24 August 1815, CO 71/51
36. Dr HAA Nicholls' notebook, headed 'Conversation with Dr Imray, 13th July 1880', Phyllis Shand Allfrey's papers in author's possession, pp1-2
37. Sturge, Joseph and Thomas Harvey, The West Indies in 1837, Dawsons, London, 1968, pp98-99
38. CO 71/50
39. Court evidence suggest that 13 people were executed following the trials; but the official lists give 11.

15 THE ROAD TO EMANCIPATION: HALFWAY TO FREEDOM

1. Henry Nelson Coleridge, Six Months in the West Indies in 1825, London: John Murray, 1832, p139
2. In fact, much of Segment 5 of the present Waitukubuli National Trail is actually part of this trace laid down by the Rangers in 1827-1828.
3. Notebook of HAA Nicholls, report by J Finlay, surveyor general, Dominica, 13 March 1828, p53
4. The Leeward Islands and Dominica Almanack 1879, Official Gazette Office, Hanover Street, Roseau, p155
5. Circular, Dominica, May 30 1823, American Historical Association Annual Report, 1932, vol 3, p139
6. Dispatches for 1825, CO 71/63
7. Lockhart to secretary of state Goderich, 30 August 1831, CO 71/72
8. DJ Murray, The West Indies and the development of colonial government 1801-1834, Clarendon Press, Oxford, 1965, p181
9. David Lowenthal, West Indian Societies, Oxford University Press, 1972, p63
10. Charles Marsh Schomberg, lieutenant governor of Dominica 1833-1834, British National Archives, CO71/78
11. ibid
12. Nicholls, pp23-26
13. Farewell address by Lt. Governor Henry Light to the joint houses of the legislature, Dominica, 10 July 1838, CO71/88

16 THE AFTERMATH: ZION, BABYLON AND THE GLOBALISED COLONY

1. Delivered by John Longley, 28 July 1838, published in the Colonist Newspaper, 30 July 1838
2. Lord Harris to Secretary of State Grey, 19 June 1848, Parliamentary Papers, 1847-48, xlvi.
3. Joseph John Gurney, A Winter in the West Indies, John Murray, London, 1841, p70-71
4. Cahier de Marronage du Moule (1840-1848), Société d'Histoire de la Guadeloupe, Basseterre, 1996
5. Rules and regulations for the management of the Treadmill, Roseau (received 25 October 1837), CO 71/02
6. An act establishing a police force in Roseau, Dominica, CO 71/85
7. Graeme Henderson, Redemption of a slave ship: The James Matthews, Western Australia Museum, 2009, p114-120
8. Lord Glenelg to Governors: Colonial Annual Reports, Blue Books, Dominica 1836, p152
9. Government of Dominica, administrator's files 30, 1836
10. Brian L Moore, Race, Power and Social Segmentation in Colonial Society: Guyana after Slavery 1838-1891, Gordon and Breach, New York, 1987, p167
11. Parliamentary Papers, House of Commons, London, 1846, p34
12. Government of Dominica, administrator's files 23,1856
13. Dominica Blue Books, 1882, p76
14. Copies or Extracts of Dispatches relating to disturbances in the Island of Dominica, Parliamentary Papers, House of Commons, 5 September 1844 and 18 March 1845
15. WH McCoy, Colonial Secretary, The Three Chains, in Dominica Almanack, 1869, Roseau
16. CO 152/186.
17. Robert Hamilton, Report of the Royal Commission to inquire into the condition and affairs of the island of Dominica, HMSO, London, 1894
18. Moyne Commission Report, Section on Windward Islands, Dominica, 1945
19. Dame Mary Eugenia Charles, Parliamentary Hansard of 19 November 1974, p30

Bibliography

Agorsah, E Kofi (ed). *Maroon Heritage: Archaeological, Ethnographic and Historical Perspectives* (Kingston: Canoe Press, 1994)

Anon. *An Account of the Effects of the Anglo-American War of 1812 and Hurricane of 1813* (Roseau Public Library, 1818)

Anon. *Sketches and Recollections of the West Indies by a Resident to James Laing, formerly of Dominica* (London: Smith, Elder & Co, 1828)

Anon. *Some Observations on our new West India Colonies* (London: 1764)

Atwood, Thomas. *The History of the Island of Dominica* (London: J.Johnson, 1791)

Aytoun, James. *Memoirs of a Redcoat in the Caribbean* (Cambridgeshire Regiment, 1982)

Bell, Hesketh. *Obeah: Witchcraft in the West Indies* (London: S Low, Marston Co, 1893)

– *Glimpses of a Governor's Life* (London: S Low, Marston & Co 1946)

Blackburn, Robin. *The Making of New World Slavery* (London: Verso, 1997)

Boromé, Joseph. 'Dominica during French Occupation 1778-1784'; 'The French and Dominica 1699-1763'; 'Spain and Dominica 1493-1647', in *Aspects of Dominica History* (Roseau: Government Printery, 1972)

Bremner, William. *The Memoirs of William Bremner*, microfilm (National Library of Scotland; the University of the West Indies, Mona, Jamaica)

Breton, Raymond. *Dictionnaire Caraïbe-Français* (Auxerre: 1665)

Buckley, RN. *The British Army in the West Indies, Society and the Military in the Revolutionary Age* (Florida: University Press of Florida, The Press University of the West Indies, 1998)

– *Slaves in Redcoats: the British West India Regiments 1795-1815* (New Haven: Yale University Press, 1979)

Burns, Alan. *History of the British West Indies* (London: Allen & Unwin, 1954)

Byres, John. *Map of Commissioners for Sale of Land of the Ceded Island of Dominica* (London: 1776)

Campbell, Susan. *Africans to Dominica: 100,000 Middle Passages from 'Guinea' to the Eastern Caribbean*, 1764 to 1808 http://da-academy.org/AfricanstoDominica.pdf

Casimir, Jean. *Social Structural Changes in Dominica* (Social Development Unit of the Economic Commission for Latin America, 1984)

Churchill, John Spencer. *The British Leeward Islands*, booklet (London: 1898)

Cohen, David and Green, Jack (eds). *Neither Slave nor Free: Freedmen of African Descent in the Slave Societies of the New World* (Baltimore: Johns Hopkins University Press, 1972)

Cohen, JM (ed). *Christopher Columbus: The Four Voyages* (Penguin Books, London, 1969)

Coleridge, Henry N. *Six Months in the West Indies in 1825* (London: John Murray, 1832)

Cracknell, Basil E. *Dominica*, in the 'Islands' series (David & Charles Stackpole Books, 1973)

Craton, Michael. *Testing the Chains: Resistance to Slavery in the British West Indies* (Ithaca, New York: Cornell University Press, 1982)

Crouse, Nellis M. *The French Struggle for the West Indies, 1665-1713,* (New York: Columbia University Press, 1943)

Davidson, Basil. *The African Slave Trade* (London: James Currey, 2004)

– *The Story of Africa* (London: Mitchell Beasley Publishers, 1984)

Davies, John. *The History of the Caribby Islands*, translation of C de Rochefort (London: 1666)

Davis, David Brian. *The Problem of Slavery in Western Culture* (Pelican Books, 1970)

Davis, ND. *One Hundred Years Ago or the Battle off Dominica* (Demerara: 1882)

De Rochefort, C. *Histoire naturelle et morale des Isles Antilles de L'Amerique* (Paris: 1658)

Dominica Chronicle. Bound volume (Roseau: Dupigny, 1825)

Du Tertre, Jean-Baptiste. *Histoire générale des Antilles habitées par les Francois*, 4 vols (Paris: 1667-71)

Eaden, John. *The memoirs of Père Labat* 1693-1705 (London: Constable, 1931)

Edwards, Bryan. *The History, Civil and Commercial, of the British Colonies in the West Indies*, 3 vols (London, 1793, 1801, 1826)

Equiano, Olaudah. *The Life of Olaudah Equiano or Gustavus Vassa the African Written by Himself*, Paul Edwards (ed). (Harlow: Longmans, 1989)

Esquemeling, John. *The Buccaneers of America* (London: George Routledge & Sons, 1926)

Froude, James Anthony. *The English in the West Indies or the Bow of Ulysses* (London: Longmans Green and Co, 1888)

Goodridge, CA. 'Dominica: The French Connection', in *Aspects of Dominica History* (Roseau: Government Printery, 1972)

Goveia, Elsa V. *Slave Society in the British Leeward Islands at the end of the 18th century* (New Haven: Yale University Press, 1965)

Gurney, Joseph John. *A Winter in the West Indies* (London: John Murray, 1841)

Hamilton, H. *Account of French Invasion, 1794-1796* (London, 1796)

Hamilton, Robert. *Report of the Royal Commission to inquire into the conditions and affairs of the island of Dominica* (London: HMSO, 1994)

Handler, Jerome. *Anti-Obeah Laws in the Anglophone Caribbean 1760s* (Virginia Foundation for the Humanities, Conference Papers, Society for Caribbean Studies, Virginia, 2011)

Harms, Robert. *The Diligent: A Voyage Through the Worlds of the Slave Trade* (Oxford: Perseus Press, 2002)

Hayter, T (ed). *The Papers of William, Viscount Barrington 1755-1778* (London: Bodley Head, Army Records Society, 1988)

Hochschild, Adam. *Bury the Chains: the British Struggle to Abolish Slavery* (London: Pan Macmillan, 2006)

Hodge, WH & Taylor, Douglas. *The Ethnobotany of the Island Caribs of Dominica* (Webbia, vol 12.no 2)

Honychurch, Lennox. *Carib to Creole, a History of Contact and Culture Exchange*. Unpublished doctoral thesis (Bodleian Library, Oxford University, 1997)

– *Dominica's Cabrits and Prince Rupert's Bay* (Dominica: Paramount Printers, 2013)

– *The Dominica Story* (London: Macmillan, 1995)

Hotblack, K. *Chatham's Colonial Policy* (London: Routledge, 1917)

Hulme, Peter and Whitehead, Neil (eds). *Wild Majesty, Encounters with Caribs from Columbus to the present day* (Oxford: Clarendon Press, 1992)

James, Arlington. *Cabrits Plants and their Uses* (Dominica: Forestry and Wildlife Division, 1986)

Jefferys, T. *Map of the Island of Dominica* (London: 1768)

Johnstone, Andrew Cochran. *Defence of Hon A C Johnstone*. Evidence at his trial, varied commentaries; letters relating (London: 1805)

Labat, Jean-Baptiste. *Nouveau Voyage aux Isles de l'Amerique* (The Hague: 1724)

Lewis, Gordon K. *Main Currents in Caribbean Thought* (London: Heinemann Educational Books, 1983)

Lowenthal, David, *West Indian Societies* (Oxford: Oxford University Press, 1972)

Lowndes, John. *The Coffee Planter* (London: 1801)

Mair, John. *Eyewitness Account of the Action of 12 April* (Jamaica National Archives, 1782)

Marshall, Bernard. 'Maronage in Slave Plantation Societies: A case study of Dominica 1785-1815' in *Caribbean Quarterly*, vol 22, no 2&3, June-September 1976 (Jamaica: University of the West Indies)

– 'Society and Economy in the British Windward Islands 1763-1823' (Jamaica: University of the West Indies, 1972)

Moore, Brian L. *Race, Power and Social Segmentation in Colonial Society: Guyana after Slavery 1838-1891* (New York: Gordon and Breach, 1987)

Morgan, RT. 'Ainslie, George Robert' in *Dictionary of Canadian Biography*, vol 7 (University of Toronto/University Laval, Toronto, 2003)

Moyne Commission Report (London: HMSO, 1945)

Murray, DJ. *The West Indies and the Development of Colonial Government* (Oxford: Clarendon Press, 1965)

Ober, Frederick. *Camps in the Caribbees* (New York: 1880)

Orde, John. Papers, 1786-1805 (National Maritime Museum, Greenwich, UK)

Pacquette, Robert and Egerman, Stanley (eds). *The Lesser Antilles in the Age of European Expansion* (Florida: University Press of Florida, 1996)

Paisa, Marina Besada (ed). *Dictionnaire Caraïbe-Français, Révérend Père Raymond Breton 1665* (Paris: Karthala Editions, 1999)

Pares, Richard. *Yankees and Creoles* (Oxford: Oxford University Press, 1956)

Parry, JH and Sherlock, PM. *A Short History of the West Indies* (London: Macmillan, 1971)

Pattullo, Polly (ed.). *Your Time Is Done Now. Slavery, Resistance, and Defeat. The Maroon Trials of Dominica (1813-1814)* (London and Dominica: Papillote Press, 2015)

Pope-Hennessy, James. *The Sins of the Fathers* (London: Weidenfeld and Nicolson, 1967)

Price, Richard (ed). *Maroon Societies: Rebel Slave Communities in the Americas* (New York: Anchor Books, 1973)

Priestly, HI. *France Overseas through the Old Regime* (New York: Appleton-Century, 1939)

Proesmans, Rev Raymond. Papers, unpublished manuscripts (Roseau: Bishop Arnold Boghaert Centre Archives)

Roberts, Loftus A. *The Negres Marron of Dominica*. Notes (Roseau Public Library)

Roberts, W. Adolphe. *The French in the West Indies* (New York: Cooper Square Press, 1971)

Robinson, Carey. *The Fighting Maroons of Jamaica* (Kingston: William Collins & Sangster Press, 1969)

Smelser, Marshall. *The Campaign for the Sugar Islands 1759* (Institute of Early American History & Culture, University of North Carolina Press, 1955)

Southey, Richard, *A Chronological History of the West Indies*, 2 vols (London: 1827)

St Johnston, Reginald. *The French Invasions of Dominica* (Barbados: 1932)

Sturge, Joseph and Harvey, Thomas. *The West Indies in 1837* (London: Dawsons of Pall Mall, 1968)

Taylor, Douglas. *The Island Caribs of Dominica* (American Anthropologist, vol 37, No2, part 1, 1935)

Troup, Jonathan. *The Diary of Jonathan Troup, 1788-90*, manuscript (Aberdeen: University of Aberdeen)

Watts, David. *The West Indies, Patterns of Development, Culture and Environmental Change since 1492* (Cambridge: Cambridge University Press, 1987)

Young, William (1st Bart). Considerations which may tend to promote our new West India Colonies. (London: 1764)

Young papers (Rhodes House, Oxford)

Zamore, Michael. *The Wildlife of Dominica* (Dominica Forestry Division, Ministry of Agriculture. 1983)

RESEARCH SOURCES
Bishop Arnold Boghaert Centre Archives, Roseau
Colonial Office files, British National Archives, Kew, UK
Elma Napier papers, Dominica (personal collection)
National Maritime Museum, Greenwich, UK
Phyllis Allfrey papers – Dr HAA Nicholls notebook (personal collection)
Rhodes House Library, Oxford University, UK
Roseau Public Library and National Archives, Dominica
Royal Commonwealth Society Library, Cambridge University, UK

MAPS
National Archives, Kew: numbers 3381-3391, all of Dominica consisting of plans of towns,
    fortifications and estates, 1765-1832
John Byers map of Dominica, 1776: National Archives, Kew, UK

Some of the events covered in this book have appeared in the general history of Dominica,
The Dominica Story, written by the author.

PICTURE CREDITS
All maps, diagrams, illustrations, paintings and photographs are by the author or in his
personal collection unless noted below:

Chapter 3. p18, by kind permission of the David Nabarro Collection of printed matter of the
    Island of Dominica.
Chapter 6. p63, Bolivar Gallery, Kingston, Jamaica.
Chapter 7. p73, Art Gallery of Ontario, Prints, Drawings and Watercolour Collection,
    courtesy The Canadian High Commission for the Eastern Caribbean, Barbados.
Chapter 8. p75, © National Portrait Gallery, London; p82, Library of Congress, Geography
    and Map Division (https://www.loc.gov/item/74695802/)
Chapter 10. p114/115,Yale Center for British Art, Paul Mellon Collection
Chapter 13. p151, Library of Congress Geography and Map Division
    (http://www.loc.gov/pictures/resource/cph.3b49565/); p161, Chronicle newspaper 1825,
    Dupigny Collection.
Chapter 14. p165, British Museum; p184, Stark's History and Guide to Barbados and the
    Caribbee Islands; Boston, JH Stark and London, S Low, Marston & Co. Ltd, 1903
Chapter 15 p190-191, Dominica National Archives.
Chapter 16. p198, Mary Evans Picture Library, London; p204, Roy Sanford/Dominica News
    Online.

Acknowledgements

A number of people contributed towards making this book become a reality and arranging for its re-publication. I am grateful to Polly Pattullo for proposing this second edition and guiding through its publication by Papillote Press. I must thank Miss Magdalene Robin and the staff of the Dominica National Archives and Documentation Centre for their ever-ready assistance and interest in accessing material on my behalf; Dr Karl Watson, for his encouragement and support in Barbados. My family: mother, sister and nieces, Marica and Petrea and her husband, Dr Garvin Seaman, for their understanding during my long absences. To Mr Gerry Aird and Mr and Mrs 'Pappyson' Francis for their hospitality in providing a haven in which to complete a large section of this book away from interruptions and disturbances. Thanks to Polly Pattullo for sharing her notes on the William Bremner Diary from the National Library of Scotland, which gave an important personal perspective on the events of 1812-1815.

Index

Versailles, 73
Trials, February and March 1791, 111-17; of
    French rebels, 131, 136; January-March
    1814, 179-81; of John Lowndes, 95; of
    Maroon women, 84; of Thornton, 147, 172
    (*see also* Maroons)
Trinidad, 5, 16, 53, 186-7, 198, 200
Trollope, Anthony, 22
Troup, Dr Jonathan, 148

United Negro Improvement Association
    (UNIA), 206
Universal adult suffrage, 205

Vespucci, Amerigo, 17,

Wadström, Carl, 47
Wai'tukubuli, 15, 17, 24
Warner, 'Carib' or 'Indian', 26-9
Warner Phillip, 27
Warner, Sir Thomas, 20, 26
Wawa (yam), 14, 113, 181
West Indies (Black) regiments, 76, 152, 155,
    161, 163, 168-9, 172, 200; deserters from,
    163, 175; emancipation of soldiers, 146-7;
    formation of 8th, 137-42; Kalinagos in, 62,
    146, 166; revolt of, 143-6, 147
Willoughby, Lord Francis, 25, 27
Winston, Charles, 56, 115
Woodford Hill estate, 10, 126, 128, 129, 131,
    160, 175, 200

Young, Sir William, 36, 44-6, 50, 58, 68, 157